ON SPARTAN WINGS

*To Greece's airmen and airwomen,
past, present and future*

ON SPARTAN WINGS

The Royal Hellenic Air Force in World War Two

John Carr

Pen & Sword
AVIATION

First published in Great Britain in 2012 and republished in this format in 2022 by
PEN & SWORD AVIATION
An imprint of
Pen & Sword Books Ltd
Yorkshire – Philadelphia

Copyright © John Carr 2012, 2022

ISBN 978-1-39901-975-0

The right of John Carr to be identified as the Author of this Work has been asserted by him in accordance with the Copyright, Designs and Patents Act 1988.

A CIP catalogue record for this book is available from the British Library.

All rights reserved. No part of this book may be reproduced or transmitted in any form or by any means, electronic or mechanical including photocopying, recording or by any information storage and retrieval system, without permission from the Publisher in writing.

Typeset by Concept, Huddersfield, West Yorkshire.
Printed and bound in the UK by CPI Group (UK) Ltd, Croydon, CR0 4YY.

Pen & Sword Books Limited incorporates the imprints of Atlas, Archaeology, Aviation, Discovery, Family History, Fiction, History, Maritime, Military, Military Classics, Politics, Select, Transport, True Crime, Air World, Frontline Publishing, Leo Cooper, Remember When, Seaforth Publishing, The Praetorian Press, Wharncliffe Local History, Wharncliffe Transport, Wharncliffe True Crime, White Owl and After the Battle.

For a complete list of Pen & Sword titles please contact

PEN & SWORD BOOKS LIMITED
47 Church Street, Barnsley, South Yorkshire, S70 2AS, England
E-mail: enquiries@pen-and-sword.co.uk
Website: www.pen-and-sword.co.uk

or

PEN AND SWORD BOOKS
1950 Lawrence Rd, Havertown, PA 19083, USA
E-mail: Uspen-and-sword@casematepublishers.com
Website: www.penandswordbooks.com

Contents

List of Plates vii
Maps ix
Preface xi
Prologue: The Man Who Said No xiv
1. 'The Most Magnificent Thing I Ever Saw' 1
2. The Icarus School 10
3. Planes for Tobacco 16
4. 'Contingency G' 24
5. And if Fate Calls 30
6. With a Little Help from our Friends 39
7. 'God Help Us' 47
8. Thermopylae Revisited 59
9. The Flight to Egypt 73
10. The Air Force that Nearly Wasn't 82
11. Back into the Fight: El Alamein 99
12. Unlucky 13 Mira 110
13. The Other Battle of Crete 116
14. Mutiny! 134
15. Back to the Balkans 143
16. Going Home 154
Epilogue: No Rest for the Weary 160
Notes 164

Appendix I: Targets and Losses of the RHAF, 1941–1944 170
Appendix II: Scores and Victories 171
Bibliography and Related Works 172
Index of Names 173

List of Plates

1. A naval cooperation Fairey IIIF seaplane, 1938. (*Hellenic War Museum*)
2. Avro Ansons of 13 Mira over Athens, autumn 1940. (*Hellenic War Museum*)
3. PZL24s of 22 Mira lined up at Sedes, 1940. (*Hellenic War Museum*)
4. A Bloch MB151 of 24 Mira just before delivery. (*Hellenic War Museum*)
5. A 32 Mira Bristol Blenheim IV being serviced between missions near the Albanian front, March 1941. (*Hellenic War Museum*)
6. Potez 63s of 31 Mira at a base near Larissa. (*G Mermingas collection*)
7. Sqn Ldr Yannis Kellas in front of an Avro Tutor at Tatoi. (*Hellenic War Museum*)
8. The engraved wallet of Sqn Ldr Dimitrios Stathakos, given to a squadron mate for safe-keeping just before his last and fatal mission over Albania on 11 March 1941. (*G Mermingas collection*)
9. A 33 Mira Fairey Battle at Nea Anchialos. (*G Mermingas collection*)
10. A Dornier Do22, its floats removed and modified for land operations, at Eleusis airbase, 1940. (*G Mermingas collection*)
11. Sqn Ldr Marmaduke St John 'Pat' Pattle. (*G Mermingas collection*)
12. Luftwaffe reconnaissance photo of the eastern end of the Corinth Canal, probably from a Heinkel He111, April 1944. (*Hellenic War Museum*)
13. A North American T6 Harvard trainer over Rhodesia, with an unidentified Greek student pilot. (*G Mermingas collection*)
14. Personnel of 336 Mira in front of a Hawker Hurricane in North Africa, 1942. Ilias Kartalamakis is standing on the far left. (*G Mermingas collection*)
15. King George II (foreground, with hat and swagger stick) inspects the Bristol Blenheims of 13 Mira in North Africa. (*G Mermingas collection*)
16. Flt Lt Sophocles Baltatzis with his Supermarine Spitfire Vb of 335 Mira, probably late 1943. (*G Mermingas collection*)
17. A 13 Mira Martin A20 Baltimore over an Italian port, probably Bari, September 1944. (*G Mermingas collection*)
18. 13 Mira's Baltimores line up at Biferno before starting the first leg of their flight home, October 1944. (*G Mermingas collection*)

19. Retired Air Marshal Constantine Hatzilakos, aged eighty-seven, at home in Athens, 2007. (*Author's photograph*)
20. Marinos Mitralexis's widow, Anna, at home in Athens, with her husband's photo on the table, spring 2011. (*G Mermingas*)

Maps ix

Map 1. Greece and Albania showing major airfields

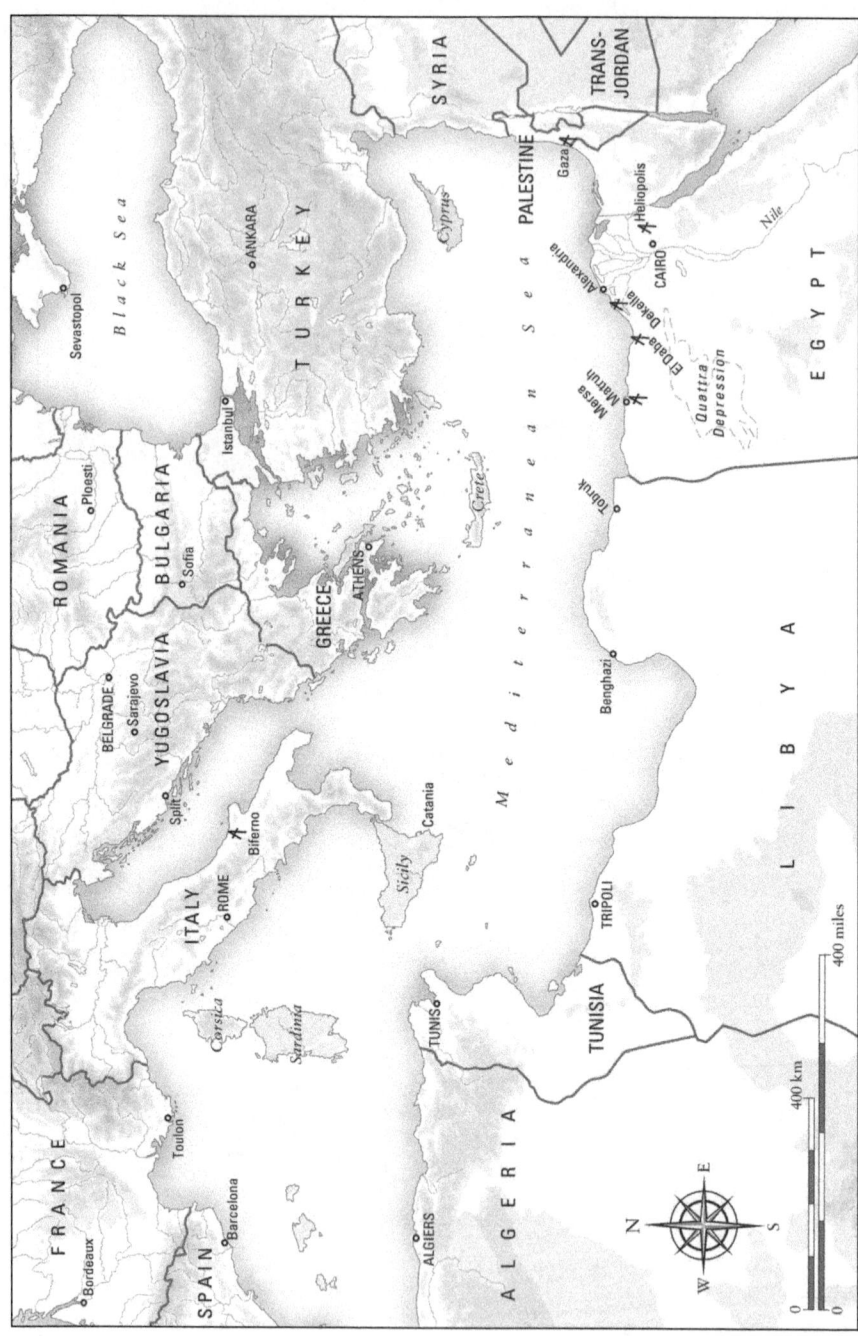

Map 2. The Mediterranean theatre showing the main airfields used by the RHAF in exile

Preface

'Soldiers and sailors in many nations,' wrote Field Marshal Montgomery of Alamein, 'are apt to forget what they owe to the air forces.'[1]

In a way, this is understandable. Whereas armies and navies have been with us for some 7,000 years, air forces are (at this writing) exactly 100 years old, a mere ripple in the great river of time. And only in the past seventy or so of those years did the aeroplane grow to become the greatest weapon of war the world had seen before the ballistic missile era. The Second World War was the motor for that stunning growth. From mere appendages of armies and navies, air forces became mighty powers in themselves, bringing with them their own theories of strategy and tactics.

Montgomery's words apply especially to Greece. Since the Greek Army fought Mussolini's invading Italians to a standstill in late 1940 and drove them back into Albania within six months, that military achievement has justly claimed pride of place in the nation's gallery of glory, up there with Marathon and Salamis. Yet the memory of that victory, perpetuated and burnished over the years by popular culture, has obscured the part played in the fight by the outnumbered and outgunned but heroic Royal Hellenic Air Force. Greece was one of those countries that in air terms had to grow up the hard way. This is that story – as gripping and moving as anything played out in the great 1939–45 conflict.

Any chronicler of the Greek air force owes an immeasurable debt to Ilias Kartalamakis, a fighter pilot in the war, whose two-volume narrative of the war years (part of a wider seven-volume history of the RHAF), is by far the most important detailed source extant. Those two volumes contain the vast bulk of aircrew recollections of the two stages of the Greek air war effort: the fight against the Italians and invading Germans in 1940–41, and the contribution to the Allied victory in North Africa and Italy from 1941 to 1944.

Inevitably, this story will contain rather more of Kartalamakis's own views and recollections than would seem to be fair to others; on the other hand, he remains our only major first-hand source, and it would hardly be fair to the reader or researcher if he were not mined to the full. Unencumbered by the rosy haze of hindsight, he pulls no punches. His accounts have the undeniable ring of authenticity – often an uncomfortable ring. He is as good at bringing to the page the atmosphere inside the cockpit of an embattled Blenheim or Hurricane as he is in teasing apart the more subtle factors at play in air power such as personal and political rivalries, and the defining influence of larger powers such as Britain's Royal Air Force.

The volumes need patience to go through. But as Mark Twain said of the memoirs of Ulysses S. Grant, they are the product of a man 'all untaught of the silken phrase-makers' and for that reason all the more valuable. Kartalamakis follows his ancient forebear Thucydides, the father of military history, in the path of realism and objectivity. He has graciously consented to my extensive use of his volumes, making the story available to the wider English-speaking world.

I also owe a great debt to George Mermingas, an aviator, reservist wing commander and expert in Greek aerial history, who made available his considerable library and archive, including many of the photographs – many never before published – in this book. He also freely gave of his judgement and expertise in cases where sources differed on key events. Retired Air Marshal Constantine Hatzilakos was also generous in providing access to his recollections and reference materials. Without the help of both, this book would have been much the poorer.

Special thanks are also due to Yannis Korodimos, the public relations director of the Hellenic War Museum, for making available the museum's photographic library and steering me towards key contacts and sources of information. The support of the following is also appreciated: Triantafyllia Katsarou of the Air Force Historical Museum, Professor Nikolaos Dimitriadis of Athens University, Air Force College lecturer Constantine Lagos and Wing Commander Panteleimon Vatakis. For valuable information on the wartime role of EEES, the Greek civil airline, thanks go to Ioanna Georgakopoulou of the University of Crete for her never-before-published research on the subject, Professor Ioannis Metaxas of Panteios University and lawyer Vasiliki Mihopoulou.

Almost from the outset the RAF played an increasingly important role in relieving some of the combat burden of the RHAF and keeping it flying. Had it not been for the RAF's help with no fewer than 265 aircraft, the Greek aerial war effort would have collapsed in short order. After the Germans occupied Greece in April 1941 and until the country's liberation in October 1944, what remained of the RHAF was absorbed into the RAF's command in the Middle East. I have not gone into too much detail on the RAF's contribution, vital as it was, as this is above all the Greeks' story. (A fuller account of the RAF's role in Greece and the Balkans can be found in Christopher Shores, Brian Cull and Nicola Malizia, *Air War for Yugoslavia, Greece and Crete*.[2])

Finally, a note on the term *mira*, the Greek term for squadron. The word derives from the ancient Spartan *mora* of about 1,000 men, instituted around the middle of the fifth century BC as part of an army reorganization. It was resurrected by the modern Greek state to denote a cavalry squadron, whence it migrated to the air force. I use 335 Mira and 336 Mira to describe what were officially known as 335 (Greek) Squadron and 336 (Greek) Squadron, RAF, as they were to all intents and purposes Greek fighting units, despite the RAF roundels on their aircraft.

This book would not have seen the light of day were it not for the steady encouragement of Philip Sidnell, commissioning editor at Pen & Sword Books, and Ting Baker, whose eagle-eyed copy-editing snagged the inevitable errors and inconsistencies that creep into even the best-tailored manuscripts.

Prologue

The Man Who Said No

In the early hours of 28 October 1940 Lieutenant Colonel Luigi Mondini, the Italian military attaché in Athens, switched on the ignition of his diplomatic car. It was a balmy night. Mondini remembered looking up at the 'myriad stars' in the clear Athenian sky. Around him the city slept – a city that in a few hours would wake up to a profound shock.

Mondini had two passengers – Emanuele Grazzi, the Italian ambassador, and an embassy interpreter. No one spoke much on the eight-mile drive through the deserted streets and out to the northern suburbs. Shortly after two o'clock Mondini drew up at the gate guard of the modest two-storey home of Ioannis Metaxas, the Greek prime minister. Surprised to see a diplomatic car arrive at that unseemly hour, the sleepy police sergeant on guard telephoned the main house that someone from the French embassy wanted to see the prime minister – in the dim light the guard had mistaken the tricoloured Italian flag above the car's front right wheel for the French one.

Metaxas emerged in his dressing gown and bedroom slippers, and ushered the three Italians into his small living room. Grazzi was, in fact, dreading what he had been instructed to do. Just hours before, resplendent in frock coats, he and the Greek prime minister had exchanged courtesies at a glittering diplomatic reception at the Italian embassy. Unknown to the guests, however, the backrooms of the embassy had been humming with the decoding of elaborate instructions – for war.

As Grazzi settled into an old brown leather armchair, he handed Metaxas an envelope. The contents were an ultimatum from Benito Mussolini: either Greece allow Italian troops to occupy 'strategic points' in north-west Greece as a 'security guarantee' against the possibility of British intervention in the Balkans, or face war.

'And what are these strategic points?' Metaxas asked, his hands trembling slightly, knowing that what he had feared for months had finally come upon him.

The unhappy Grazzi shrugged and admitted he didn't know. Metaxas knew he had no way out but the honourable one. '*Alors, c'est la guerre*,' he replied, in the French in which the meeting had been conducted. ('Well then, it's war.') Grazzi half-heartedly protested that it need not necessarily be so, but the Greek leader cut him off and escorted him and Mondini back to their car. Two hours later, Italian forces surged over the Albanian border, plunging Greece into the Second World War.

Trouble with Italy had been brewing for a long time. Though Metaxas was essentially a dictator on the southern European model of Mussolini or Spain's Franco, he had cast his lot with the British and French rather than the Axis. This attitude mystified Mussolini, who never quite seemed to be able to decide what to do with little Greece. Fearing that Metaxas might be getting too comfortable with the British and French, he was in the habit of blowing hot and cold on Greece as the mood took him, frustrating well-meaning diplomats on both sides. As for Metaxas, he was under no illusions. Much as Mussolini might periodically reassure Athens of Italy's good intentions, the Greeks knew better. As 1940 progressed, every Greek from King George II and Metaxas on down became chillingly aware that Italy was growing more hostile by the week. Metaxas's policy was to avoid irritating the Duce until Greece could pull together the military clout to confront him if he attacked.[1]

The fall of France in June threw a further shadow over Greece. There was now nothing to stop Italy from aggressing in the east if it so wished. Italian aircraft based in Albania were already making a habit of poking their noses over the Greek border with impunity. Other Italian planes harassed Greek merchant vessels in the Adriatic and Ionian seas. The crews of Ala Littoria, the Italian airline, were enlisted as spies in Rome's service when they flew on routes to the Italian-held Dodecanese islands in the southern Aegean Sea. (Many of the Ala Littoria pilots, overeager to help the national fascist cause, returned with fanciful reports of Greek island ports teeming with British warships.[2]) Italy manufactured incidents on the Albanian border, further heightening tensions. 'Will everything collapse?' Metaxas in a black mood confided to his diary in June. 'If so I'll go with the army and seek to be killed.'

On 15 August 1940 an Italian submarine torpedoed the Greek destroyer *Elli* moored at the island of Tinos during a religious festival. The loss of life was minimal but the psychological impact was tremendous. The attack had taken place on one of Greece's holiest days. Italy denied the action, even when Italian markings were found on recovered torpedo fragments. Two weeks later Metaxas received an encouraging message from Britain's Winston Churchill citing Greek valour on the ancient battlegrounds of

Marathon, Thermopylae and Salamis. The message was distributed to the press. Coming from a man whose own nation at the time was desperately fighting off waves of Luftwaffe raiders, it was a particular boost to Greek morale. Yet Metaxas kept a level head. That week he quietly ordered a call-up of the reservists of the Army's 8th and 9th Divisions.

Greece's rearmament programme was still far from complete when Grazzi delivered his midnight ultimatum. But Metaxas, fortunately for his country, had not been an overly harsh dictator. Four years into his rule, he still enjoyed a good deal of public support. After his famous riposte of 28 October 1940 that support turned into adulation. By dawn that day, bells all over Greece were ringing and young men were flocking to the colours, confident of giving the 'macaroni boys' (*makaronades*) a pasting in the mountains of Epiros.

For Prime Minister Metaxas, as he bade his midnight visitor a cold farewell, there could, of course, be no question of going back to bed. Grabbing the phone, he ordered an immediate general mobilization. One of his first calls was to Major General Panayotis Ekonomakos, an Army officer serving as the Undersecretary of State for Air. Metaxas was one of the few Greeks in high places keenly aware of the growing importance of strategic air power, and wisely kept the post of Air Minister for himself. The highest-ranking wearer of the blue RHAF uniform, Air Vice-Marshal Vasilios Tsarpalis, served as Chief of the Air Staff under Ekonomakos. Third in line in the air hierarchy was Group Captain Stergios Tilios, the head of the Higher Army Air Corps Command (ADAS), an unusual joint army-air force post, reflecting the dominant concept of Army hegemony over air operations.

On the way downtown to his office Metaxas woke up the British ambassador, Sir Michael Palairet, and through him asked Churchill for urgent air reinforcement. A year and a half before, Britain had pledged to stand by Greece if attacked, and now Metaxas was calling in the debt. By five o'clock he was chairing an emergency cabinet meeting. At first light, joined by King George II, Metaxas took a short walk through central Athens, already awash with cheering crowds. Not since Leonidas's famous riposte at Thermopylae in 480 BC had a Greek leader thus thrown down the gauntlet to a menacing superior power. But Metaxas, like the Spartan king, was under no illusions. 'God help us,' he confided to his diary.

Chapter 1

'The Most Magnificent Thing I Ever Saw'

At about lunchtime on 2 November 1940, five days after the declaration of war, Pilot Officer Marinos Mitralexis of the Royal Hellenic Air Force's 22 Pursuit Mira climbed nervously into his Polish-built PZL24 fighter. This was the opening scramble, the baptism of fire for him and his squadron's seven other pilots based at Sedes near Thessaloniki in northern Greece. An incoming formation of Italian raiders was just five miles away. As Grazzi returned to his embassy after delivering the Duce's ultimatum, Italian forces were already crossing the Albanian border into Greece and the Italian air force, the Regia Aeronautica, was on its way to bomb Greece's cities.

One by one, the eight PZLs climbed into the air. Friendly fire caused the RHAF's first war casualty. As the fighters droned overhead, jumpy anti-aircraft units around the port of Thessaloniki opened up, hitting one and seriously wounding the pilot, Sergeant Dimitrios Filis. The Italian bombers were at about 20,000 feet and at the very limit of the PZLs' operational ceiling. Mitralexis fixed a CantZ1007bis of 50 Gruppo of the Regia Aeronautica in the gunsight nestling between the fighter's gull wings. An initial burst seemed to have some effect, and he squeezed the button of his four Skoda 7.92mm machine guns again. Moving in for what he hoped would be the kill, Mitralexis found himself out of ammunition. He'd made the novice's mistake of firing too quickly with long bursts. Cursing his luck, he dithered. To let the enemy raider escape, after he had come so close to a kill, was unthinkable in the heat of battle. Mitralexis pulled back the stick to gain height. His wingman, Flight Sergeant Constantine Lambropoulos, saw what happened next.

'I was quite close to Mitralexis and saw him simply dive his plane straight into the Italian bomber,' he wrote in his mission report. 'Both planes went down. It was the most magnificent thing I ever saw.'

The nose of Mitralexis's PZL caught the CantZ's tail section, slicing off a part of the bomber's rudder and sending the plane into a spin. It also knocked out Mitralexis's engine. The four surviving Italian crew members (the pilot had been killed in the first bursts of fire) baled out to be met on the ground by a mob of angry peasants armed with scythes and pickaxes. They heard a shout and saw a diminutive Greek air force officer in flying uniform drawing his pistol and warning the villagers away. This was none other than Mitralexis, who had glided his PZL to earth with nothing worse than a bent propeller. He personally drove his dazed prisoners to Sedes in a staff car.

That wasn't the end of the day's action for the RHAF. There was a second scramble for 22 Mira in the afternoon to meet twenty-seven Italian bombers escorted by eighteen Fiat C42 biplane fighters. Lambropoulos went up and, as he wrote in his report later, was rattled by the size of the attacking force. But when five Fiats dived on two Greek PZLs, he 'stopped thinking and went straight into' the dogfight. He sent one Fiat spinning down, and then found himself in the fight of his life. 'Just when I thought all was lost,' he wrote, 'I tried a repeat of what I'd seen Mitralexis do that morning.' But an agile, wheeling Fiat was a harder target to hit than the bigger CantZ.

> I stalled, and the Fiats were all around me, firing. I got hit on my right side, right arm and right leg. My plane caught fire and I lost consciousness, reviving to find myself in a spin. With all my remaining strength I pulled the plane back on an even keel, then turned it upside down to bale out more easily.

But the battered Gladiator wouldn't give up its pilot. The lace on Lambropoulos's left flying boot got caught in the seat frame. He couldn't get out. The plane continued to spin earthwards, with its pilot pinned against the fuselage outside the cockpit and unable to move. Just when it seemed that he would plunge straight into the ground, a shell exploded near his trapped foot. A fragment sliced through the bootlace and freed him. Barefoot, he found himself in the air. 'A few moments later, before my parachute could open, my plane broke into a thousand pieces.' Even then he was not out of danger. The Italians kept on shooting at Lambropoulos as he drifted down. They didn't hit him, but his recovered parachute was found to have fifty-two holes in it.[1]

Mitralexis's feat took Greece by storm. The Icarus School, the Greek air force academy based at Tatoi, north of Athens, was swamped with volunteers. The cadets themselves became the heroes of the hour. 'None of us could wait to finish our training and get into the fight – morale was superb,' recalled one of them, Constantine Hatzilakos.[2] Serving pilots yearned to be able to repeat the stunt and slice off an Italian tail section. But no one else seemed to be able to manage it. One who tried it against a formation of Savoia-Marchetti SM79s found that turbulence in the bombers' wake made it hard for the PZL to keep a stable course and exposed it to defensive fire from the bomber.

The pilots knew they were a precious few, fewer even than the Few of the Battle of Britain. Yet like their RAF counterparts, they were given strength by that very realization. 'We are all ready to do our duty,' wrote Squadron Leader Anargyros Koudounas, the CO of newly formed 33 Bombing Mira, to his wife on the day war was announced. (He had no way of knowing it yet, but his squadron was destined to do more than its share on the Albanian front.[3])

Athens received its first taste of enemy bombing that same day. A formation of Regia Aeronautica Savoia-Marchetti SM81s had taken off from bases in southern Italy before dawn and by late morning appeared at 20,000 feet over Tatoi. As the fine art of aircraft recognition had not been part of the Icarus School curriculum, the raiders were at first mistaken for RHAF or RAF Blenheims. The school commandant, Group Captain George Falkonakis, hesitated to give the order to the anti-aircraft batteries to fire (a hesitation that would later send him before a court martial), and only when the first bombs came whistling down did he realize what was happening. The bombs went wide. A flight of Bloch MB151s under Flying Officer George Doukas was finally sent up, but by that time the raiders were well away.[4]

Cadet Hatzilakos, barely twenty years old, had already displayed a form of rare courage by enrolling in the Icarus School as a flying cadet after his elder brother Ilias, also a cadet, had perished in a training accident. 'The air raid sirens sounded, and we were ordered to put on our tin hats and man the anti-aircraft guns,' Hatzilakos recalled. 'We hadn't been trained for it, but none of us complained. All we wanted was to get into the fight.'[5]

Doros Kleiamakis, a newly minted pilot officer, was in the air checking out an old Breguet XIX, the faithful workhorse of the RHAF in the 1930s. He hadn't noticed the bombing, and when he was making his final approach to Tatoi he wondered at the anti-aircraft bursts pock-marking the sky around him. He didn't have to wonder long. He and Doukas's Bloch MB151s belatedly managed to land without being hit. It was the second time within a few months that Kleiamakis had narrowly escaped death; that summer, a pupil he was instructing had mishandled a manoeuvre near Marathon and sent the plane into a shattering crash-landing, 'turning it into toothpicks' in the rueful phrase of the time. Neither man had been seriously injured.[6]

After Tatoi the raiders turned south to unload a few more bombs on the port of Piraeus, moving on to the strategic Corinth Canal and then the western city of Patras, where many civilians were killed. Greek ground fire managed to wing one SM81, but failed to bring it down. Another Italian bomber formation, returning after having attacked the eastern port of Volos, was intercepted by the PZLs of 23 Pursuit Mira based at Larissa. Flying Officer Patroklos Bousios strained to gain height, followed by his wingman, Sergeant Yannis Kouyoumtzoglou. But Kouyoumtzoglou tried to climb a little too steeply after take-off and stalled, sending the plane skimming into the Pineios River and onto a mud bank. Kouyoumtzoglou survived, but was badly injured. Bousios, now alone in the air, saw the retreating Italian bombers outpacing him and felt himself 'physically trying to push his PZL faster'. Desperate to do something, he fired a few bursts at long range but in vain.[7]

Bad weather over north-west Greece on 29 October held up air operations except for a small Italian raid on Metsovo and a few reconnaissance flights by Greek Potez 63s. On 30 October the clouds cleared and a handful of Henschel Hs126s of 3/2 Flight of 3 Observation Mira took to the skies. Before they could locate any Italian Army columns they were jumped by five Fiat CR42s of 393 Squadriglia in the first real air battle of the campaign. One of the Henschels was riddled with bullets and crashed, killing its observer, Pilot Officer Evanghelos Giannaris, the first Greek airman to die in the war. Giannaris had volunteered for the mission in place of an Icarus School classmate who had just arrived at the squadron and had yet to find his bearings. Another Henschel was downed over Mount Smolikas, killing its crew, Pilot Officer Lazaros Papamichail and Sergeant Constantine Yemenetzis. That same day, the battered city of Patras took another pounding.

The weather closed in again on 31 October, but that didn't prevent a Blenheim of 32 Bombing Mira, based at Trikala in central Greece, from trying to photograph the Italian airbase at Korce. The whole squadron turned out to watch as the Blenheim, flown by Flying Officer Dimitrios Papageorgiou, with Pilot Officer Kleanthos Hadjioannou as navigator/observer and Warrant Officer George Sakis as gunner, gunned its engines for take-off. But heavy rain during the night had turned the runway into a quagmire, and the Blenheim's wheels refused to come unstuck. The 32 Mira CO, Squadron Leader Haralambos Potamianos, was determined that the mission should go on, and ordered one of the squadron's crack pilots, Flying Officer Alexander Papaioannou, into the pilot's seat in place of Papageorgiou.

Papaioannou decided to take off unconventionally, with the help of a tailwind to sweep him off the ground. As he slammed the throttles forward at full strength and raced down the strip, he recalled the mud spattering up from the undercarriage making 'a hellish noise' against the fuselage. Still the nose wouldn't lift. He was on the verge of aborting when the Blenheim finally came unstuck with a loud groan. After circling the base once, Papaioannou set course for the Albanian border.

The flight was tense. As the plane was unescorted, for all the crew knew the Regia Aeronautica could easily blow them out of the sky. They landed back at base without incident, but when the film was sent for developing it was found to be completely blank. The cameras hadn't worked. (They were later replaced by more efficient British-made Eagle cameras.) One source of satisfaction for 32 Mira, though, was the fact that it had gone up against the enemy, and the enemy hadn't fought back.[8]

The RHAF's mission was officially to provide air cover for the Greek 8th Division, which was bearing the brunt of the Italian land incursion. Lieutenant General Alexander Papagos, the Greek commander-in-chief, had his hands full with the ground war from the outset and pretty much left air operational tactics to Group Captain Tilios, who didn't have very much leeway for initiative. Tilios and other senior air officers were essentially army officers in blue, restricted entirely to carrying out orders from the General Staff, which concentrated on supporting ground operations. The air force followed the prevailing European model of acting as long-range artillery. The use of dive-bombers in the Germans' recent *blitzkrieg* tactics against Poland and France – a matter of smashing through the enemy lines and fortifications – typified the thinking of the time. On the contrary, the lessons from the Battle of Britain, where for the first time opposing air fleets had to work out aerial tactics against each other, had yet to reach Greece.

To be fair, the first days of the war didn't leave the Greeks much time for thinking. Tilios was thrown in at the deep end by the immediate need to repel the incoming bomber raids as well as make squadrons available to support the ground war. As there had been no serious preparation for such an eventuality, the script had to be improvised day by day.

The initial problem was that the Italian bombers were coming in at high altitude – at least 20,000 feet, the limit of the PZL's operational ceiling. As three Italian divisions, the Siena, Ferrara and mechanized Centauro, trundled towards their first objective of Ioannina, the RHAF could only make pinpricks against the Regia Aeronautica's bombers. 'We didn't know how to fly then,' recalled Doukas. 'We couldn't even shoot. We knew nothing of firing distances or angles of attack. We went to war in close formation, as if we were on parade. Only later, and from the British, did we learn about evasive manoeuvres.' For example, when two formations of nine PZLs each flew over Trebesina in Albania in impeccable V-formation, they were easy meat for the enemy. On that mission two pilots died and a third was wounded. 'We were blown out of the sky,' Doukas said.[9]

Two Potez 63 bombers of 31 Mira were ordered into action on the second day of hostilities to carry out a reconnaissance of the Italians' main supply routes through the mountain valleys of southern Albania. The narrow and winding roads through these valleys were vulnerable, but on the other hand often shrouded in mist. An aerial attack on such terrain was filled with hazards. The squadron CO, Flight Lieutenant George Karnavias, skippering the lead plane, was well aware of the dangers. But he and his wingman, Flight Lieutenant Lambros Kouziyannis, trusted the abilities of the fast and manoeuvrable Potez 63. Flak got Kouziyannis's plane as it dived below cloud cover at 600 feet. Shrapnel peppered the fuselage and a 37mm shell penetrated the cockpit, rolled between the feet of the navigator/observer, Pilot Officer Nikolaos Troupakis, and exploded inside the camera mechanism. Though Troupakis was miraculously unhurt, a shell fragment hit Kouziyannis in the head, stunning him. With the cockpit canopy blown to bits, the Potez lurched into a spin. Cold air rushing into the cockpit revived Kouziyannis, who pulled the bomber level.

Bleeding and fighting off dizziness, Kouziyannis sought the refuge of cloud cover. Emerging from the cloud, he narrowly missed flying into a mountain peak near Metsovo. 'A little more to the left, and we wouldn't have had the chance to learn where exactly we had been killed,' he recalled later, with the sepulchral humour typical of Greek pilots of the time. As he was trying to recover from that second shock, Troupakis calmly informed him that five Fiats had passed blithely overhead. Kouziyannis managed to land at the 31 Mira base at Niamata near Larissa, slumping in a dead faint as soon as he came to a stop. A squadron surgeon found that the shell fragment had come within millimetres of penetrating Kouziyannis's brain. What had saved him was the plane's camera, which had absorbed the shell's impact.

The squadron was ordered into action again on 1 November to bomb enemy artillery positions and mechanized units at Doliana and Kalpaki, inside the Greek border. The Italians were advancing and it was imperative that they be halted before they got within shelling distance of Ioannina, the first key city in their path. Metaxas, the prime minister, telephoned Group Captain Stephanos Philippas at RHAF bomber headquarters at Larissa. 'Listen, Philippas,' Metaxas barked in his Germanic, no-nonsense style, 'send planes to bomb the column at Doliana even if none of them comes back.'[10] There was one snag – the operation would have to be done at night.

As Karnavias was preparing three Potez 63s for the operation at Niamata base, Troupakis approached him. 'We don't mind going in, sir,' Troupakis said, 'but what about coming back? We've never flown at night before.' The CO didn't need reminding of that uncomfortable fact. He had no answers. But Metaxas had ordered it, and that was that. As a CO should, he put on a brave face.

'Do it for me, lads,' Karnavias said. 'Do it for your commanding officer. I trust you, you'll pull off this thing.'

The sun was about to set when Pilot Officer Anastasios Vladousis led off the first Potez, followed by Troupakis, this time on pilot duty. Kouziyannis, his head bandaged, wanted to skipper the third plane. Karnavias tried to dissuade him, but he insisted. 'I've got to fly while I still can,' Kouziyannis told his CO. 'The target won't wait.' He got his way.

At that moment Vladousis was droning at 12,000 feet over a blacked-out landscape. Only the feeble lamplights of a monastery perched on top of the Meteora cliffs were visible. Presently the town and shimmering lake of Ioannina passed beneath, and soon the lights of the lead Italian columns at Kalpaki came into view north of the city. Vladousis pushed the Potez into a steep dive and released his bombs, bucking the shock waves as he levelled out at a very low height. Troupakis bombed next, guided by the fires and the string of vehicle lights indicating where the column was. Streams of fiery flak tracer criss-crossed the sky. Kouziyannis arrived over the target after a twenty-seven-minute flight by instruments alone and dazzled by the glare of the Potez's exhausts over the wings. When he saw the burning column he dived through a hail of flak and bombed where he could. On the climb-out his navigator/observer, Pilot Officer Spyros Kovatzis, suddenly began firing his single defensive MAC 7.5mm machine gun. Kouziyannis ordered him to stop, as there was no apparent target in sight and the shooting could give away their position.

'Let me shoot, sir,' Kovatzis replied. 'How can I go back without firing a single bullet?' Caught up in the spirit of combat, he couldn't bear sitting in the back of the cockpit without doing anything.

The trip back was fraught with hazard. Vladousis was relieved to see the winking candles of the Meteora monastery again; it meant that Niamata wasn't far off. Troupakis thought he saw the same light, but somehow failed to see the Niamata runway lights – a wing probably obscured them – and presently found himself over the Aegean Sea off the east coast. He turned round, saw the lights, and as soon as he landed and taxied in his port engine cut out, starved of fuel. Karnavias, overwrought with anxiety over his men's fate after their first night mission, rushed out and hugged Troupakis. Only Kouziyannis hadn't yet arrived. As the anxious minutes passed, Karnavias asked the Larissa air defence chief, an Army colonel, to switch on his searchlights to help Kouziyannis to find his way to base. The colonel refused; he didn't want to light up Larissa for the benefit of any enemy bombers that might be on the way.

Droning through the blackness on his way back, Kouziyannis realized he was lost. Keeping an anxious eye on his fuel gauge, he decided to head south for the familiar coastlines of the Gulf of Corinth and the Athens area to get his bearings and hopefully land at Tatoi. The lights of the coastal fishing villages and towns guided him until, over the island of Salamis and its strategic naval base, he was blinded by searchlights. Kouziyannis signalled an SOS with his navigation lights, and luckily the Salamis anti-aircraft guns didn't open up. At 12,000 feet over the Athens seaside suburb of Faliron, his fuel gauge touched zero. 'You'd better prepare to jump,' he told Kovatzis. 'Don't worry. You'll reach the ground sitting on a deck chair. I'll keep the plane level to give you time to get out.'

The news came as a shock to Kovatzis. He'd no idea what was happening, as until now Kouziyannis had kept their predicament to himself. 'What's wrong, skipper?' Kovatzis said. 'Haven't we got to Larissa yet?'

By way of reply, the Potez's engines cut out and the bomber dipped its nose in a glide. There was no question of baling out now, as Kouziyannis, a former instructor familiar with the fine art of forced landings, nursed the powerless bomber over blacked-out Athens towards Tatoi, which by now had been alerted. Guided by the runway lights, which took an agonizingly long time to grow in his sight, Kouziyannis only just cleared the airfield perimeter and dropped to a landing. He had just breathed a fervent, 'Thank you, Virgin Mary,' when a jarring crash shook the plane. A parked Avro Tutor had been in the way. The collision slewed the Potez off its course, snapping off its undercarriage. When the plane finally came to a stop, Kouziyannis was paralyzed by a sudden violent pain in his lower back. In the hospital they found two broken vertebrae, which left him a cripple for the rest of his life.

That day, the fourth day of hostilities, the Greek Army II Corps was holding the hard-pressed Metsovo sector. The corps command needed an aeroplane to drop tactical orders to the front-line units. An initial attempt to do so resulted in the plane running into a fusillade of friendly fire and having to abort the mission.[11] At about the ssame time, the Regia Aeronautica's bombers took their first crack at Thessaloniki. Leading the raid was the Italian foreign minister himself, Count Galeazzo Ciano, who had been in Albania waiting for the weather to clear so that he could earn himself a combat medal – something apparently missing from his formal dress tunic. 'A spectacular bombing,' Ciano wrote in his diary, with perhaps a touch of exaggeration. 'Attacked by Greek aircraft on the way back. All went well. Two were shot down, though I must confess that it was the first time I had them behind me and I felt very uncomfortable.' The RHAF, on the contrary, reported no fighters lost that day. Ciano, in fact, had narrowly missed destroying a building containing Italian consular staff and their families in the process of being shipped out as enemy aliens.[12]

Thanks to Metaxas's determination and foresight, the Greek fighter force had been dispersed to bases around the country. Until 1940 the bulk of the force had been concentrated at Sedes, as the main threat to Greek security was viewed as coming from neighbouring Bulgaria. With the Italian occupation of Albania, 21 Mira was moved south to Vasiliki near Trikala, in the shadow of the mountains of Epiros, while 23 Mira moved to Larissa to guard the eastern port of Volos. Moreover, Ala Littoria, the Italian civil airline, used Sedes on its eastern routes and undoubtedly its crews took accurate note of the fighter strength they saw. 22 Mira was left to guard Thessaloniki, whose factories and port were a prime target for the Italians. It was also from there that Greek infantry units were processed to the Albanian front.

The first wave of SM79s of 107 Gruppo and 262 and 263 Squadriglie based at Grottaglie in southern Italy was followed by another of CantZ1007s of 47 Stormo. Bruno and Vittorio Mussolini, the Duce's two sons, were among the pilots of the latter formation earning their own baptism of fire – which wasn't much. 21 Mira scrambled to meet the raiders, but all it could accomplish was one 'probable' victory which, however, does not appear in the Italian records. The Greeks suffered no losses, though Italian bombs killed scores of people in Thessaloniki and Larissa.

A formation of Blenheims of 32 Mira under Flying Officer Constantine Margaritis took off from Athens and, evading Italian formations coming the other way, bombed the operations headquarters of Korce airfield well inside Albania. One bomb smashed through the roof of the Korce ops room where Italian aircrews had gathered for a pre-mission briefing, killing nineteen airmen and wounding twenty-five. Two Italian fighters, one CR32 and one CR42, were damaged trying to land on the cratered runway after failing to stop the Greek raid.[13]

As a measure of how ill-equipped to fight a war most Greek squadrons were, the pilots of the Fairey Battles of 33 Mira, for example, could communicate with their gunner/observers in the back only through a speaking tube. And even then the speaking tube was virtually useless, as the engine noise would drown out anything being said. At the outbreak of war the squadron had only one map of southern Albania, to be rotated among the crews. On one mission, Flying Officer Sarandis Skatzikas wanted to ask his gunner for the map, but found no way to do it. 'I couldn't even find a piece of paper and pencil to write to him,' he recalled later.[14]

Chapter 2

The Icarus School

In Greek mythology Icarus was the son of Daedalus, a skilled craftsman who built the Labyrinth for the Cretan Minotaur and did the job so well that the half-bull, half-human Minotaur wouldn't let Daedalus return to his native Athens. Daedalus, though, figured that if he couldn't go home by sea, he would go by air. So, the myth goes, he fashioned a pair of wings out of wax and feathers, and bound them with linen fastenings.

After making another pair for his son, both of them set out (we are not told how they took off) and were soon over the blue Aegean Sea. Daedalus had warned Icarus not to fly too high as there was a risk that the sun would melt the wax and he would crash. But in his youthful exuberance Icarus recklessly gained altitude, only to suffer what his father had feared and plunge into the sea. In the minds of those who set up the RHAF flying college in 1931, Icarus, with his adventuresome spirit and disdain for death, was a better role model for Greece's modern aerial warriors than his more cautious father. Since before the Second World War the college has become known as the Icarus School.

It was fitting that the aerodrome at Sedes, where 22 Mira was based, should figure prominently in the opening days of Greece's air war in 1940. Sedes was a village outside Thessaloniki where, almost exactly thirty years before, on 18 October 1910, a French pilot had carried out the first known display flight in Greek history. In 1912 the space was expanded to accommodate a Hanriot captured from the Turks in the First Balkan War. The following year Sedes became the home base of the Greek Army's 'Air Company,' a department of the Engineer Corps, with one Henri Farman HF20 and two Maurice Farman MF7 trainers on its strength.[1]

Greece had received its first taste of air warfare as early as 1912, when a Greek army under Crown Prince Constantine was on the march in the mountains of Western Greece. Their goal was the city of Ioannina, held by the Ottoman Turks for more than half a millennium but Greek in population and sentiment. The Second Balkan War was nearing its climax.

By December 1912 the Greeks had slogged their way northwards through snow and mud to Emin Aga about twenty miles from Ioannina.

The Turkish defences around Ioannina were considerable. The staff of the Greek 2nd Division, charged with assaulting the city, wanted to find out where the strong points were. On 5 December Lieutenant Michalis Moutousis was ordered aloft from a rough field at Preveza in his Henri Farman HF20, one of three that the Greek Army operated, to take a look. The soldiers cheered him on his way as he flew over their lines on take-off and climbed to 4,200 feet, guided on course by the long mass of Mount Xerovouni on his right. At Bizani, just south of Ioannina, he dropped to 2,000 feet for a good look at the Turkish defences. Going one step further in the military use of aircraft, he lobbed a few hand grenades on a Turkish column. The Turks fired back. He landed back at Preveza with three holes in the Farman's wood and fabric – and a hero's status among the army rank and file. Four days later Moutousis repeated the stunt, carefully noting positions and again getting shot at for his pains. This time the enemy bullets merely grazed the landing gear.[2]

Moutousis's brief mission was the second bombing raid in history. He had been pipped by a matter of five weeks by Giulio Gavotti, a second lieutenant in the Italian Army air corps, who retains the distinction of being history's first bomber pilot. Gavotti had dropped four explosive devices on Turkish held-bases in Libya on 1 November 1912. It's a curiosity of history that a Greek and an Italian airman independently made an identical great stride in aerial warfare, two years before the outbreak of the First World War, and that less than three decades later, the airmen of both countries were pitted against one another.

Greece managed to stay neutral during most of the First World War thanks to the pro-German sentiments of King Constantine I, who as crown prince had led the Greeks to victory in 1913. Constantine was a brother-in-law of Kaiser Wilhelm II and could perhaps be excused his family feeling. But those were not the sentiments of Eleftherios Venizelos, a capable politician who had become prime minister in 1915 and strongly favoured the British and French. After a dispute with the king that almost triggered a civil war, Venizelos moved to Thessaloniki to set up a separate pro-Entente government. There, with French help, Greek military aviation received its first real boost. On 4 September 1917 a formal flying training programme began at Sedes, with thirty officers and ninety-three enlisted men on the staff. Pilots and observers were qualified after three months of instruction.[3]

By the time the Greek Army was able to join the final Allied assault on the Macedonian front in September 1918, it could boast its first proper squadron. This was 532 Reconnaissance Mira, equipped with Breguet XIVs, the mainstay of Greek air power throughout the 1920s. Joining this unit were 531 Pursuit Mira with the Nieuport 24bis and Spad VII and VIII, while 533 and 534 Mirai were assigned to patrol the northern Greek border area against the constant threat of Bulgaria seeking an outlet to the Aegean Sea. After the Armistice, 531 Mira was disbanded. Greece's first flying fatality occurred at Sedes on 27 February 1919 when Lieutenant Dimitrios Anninos lost control of his aircraft during an air show.

Because of its geographical position, Sedes became the focal point of developments in Greek military aviation throughout the 1920s.[4] By 1927 the aerodrome had evolved into a proper flight training base equipped with new hangars and Potez 25 and Morane-Saulnier MS137 advanced trainers – a testimony to early French control over the birth of Greece's air power. At that time Sedes also began to share civil aviation duties with the country's emergent domestic airline, the Hellenic Aerial Transport Company (EEES).

Alexander Zannas was a precocious officer who had learned much from the French at Sedes. In the 1920s he was one of those relatively few Europeans who foresaw that the military aeroplane would come to dominate warfare. He caught the attention of Venizelos, who served several times as Greece's prime minister in the inter-war years and is credited with raising the country's aerial profile. A drive to upgrade the fledgeling air force was begun in 1925, and four years later an Air Ministry (*Ypourgeion Aeroporias*) was set up. Zannas seemed the natural choice to head the ministry. But given the unstable Greek politics of the time, he preferred to operate behind the scenes instead of in the fickle public eye; he talked Venizelos, the prime minister, into heading the Air Ministry himself, ensuring that decisions in that sector would have clout.[5]

Thanks to the efforts of those two men, in 1931 the Greek Air Force College was set up. That year's cadet intake – all of eleven men out of some 250 applicants – were among the first to wear the new blue RHAF uniform, consciously modelled on that of the RAF. In this the air force followed the Greek Navy, which had been pro-British since its inception, as opposed to the Army, which retained French-style *kepis* for the officers. The similarity in uniform, rank stripes and insignia would subconsciously help weld Greek and British airmen together in a common cause when the crunch came.

Life in the newly minted RHAF officer corps was no means easy. Zannas had more than enough of a task on his hands melding Army and Navy fliers into a single service and placating the intense rivalry between the two senior services, not always successfully. For some time, officers derived from the Army and Navy were allowed to wear their own service uniforms and badges of rank along with the RHAF ones. This caused some confusion among gate guards, who didn't know whether to demand the Army or Navy password when such a confusingly bedecked officer showed up! The Army and Navy (not surprisingly) had differing approaches to everything, including air training methods. The result was a continuous compromise process that did nothing to advance the concept of independent air force tactics. It was a lack for which the RHAF would pay heavily when war came.[6]

Politics was a constant menace. At one point in 1932 it looked as if the air force would have a brief life indeed when Venizelos was unseated as prime minister and his opponents pandered to the fears of the Army and Navy chiefs, ever disdainful of the upstart RHAF, that an independent air force might usurp their own influence and even, heaven forbid, form its own power centre. One otherwise reasonable senior admiral dismissed the air force as 'a stunted child born of misshapen parents and raised by ignorant guardians.'[7] The new government, to its credit, resisted these pressures. But the air force college only just managed to stay in business when its commandant, Wing Commander Panayotis Vilos, a former Navy man trained in Britain, threatened to resign. The college intakes of 1932 and 1933 reflected the crisis – just nine and seven flying training cadets respectively, the lowest number in its history.[8] Yet they were enough to keep it going.

Lingering rivalry, often escalating into bitter enmity, between the Army and Navy traditions would continue to plague the RHAF until well into the war. Yet neither senior service was above using the tiny air force for its own purposes when the occasion arose. Two attempted *coups d'état* by disaffected Army generals in the 1930s resulted in a crippling purge and subsequent reinstatement of some RHAF officers. A key step out of this predicament was taken in August 1934, when the General Air Staff was set up to reduce the airmen's dependency on the politically volatile Army. Partly as a result, the Air Force College intake numbers began to rise – sixteen in 1934, twenty-eight in 1935, eighteen in 1936 and twenty-seven in 1937. In fact, it might well be argued that the constant struggle to maintain a service identity against unstable politics and attacks from the other services helped the RHAF forge a strong and independent core. Yet by the outbreak of war, pilots deriving from the Army and Navy still heavily outnumbered the 'real' air force types.[9]

The officers' training course at Tatoi lasted three years. Flying training began in the third or fourth week on Avro 621 Tutors assembled at a local branch of Britain's Blackburn aircraft manufacturers at Faliron by the Athens seaside. A cadet could go solo after a minimum of twelve and maximum of twenty hours' instruction. Advanced training was done in the Morane-Saulnier MS320, a high-wing monoplane with a rakish sweep-back. The three-seat Avro 626 was used for aerial gunnery practice.

Despite the strict methods of the French – and later British – flight instructors, Greek pilots from the first displayed a sometimes invigorating, sometimes alarming, propensity for flying on the wild side. Not for nothing did they hold up their mythical forebear Icarus as a role model. Naturally, training accidents multiplied. The first college intake lost one cadet in an accident and another who was washed out during the course, but it managed to graduate more or less intact on 12 October 1934 – the first nine men to wear the RHAF wings under exclusive air force training. A few of these nine were to take their 'purist' air force college status somewhat too seriously in the war years, forming the core of a movement to rid the air force of its 'alien' Army and Navy aviators – but in the process hamper the RHAF's contribution to the Allied cause.

In October 1935 the Air Ministry reorganized flying training along tighter schedules and safety rules. In that year a veteran airman named Dimitrios Kamberos, one of the country's very first fliers with a record in the Balkan Wars, proposed that the air force college be unoffically named the Icarus School. The name somehow stuck, is now official, and for nearly eighty years has shown no signs of changing. The first eight intakes of the Icarus School from 1931 to 1938 produced the RHAF's first solid, professional cadre of officers – some 130 men – that despite the simmering resentment over the preponderance of Army and Navy fliers would see the service competently through the Second World War and fill its senior posts into the 1970s.

In the mid-1930s Greek rearmament concentrated naturally on the Army and Navy, with the poor-sister air force left panting behind. The RHAF may on paper have been a separate service, but it remained firmly under the thumb of the senior service staffs. Besides five observation *mirai* directly under Army control as army cooperation units, the three bomber and four pursuit *mirai* were administered by the Higher Army Air Corps Command (ADAS). Three seaplane *mirai* operated under the Higher Naval Aviation Command (ADAN.) All the Air Ministry actually administered were the main air bases, the Air Force College and other flying schools, the anti-aircraft batteries, the aircraft assembly and repair factory at Faliron and miscellaneous stores.

It took the accession to near-absolute power of Ioannis Metaxas in the summer of 1936 for Greece to finally acquire a rearmaments programme worthy of the name.

Metaxas, though a brilliant product of the German school of military and national discipline, never made any secret of his conviction that Greece, with its hundreds of islands and long and convoluted coastline, should be a natural ally of Great Britain, the dominant naval power in the Mediterranean. In early 1939, as the war clouds gathered, he insisted on hardening Anglo-Greek friendship into a formal alliance. But Sir Neville Chamberlain, the British prime minister, was into his Axis-appeasement stage and shied away from anything more binding than an informal promise.

Since May, Metaxas had been unobtrusively decentralizing the RHAF's pursuit and bombing *mirai* from the main base at Sedes to more scattered stations. Neither had he been idle on the diplomatic front. Having rather better relations with the Germans than with Fascist Italy (he had been top of his class in the Imperial German War Academy in 1903), he hoped he could talk Hitler into restraining Mussolini. The Fuehrer himself suspected that the Duce was toying with the idea of invading Greece and didn't approve. At a time when the issue over the skies of Britain was far from decided, and an invasion of Britain was still on the cards in Berlin, Hitler believed action against Greece would be a waste of Axis manpower and energy. But the stream of grim cables from the Greek embassy in Rome – partly the result of sloppy Italian security – left Metaxas and the Greeks in no doubt about what was going to happen. The countdown to war was now irreversible. The Greeks prepared for war, according to a noted British historian, 'with efficiency and a heroic confidence in their still unwritten alliance with Britain.'[10]

Chapter 3

Planes for Tobacco

The RHAF entered 1940 with no developed operational doctrine apart from the subordination to ground and sea warfare demands. Moreover, it couldn't quite shake off a dilettantist image as a flying club for well-to-do and restless young men. The Icarus School was good at teaching pilots how to keep an impeccable parade formation but not how to fight an enemy in the air. The senior services still rested on the laurels of their successes in the Balkan Wars nearly three decades before. The brief Greek experience of the First World War and the tragic outcome of the Asia Minor War with Turkey (1920–22), had a discouraging effect on any innovative military thinking. In the inter-war years the Navy – less tainted by the Asia Minor debacle than the Army – attracted more talent, including that of the flying sort. On land, the Army stuck to a strictly defensive policy. It had considerable faith in the 'Metaxas Line' along the Bulgarian border, built on the model of the Maginot Line – a fortification that was destined to collapse as completely as its fabled French counterpart under the German assaults.

And so Greece was dragged into the Second World War, according to a modern air historian, with 'a small air force equipped with mostly old and obsolete aircraft'.[1]

The bell-ringing and cheering on 28 October couldn't hide the stark fact that rarely has a European air force been in a worse shape to fight a modern war as the RHAF was on that date. With barely one-sixth of the strength of its opponents, it could field 128 operational aircraft – though by no means all of these were ready for service – out of a total of 158. This was all that Group Captain Tilios had to work with as he ordered the five Army cooperation *mirai* to locate invading columns and the four pursuit *mirai* to repel the expected Italian bombing raids. At the same time, the three bomber *mirai* were to go for Italian supply lines and troop concentrations, plus enemy air bases inside Albania at Tirana, Berat, Gjirokaster, Sarande and Vlore. The four Navy cooperation *mirai* were to remain on alert for the time being.[2] The country's aviation fuel stock of 1,500 tonnes was deemed enough for twenty-five days of operations.[3] The country's total aircrew, officers and

NCOs, amounted to about 300.[4] The front-line battle strength of the RHAF at the outbreak of war consisted of:

- 1 Observation (or Army Cooperation) Mira under I Corps command, with Breguet XIXs, based at Perigiali near Corinth.
- 2 Observation Mira under II Corps command, with Breguet XIXs based at Larissa and Kozani.
- 3 Observation Mira under III Corps command, with Henschel Hs126s based at Thessaloniki and Veria.
- 4 Observation Mira, partly under IV Corps command, with Potez 25s based at Veria and Florina.
- 2828 Independent Observation Flight under 8th Division command, with Breguet XIXs based at Dekeleia and Tanagra near Athens.
- 11 Naval Cooperation Mira with Fairey IIIF seaplanes, based at Trikeri near Volos.
- 12 Naval Cooperation Mira with Dornier Do22Kg seaplanes, based near Athens.
- 13 Naval Cooperation Mira with Avro Anson Mk Is, based first at Araxos and later near Athens.
- 21 Pursuit Mira with PZL24s and Gloster Gladiator Mk IIs, based first at Sedes and later at Trikala.
- 22 Pursuit Mira with PZL-24s, based at Thessaloniki.
- 23 Pursuit Mira with PZL-24s, based at Larissa.
- 24 Pursuit Mira with Bloch MB151s, nominally independent but in actuality under Army control, based at Sedes.
- 31 Bombing Mira with Potez 63s, based first near Athens and later at Larissa.
- 32 Bombing Mira with Bristol Blenheim IVs, based at the same locations as 31 Mira.
- 33 Bombing Mira with Fairey Battle Mk Is, based first near Athens and later at Nea Anchialos.

A standard *mira*, similar to an RAF squadron or Luftwaffe *Geschwader*, was made up of twelve aircraft. The RHAF had no larger unit such as a wing or a group. In terms of numbers, the total RHAF strength at the outset was:

- 18 Breguet XIXs (nine of which were unserviceable)
- 15 Potez 25s
- 16 Henschel Hs126s
- 11 Potez 63s (three unserviceable)
- 12 Bristol Blenheim IVs (one unserviceable)
- 12 Fairey Battles (two unserviceable)

- 35 PZL24s (at least seven unserviceable)
- 9 Bloch MB151s (three unserviceable)
- 9 Fairey IIIFs
- 12 Dornier Do22Kgs
- 9 Avro Anson Mk Is
- 6 Avia B534s
- 2 Gloster Gladiator Mk IIs
- 6 Hawker Horsley IIs
- 20 Avro Tutors
- 22 Avro 626s
- 3 Junkers Ju52s, pressed into service from civil aviation
- 4 Junkers G24s, similarly requisitioned

This confusingly mixed bag of equipment reflected the erratic procurement procedures of the 1930s. There were two main reasons for this. First Greece, anxious to stay on the good side of the major aircraft-producing powers, had ordered some from each. Second, as the decade progressed, Metaxas was pressed to seek aircraft from any available source.[5] To help meet the needs of the air force, the poor and neglected sister in the Greek military family, the Federation of Greek Industry in 1937 decided to pass the hat around the captains of industry for contributions to build up national air strength. A considerable sum was raised that way. Then an investigation by a financial newspaper found that those industrialists who earned the biggest profits had contributed the least. True or not, the report was believed by Metaxas who sacked his national economy minister. But the money raised was enough for the government to confidently begin ordering new aircraft.[6]

The first stage of aerial rearmament was a contract for the purchase of thirty-six PZL24s from Poland's Panstwowe Zaklady Lotnicze in return for the equivalent value in Greek tobacco – a profitable exchange, if ever there was one. A quantity of Bristol Blenheim IVs – one of Europe's most modern bombers at the time – was also ordered. By 1939 Greece had also placed firm orders for thirty-four Supermarine Spitfire Is, thirty Grumman F4F3A Wildcats, thirty Curtiss P40 Tomahawks, forty-eight Martin Maryland bombers and twenty-four Bristol Blenheim IIIs, plus an undetermined number of French-built Liore-et-Olivier 451Gs, a high-altitude bomber advanced for its time; the outbreak of war cancelled all scheduled deliveries, leaving the RHAF short of 107 modern aircraft that would have at least doubled its strength in the battles that would soon be upon it.[7]

Among the deliveries from Britain were twelve Fairey Battle Mk I bombers, with an option for twelve more. The Greeks appreciated the dive-bombing capabilities of the Battle, especially in mountainous terrain, which could compensate for its low speed and relative lack of defensive armament.[8] At the same time wealthy Greeks abroad donated four machines. Yet by 1940, *Jane's All The World's Aircraft* of that year could devote just six brief paragraphs to a description of Greece's service aviation, while Italy's took up six pages.[9] At least three of the six ageing Yugoslav-built Avia B534 fighters had been donated by a rich Greek-American businessman, while another paid for the only two Gloster Gladiators in RHAF service. The PZL24s were destined to stoutly bear the brunt of fighter operations on the Albanian front.[10]

As hostilities proceeded Britain would send considerable help. The RAF would pitch in with dozens more aircraft and aircrews and vital air combat know-how. But that was still in the future as the puny RHAF braced to meet the onslaught of the hundreds of shiny new fighters and bombers of Italy's Regia Aeronautica, one of the strongest air forces in Europe at that time, with pilots who had honed their air combat skills in the Spanish Civil War. The exact number of combat-ready aircraft that Greece had on hand when Metaxas turned down Mussolini's ultimatum is disputed. Official records differ. But it would be safe to put the number at around ninety-five, with seventy-nine ready for action.

In the tense summer of 1940 new sources of aircrew had to be found. One involved a scheme to build up a supply of commissioned and non-commissioned aircrew reservists. Other reservists came from the ranks of the National Youth Organization (EON), set up on the German and Italian model. The handful of private civil pilots in the country were offered air force commissions, but there is no record of any Greek combat pilot coming from that quarter. Yet enthusiasm helped make up for the lack of numbers. There was certainly no lack of applicants for the Icarus School at Tatoi. But from the first day of the war the college proved vulnerable to bombing raids, and so in December the college was disbanded and transferred to Argos, about a hundred miles south-west of Athens, to be renamed the Flight Training Centre (EKI). This centre had the task of turning out as many aircrew as possible in a condensed four month training course. The 1938 intake of the Icarus School was hurriedly graduated a year early, but those of the 1939 intake weren't as lucky. Besides having to settle for NCO status because their course was interrupted, they had to start their basic training on Avro Tutors all over again!

Thirty-six PZL24 monoplanes, in service since 1938, were allocated among 21, 22 and 23 Pursuit Mirai, but only twenty-four of these were airworthy on 28 October. It proved to be a machine popular with its pilots. With its high gull wing giving the pilot a clear field of vision for firing, it was fast for its time at 430kph. Its robust all-metal construction made it trustworthy in a hard dive. 'The PZL24 was great at aerobatics,' Hatzilakos recalled. It also sounded good. 'In a dive it gave out a hell of a whine. We all wanted to hurry up and qualify and get into it.'

The PZL's main shortcoming was its fixed undercarriage, a definite disadvantage in 1940 but nowhere inferior to the Italian fixed-undercarriage biplanes it would soon confront. The sturdy little fighter had acquitted itself well in the German invasion of Poland, even against an adversary such as the Messerschmitt Bf109. In Greek hands it would give the opposing Fiat CR32 and CR42 biplane fighters as good as it got. But spare parts had stopped arriving after the German conquest of Poland a year before, and thus the useful days of the PZL24 were clearly numbered. None of this mattered to the cadets who were itching to get into the cockpit of a PZL after their dull and docile Avro Tutors.

The newest aircraft in Greece's fighter force were nine French-built Bloch MB151 monoplanes in 24 Pursuit Mira, the only ones delivered out of twenty-five ordered, as the fall of France cancelled the rest. The Bloch MB151 had the appearance of a sleek, modern fighter, but it had a slow rate of climb and was heavy at the controls. Yet it manoeuvred well and could take considerable punishment. Its armament consisted of two 20mm Hispano 404 cannon and two 7.5mm MAC machine guns. Its main drawback was the 900hp Gnome-Rhone engine that was prone to overheating. The Bloch was not a favourite of the crews of 24 Mira, who would joke that its main value was that jumpy Italian pilots would sometimes mistake its humped profile for a feared RAF Hawker Hurricane and make themselves scarce!

The two Gloster Gladiator Mk IIs were allocated to 21 Pursuit Mira. By December the RAF would donate fourteen second-hand Gladiators to Greece. They were welcome, even though many were worn out and lacked vital parts. Unlike the RAF version, the underpowered and fatigued Greek Gladiators, even with their four Browning .303 machine guns, were a poor match for the the Italians. The RHAF's Avia BH33Es and two Avia B534 biplanes, adequate for the mid-1930s, were virtually useless by 1940. The BH33Es had been hurriedly acquired in 1935 to help put down an attempted military coup in northern Greece. They reverted to an advanced training role and were never involved in combat.

Greece's bomber force was wafer-thin – a mere thirty-five front-line aircraft. This in part reflected long-term Greek strategic thinking. Governments in Athens in the 1920s and 1930s, chastened by the Asia Minor defeat, never viewed their country as an offensive power that could one day bomb targets in other lands. Turkey, the Greeks' traditional foe, intent on its own internal development under Kemal Atatürk and his successor, had little inclination for foreign adventurism. There remained Bulgaria, still smarting since the Balkan Wars over its failure to acquire an outlet to the warm Aegean Sea. Protection against a possible Bulgarian attack underlay Greece's defence doctrine under Metaxas. In the air sphere, this translated into a defensive emphasis on fighters and observation aircraft.

The backbone of the RHAF bomber force was the Bristol Blenheim IV, twelve of which were acquired in 1939 and went to equip 32 Bombing Mira based initially near Athens and later at Larissa. These were just half of an order for twenty-four, the rest of which were never delivered because of the outbreak of war. The Blenheims that were shipped to Greece often lacked basic features such as bomb-aiming equipment. The ground crews of 32 Mira performed miracles of improvisation, rigging up rudimentary bombsights by tying lengths of string at certain angles inside the glazed nose. On low-level bombing runs this home-made arrangement seemed to work. The Blenheims also lacked the necessary bomb bay attachments, and so metal barrel hoops were pressed into service to hold up the hardware. (Britain would supply six Blenheim Is in February 1941 to replace losses, which for the type were high.[11])

Eleven single-engined Fairey Battle Mk I light bombers equipped 33 Bombing Mira based at first near Athens and later at Nea Anchialos. Already obsolescent when acquired in 1939, the type was nonetheless liked for its reliable engine, steady flying qualities and dive-bombing ability. Greece had ordered twelve, but the fate of the twelfth remains a mystery. The official story is that the ship ferrying it was sunk, but more recent research suggests that it could have been inadvertently left in Turkey.[12] The Battles went to equip the hastily organized 33 Mira in July 1940. Between that date and the outbreak of war there wasn't enough time for the adequate training of either air or ground crews. The squadron's new airfield at Nea Anchialos was a desolate place – 'just a strip shaved out of a field and [full of] mole holes that could prang an aircraft,' according to Flying Officer Skatzikas.[13]

Eleven twin-engined Potez 63 medium bombers equipped 31 Bombing Mira based at Larissa. Like the Blenheims, they were half of an original order for twenty-four, and one had been lost in an accident. With a crew of two, the Potez 63 was versatile enough to act as a fighter-bomber and reconnaissance plane as well as a pure bomber. Crews liked its top cruising speed of 400kph, its forgiving flight characteristics and its ability to absorb punishment.

The Greek roster of fifty-one army cooperation aircraft was divided about equally among the German-built Henschel Hs126, the Breguet XIX and Potez 25, all obsolete except for the Henschels, which were the most trustworthy, equipping 3 Observation Mira under the command of the Army's

III Corps charged with defending the vulnerable central sector of the northern Greek frontier. The Henschel was a hefty, durable high-wing monoplane with good pilot vision between the wings and a sturdy fixed and spatted undercarriage ideal for take-offs from short and bumpy strips. The Army had originally hoped to acquire forty-eight Henschels from Hitler's Germany, though only sixteen had been delivered when Greece entered the war on the Allied side. Plans to assemble more at the Blackburn works at Faliron foundered on the lack of parts. When the Luftwaffe poured into Greece in April 1941 it, too, employed Henschel Hs126s in the observation role, resulting in some confusion in the skies.

The Breguet XIX should already have been retired. This lumbering antique had been in service since 1925, its only distinguishing achievement since then being the bombing of the northern town of Serres in 1935 during an abortive attempt at a military coup. Nine of them were operational at the outbreak of war, equipping 1 and 2 Observation Mirai and 2828 Independent Observation Flight based in central and northern Greece. The Breguet was to outlast the hostilities for a surprisingly long time and be the protagonist, as will be seen, of a key tactical victory. The Potez 25 was an unremarkable little plane, similar in size and function to a de Havilland Tiger Moth. Though it performed some respectable service with 4 Observation Mira, its operational days were already over.

Greece's naval cooperation arm numbered thirty-six aircraft. Twelve German-designed and Swiss-built Dornier Do22Kg seaplanes equipped 12 Naval Cooperation Mira based near Athens. Sleek and racy-looking, with a cruising speed of some 310kph, the Dornier was popular with its crews. It was also highly versatile. Soon after mobilization, eight of 12 Mira's Dorniers had their floats removed and were towed through the centre of Athens – attracting considerable public attention – to serve as a landplane reserve at Eleusis.

Nine British-built Fairey IIIF seaplanes equipped 11 Naval Cooperation Mira based at Trikeri, on the tip of the Magnesia peninsula curling south of the eastern port of Volos. Having been in service for more than a dozen years, they were worn out and unpopular with crews, who viewed them as accident-prone. Their wartime role of escorting Greek and Allied convoys would prove to be short-lived. To modernize the naval air arm, twelve Avro Anson Mk Is had been acquired from Britain in 1939. As with so many types on order, the outbreak of war interrupted planned further deliveries. In the hands of 13 Naval Cooperation Mira based near Athens, the Ansons stalked Italian submarines in the Aegean Sea. Scattered through the naval air arm *mirai* were a half dozen 1920s-vintage Hawker Horsley II light bombers whose role in the war was minimal.

For transport aircraft the RHAF commandeered all seven civil aircraft belonging to Greece's airline of the time, the Hellenic Aerial Transport Company (EEES). Three of these were relatively modern Junkers Ju52 trimotors, one of the toughest and most reliable aircraft of the era. The other four were older and smaller Junkers G24s, which would do their part in the uneven battle to come.

Chapter 4

'Contingency G'

It seemed in Athens in those anxious days of October 1940 that a great steel-tipped Italian juggernaut was about to roll over Greece, crushing anything in its path. The reality across the Adriatic, however, was rather different.

In the middle of the morning of 15 October the telephone rang in the Rome office of General Mario Roatta, the deputy chief of staff of the Italian Army, summoning him to an urgent meeting with Mussolini. Roatta arrived at the Duce's palatial headquarters in the Palazzo Venezia to find a high-level war council underway. Present were a galaxy of high officials, including Ciano, the foreign minister, Marshal Pietro Badoglio, the Chief of the General Staff and General Sebastiano Visconti Prasca, the commander of the Italian forces in Albania. Roatta sat and listened, and what he heard filled him with growing alarm.

The Duce had finally come to a decision on Greece. Tired of acting as second fiddle to Hitler in the Axis pecking order, he had resolved on an invasion of Greece to show his senior partner that Italy, too, could flex muscles of steel when it had to. But this, of course, was not the explanation he gave to his military chiefs. For months, the Italian General Staff had been working out an exercise on paper dubbed *Esigenza G* – Contingency G – detailing a proposed invasion and occupation of Greece and outlining the pretexts that Rome would need for such an action. The previous month, as the Duce mulled the issues, the plan had been placed on the back burner. Now, suddenly, it was a strategic priority. The date for the invasion was set at 26 October – eleven days away!

Roatta was not the only one appalled. So was Badoglio, who was in the best position of all to know that the Italian Army was in poor shape to fight a hard campaign against a determined foe in the rugged terrain of Albania and north-west Greece. The nine Italian divisions in Albania were lamentably short of mobile armour and field hospitals. Reinforcement and resupply would be a slow process, as Albanian ports were too shallow for large supply ships and troop transports. As France had been knocked out of the war, Badoglio, in fact, had just ordered the demobilization of 300,000 men.

Only one senior military figure actively encouraged Contingency G (often referred to as *Emergenza*, or Emergency, G). That was Visconti Prasca, a vainglorious and ambitious general who longed to be made a *Maresciallo d'Italia* (field marshal). He believed – or appeared to believe – the regime's own propaganda that the demoralized Greeks would break and surrender at the first blow – in contrast to the precise opposite messages emanating from Grazzi in Athens, who since August had been sending regular reports on the stiffening resolve of Metaxas and the Greeks in general and the gradual mobilization of the Greek war machine. Brushing such inconvenient facts aside, Visconti Prasca envisioned a two-pronged land attack over the Albanian border into the Greek province of Epiros, to trap the defending Greeks in a pincer movement around Ioannina and then move on Athens with five or six divisions in a *passeggiata* – a walkover. It was Visconti Prasca who had the Duce's ear, and so more cautious views were ruled out of order. Badoglio hardly spoke at the 15 October conference, perhaps already beginning to sink into the depression that would cost him his job before the year was out. Roatta dared not voice any objections. Boot heels clicked, fascist salutes were raised, and the meeting broke up to put together a major campaign at eleven days' notice.

Where was the Italian air force, the Regia Aeronautica, in all this? General Francesco Pricolo, the air force Chief of Staff (*Capo di Stato Maggiore dell'Aeronautica*), had not even been invited to the Duce's meeting. It wouldn't have made much difference if he had. Though Mussolini was himself an aviator, and could be expected to have a soft spot for the air force, that soft spot turned into a blind spot where the Regia Aeronautica's strategic importance was concerned. The events of October give the unmistakable impression that the air force (like the Italian Navy) simply didn't enter the calculations of the senior planners. Planes and ships, it was automatically assumed, would be available for use as if they were lorries or bullets. As a final finessing of Contingency G, the invasion date was put back two days, to 28 October. On that date Mussolini was due to confer with Hitler in Florence and announce that he, too, was a conquering warlord.[1]

In sheer numbers, the Regia Aeronautica was a formidable force, outnumbering the RHAF's front-line strength by three to one. Some of its aircraft were among the most advanced machines in the sky, such as the Fiat G50bis *Freccia* (Arrow) monoplane fighter, the Macchi C200 *Saetta* (Lightning) fighter, the CantZ1007bis bomber and the trimotor Savoia-Marchetti SM79 and SM81 bombers, bristling with defensive guns. Unlike the Greeks, many Italian airmen had the opportunity to acquire ample real-time combat training in the Spanish Civil War. At home, design teams had been developing new types throughout the 1930s. Mussolini's attempts to transform the Italians into a warlike nation like the Romans of old had triggered a surge of air sports and public air-mindedness.

In existence as a separate service since 1923 (a year after Mussolini seized power), the Regia Aeronautica had been fortunate to have the likes of men such as Major Giulio Douhet and Marshal Italo Balbo. As early as 1927 Douhet had worked out the foundations of the strategic bombing doctrine that would dominate Second World War operations. Balbo, in between his highly publicized show flights, had refined Douhet's theory with the idea of a close-formation massed bomber force to strike the enemy heartland like a mailed fist. With such brains and tradition behind it, the Regia Aeronautica in 1940 was at the pinnacle of its power. Among its star pilots were Ciano himself and the Duce's own sons, Bruno and Vittorio, all of whom skippered bombing raids on Greece.

Mussolini boasted to a meeting of fascist party leaders on 18 November:

> The Italian air force is always at the peak of its task. It has dominated and continues to dominate the skies. Its bombers can reach the most distant of objectives, its fighters are making life quite difficult for the fighters of the enemy. Its men are truly men of our time: their characteristic is a calm intrepidity.

The Duce wasn't far wrong. The Regia Aeronautica looked good and was good in terms of number of wings and firepower. But it wasn't positioned for a specific campaign. Some fighters were stationed as far away as Belgium, seconded to the Luftwaffe in its battle against the RAF. Other squadrons were scattered in bases in Sardinia, Sicily, Libya, East Africa and the southern Aegean Sea. Pricolo, moreover, chafed at the air force's subordinate status. Though not a very imaginative officer, he was nonetheless competent enough to realize that Contingency G was based on the extremely shaky premises that the Greeks were militarily weak and their morale was about to collapse. Yet he was not about to risk his job, and by way of helping out, suggested that Ala Littoria crews fly over the Albanian border photographing Greek troop positions. Mussolini vetoed the idea on the grounds that it would remove the supposed element of surprise. On the very day before the critical meeting at the Palazzo Venezia, Roatta had given Pricolo the comforting impression that Contingency G would stay on hold 'for the moment'. When he was abruptly disabused the following day, Pricolo protested that he couldn't possibly put together an offensive air campaign before the first week of November. 'The reply was always that it would be enough to just reinforce the existing air units in Albania, as an excessive use of force would not be necessary,' he wrote later.[2]

The Regia Aeronautica in Albania numbered 225 bombers, 179 fighters and 59 reconnaissance patrollers. The main forward bases were at Tirana, Korce, Gjirokaster, Berat, Sarande and Vlore (Valona). Other squadrons could reach the battle area from bases in the heel of Italy such as Lecce, Bari and Grottaglie. Some eighty aircraft were based in the Dodecanese islands, though these played no part in the Greek campaign. The Regia Aeronautica battle order on 28 October was:

- 160 Fighter Gruppo, consisting of 393 and 394 Squadriglie (Fiat CR32s and CR42s) and 395 Squadriglia (Fiat G50s), based at Drenova.
- 24 Fighter Gruppo, consisting of 363, 364 and 365 Squadriglie (Fiat CR42s), based at Tirana.
- 150 Fighter Gruppo, consisting of 354, 355 and 361 Squadriglie (Fiat G50s), based at Tirana.
- 104 Bomber Gruppo, consisting of 252 and 253 Squadriglie (Savoia-Marchetti S79s), based at Tirana.
- 105 Bomber Gruppo, consisting of 254 and 255 Squadriglie (Savoia-Marchetti S79s), based at Tirana.
- 72 Reconnaissance Gruppo, consisting of 25, 42 and 120 Squadriglie (Meridionali Ro37s), based at Gjirokaster.
- 39 Gruppo (of 38 Stormo), consisting of 51 and 69 Squadriglie (Savoia-Marchetti S81s), based at Vlore.
- 40 Stormo, consisting of 202 and 203 Squadriglie (Savoia-Marchetti S79s and S81s), based at Vlore.

About half the Italian fighter force consisted of sixty-four Fiat CR42 *Falco* (Falcon) biplanes and 23 Fiat CR32s, the latter already outdated. With its four Breda 12.7mm guns, the CR42 was about a match for the PZL24 and the Gloster Gladiator. Much more effective was the Fiat G50bis, Italy's first all-metal fighter, fast and rugged, eighty of which were available at the opening of hostilities. Twelve examples of the newer Macchi MC200 were also available. Although fast at 500kph, some pilots considered the MC200 underpowered for its role.

The bulk of the Italian bomber force was made up of the menacing-looking three-engined Cant Z1007bis *Alcione* (Halcyon), sixty of which all but ruled the Greek skies in the opening stages of the campaign. Though of wooden construction, they could take a lot of punishment and were highly manoeuvrable. Fifty examples of the Cant Z506B *Airone* (Heron), a seaplane version of the Cant Z1007, were also in service. Also lined up on Albanian airfields were seventy-two Savoia-Marchetti SM81 *Pipistrello* (Bat) bombers. A veteran of the Spanish Civil War, the SM81 was already facing obsolescence because of its drag-inducing fixed undercarriage. It was rapidly being superseded by the sleeker Savoia-Marchetti SM79 *Sparviero* (Hawk), another trimotor, whose steel tube, timber, aluminium and fabric construction gave it unusual endurance. But its meagre defensive firepower made it an easy target for the Greeks. Of the thirty-one in Regia Aeronautica service on the Albanian front, one was later captured by the Greeks and given a new job in the RHAF. Supplementing the force were eighteen Fiat BR20M *Cicogna* (Stork) twin-engined bombers.

Twenty Junkers Ju87 Stuka dive-bombers were based at Brindisi, also the home of sixteen *squadriglie* of bombers of various types under the Regia Aeronautica's Fourth Air Force. As the Greek campaign wore on, many of these would reinforce the aircraft in Albania. But impressive as it was on paper, this air fleet suffered from much the same problems as the RHAF. The biplanes, for example, were fast becoming obsolete, and the sheer variety of aircraft types unnecessarily burdened the supply and repair services.

An Italian *squadriglia* was slightly smaller than an RAF squadron or Greek *mira*, fielding nine aircraft. Three *squadriglie* made up a *gruppo* (somewhere between a squadron and a wing), and two *gruppi* made up a *stormo*, or wing. A larger *ad hoc* unit was the *squadra aerea*, a flexible formation of no fixed number, organized according to the nature of a particular operation.[3]

The Regia Aeronautica's aircraft were top-class and the aircrews well trained. But the same cannot be said of the service's leadership. Pricolo was hesitant and pessimistic. One feels that had he been more assertive, he could have accomplished much. To his detriment he had been caught up in high-level power jockeying and given to unduly worrying about his insecure position within the Duce's inner circle. He had already received a bit of a shock some weeks before, when his regional commander in Albania, General Ferruccio Ranza, asked him what the air support plans were for the planned invasion of Greece. Rather naively, Pricolo replied that since he hadn't been at any high-level conferences, he assumed that the plans had been shelved.

Not long after the 15 October meeting, Mussolini deigned to update his air force chief. The dialogue, as recorded by Pricolo afterwards, is revealing of the state of mind of both men.

'We've got to be [in Greece] before the British turn it into a base against us,' the Duce said.

'Is there proof that Britain has such intentions?' Pricolo said.

'Of course,' Mussolini replied, without elaborating.

'It would be in our interest, rather, to take the island of Crete,' Pricolo said, displaying a spark of independent strategic thinking.

'We'll take that, too.'

'Then we need to have the proper dispositions in time.'

'Naturally,' Mussolini replied airily, and that was the extent of the thinking about the air offensive.[4]

To Pricolo, Mussolini was rationalizing the planned attack on Greece as a move to knock a pro-British prop away from the Mediterranean. In the process the Duce nursed specific plans to give all the glory to the Italian Army, leaving the air force (and navy) to feed on the leftover scraps. Pricolo wasn't a strong enough character to either voice a strong objection (and possibly resign) or insist on a bigger role for the air force. He merely wanted to keep his job. The most he could suggest, to show that he wasn't being disloyal to his boss, was to have the Ala Littoria airliners act as spy planes. Pricolo wasn't even told of Grazzi's ultimatum to Metaxas. Throughout the Greek campaign, in fact, he gave the impression of a rubber-stamp air commander on the sidelines, leaving the battle decisions to his subordinates.

The result was an unimaginative air offensive, mimicking the Luftwaffe's – ultimately unsuccessful – strategy in the Battle of Britain. Groups of bombers were sent at high altitude to bomb civilians and industrial centres, a tactic that signally failed to produce any strategic result beyond stiffening the Greek will to fight. A good deal of air power was wasted this way, when lower-flying attack bombers, for example, might have been better employed tactically against the Greek troops in the mountains.[5] The bombers, moreover, proved vulnerable to aggressive attacks by Greek fighters. It was in the icy skies over Epiros and Albania that the real test would come.

Events now moved quickly. On 23 October a prominent Italian journalist called on Grazzi at the Athens embassy. He told the diplomat he had just come from Ciano, who had the following message: 'Tell Grazzi he can write what he likes – I'll make war on Greece all the same.'[6] If Grazzi had any lingering illusions that peace with Greece could be maintained, this message shattered them once and for all.

Moreover, on 27 October, Papagos, the Greek commander-in-chief, convinced that an invasion was imminent, summoned Mondini to warn him that the frontier was strongly guarded 'metre by metre.' And so it was that, hours later, a very unhappy Grazzi was driven up to Metaxas's home to deliver the fatal message.

Chapter 5

And if Fate Calls . . .

On 2 November an unidentified three-engined plane was reported approaching the Trikala base. Three fighters of 21 Mira took off to intercept what turned out to be a Junkers Ju52. Fired on, the plane made a forced landing on the bank of the Pineios River. It was actually a civil airliner belonging to the EEES, Greece's national airline. That near-tragedy pointed up the woeful lack of an adequate air defence warning system. The Greeks had no radar to detect enemy raiders before they crossed the border. Aircraft recognition was a hit-and-miss affair, very much depending on what a later generation of warriors would call the 'mark one eyeball'.

The pilots who were partly responsible for the gaffe were eager to make amends. On their second sortie of the day they were sent to provide cover for the 8th Division trying to hold back the Italian advance on the northern approaches to Ioannina. Pilot Officer Yannis Katsaros found himself facing a 'very strong enemy air force' and prudently turned back. The other two were shot down and killed. One of them, Flying Officer Yannis Sakellariou, had been sitting at a cafe in Ioannina a few days before and was overheard singing softly to himself. It was a popular air force song, one of whose lines went:

And it fate calls, one day I'll die.

'Why do you keep singing that?' someone asked him.

'Of course I want to come back, so I can fight again,' Sakellariou replied. 'But if I thought about coming back I wouldn't be doing a good job. This song is a shot in the arm. Whoever wrote it knew what he was talking about. Anyway, I wouldn't want to die in my bed of a cold.'[1] (The third fatality was a Sergeant Papadopoulos.) Of men with that noble and courageous attitude the RHAF had more than its share.

That same day, one of Mussolini's crack units, the Julia Alpine division specialized in mountain fighting, had punched a salient near Metsovo and appeared to be on the way to outflanking the Greek defence from the east. The Greek 8th Division was momentarily seized by panic. For

Papagos, locating the Julia division became a matter of the utmost urgency. More by chance than anything else, an ancient 2 Mira Breguet XIX, piloted by Sergeant Yannis Katsoulas with Pilot Officer Dimitrios Karakitsos as observer/gunner, stumbled on the lead columns of the Julia in a mountain pass near Metsovo. Thanks to that intelligence the Greeks were able to entrap the entire division and knock it out of the fight – and, incidentally, drape the end of the venerable Breguet XIX's career in a mantle of glory. In other actions of the day, SM81s of 202 Squadriglia bombed Corfu, Thessaloniki and Patras, killing eighty-six civilians. One of the bombers was lost to flak over Doliana.

With the Julia division reeling back, three Breguets were sent up to monitor its retreat and attack it where possible. Led by Flight Lieutenant Ilias Koutsoukos, the flight threaded through the beetling ravines in line astern, bombing and strafing the weary and mud-caked Italian troops whenever they came into view. On the way out Karakitsos, flying as Koutsoukos's observer, turned his head to see three Fiat CR42s diving on them and spitting tracer. At that moment his ring mount jammed, forcing him to lean almost out of the plane to get a bead on the attackers. He emptied his magazine into one Fiat's wing but to no effect.

He stooped to get the reserve magazine out of its wooden crate, but it wouldn't budge. The lid had swollen in the humid conditions and was stuck tight. He tugged with all his might, but the crate handle came away in his hands. All this time, the Fiats were pouring bullets into the Breguet XIX, which was a tough old bird and managed to absorb most of the punishment. Karakitsos, in desperation, was about to draw his pistol, First World War style, when an explosive bullet hit him in the thigh, taking out a chunk of flesh. Koutsoukos shook off the attackers by diving into a ravine.

But the old Breguet was fatally wounded. The instrument panel had been shattered, fuel and oil lines had been severed, the water coolant had gone and the antiquated Renault engine was sputtering. Koutsoukos fought to stay in the air, finally making a forced landing in a field near the base at Kozani. Taking advantage of a wagon full of hay that happened to be standing by, he loaded his wounded observer into it and trundled him to a hospital. The second Breguet of the mission, flown by Pilot Officer Alexander Sarvanis with Pilot Officer Friderikos Katasos as observer, was shot down; both men were probably dead before the plane hit the ground. The third aircraft, though badly shot up, returned to base.

The ignoble end of the Julia Alpine division came as a shock to the Italian command. A single old biplane had thwarted Visconti Prasca's overambitious pincer scheme. General Carlo Rossi, one of the Italian corps commanders, complained bitterly of the lack of air cover from the Regia Aeronautica. Pricolo, the air force chief, happened to be at the front at the time. But in the accounts he appears as a mere staff officer carrying dispatches from Mussolini, and merely administering rather than directing air operations.[2] In view of Italy's undoubted air superiority, cooperation between the Italian Army and Regia Aeronautica was, in fact, lamentably poor. Much later an Italian military historian would find it 'incredible' that there was not even a functioning telephone line between General Ranza, the Italian air chief in Albania, and the Fourth Air Force headquarters on the Italian mainland.[3]

This was very much Visconti Prasca's show, even in the air. He wasn't unduly put out when much of his air strength found itself grounded by bad weather on the key day of 28 October. Whatever operations did take place started from mainland Italian bases. That day, according to War Bulletin 144, 'Our air force, notwithstanding adverse atmospheric conditions, has repeatedly bombed its assigned military objectives.'[4] Pricolo seems to have had little to do with those operations. In fact, the commander-in-chief's habit of ordering vague and impracticable bombing attacks on a whim got seriously on his nerves. But as long as Visconti Prasca enjoyed the position of court favourite, Pricolo judged it best not to rock the boat but to feed his planes and crews into the fray as he was told. It is to those crews' credit that, despite the lack of effective leadership at the top, they flew and fought as well as they did.

The RHAF leadership and crews, of course, knew nothing of this. All they could see were the waves of bombers and fighters droning in from the north-west, triggering scramble after scramble and leaving little time for any thoughts except those of repelling the raiders. At about the time Mitralexis was slicing the tail off his enemy bomber, the whole Greek fighter force was under constant attack from squadrons of Fiat CR42s. Katsaros escaped a potentially fatal confrontation by throwing his PZL24 into a spin from which he recovered only metres from the ground. In this melee two Fiat CR42s and two PZL24s were lost, and one probable CantZ1007 of 201 Squadriglia. To round out the full day of action on 2 November, Blenheim IVs of 32 Mira delivered a load of high explosive on Korce airbase in Albania, while three Potez 63s of 31 Mira inflicted some damage on an Italian mechanized column near Metsovo.

On land the invading Italians soon found themselves up against a determined foe as stiff Greek Army resistance stalled the Duce's offensive within days. Greek Blenheims and Potez 63s carried out long-range artillery duties by hammering the Italian lines. On 6 November Blenheims of 32 Mira bombed the Albanian port of Vlore, the Italians' main supply point, losing one aircraft. By the end of the second week in November the tide on the ground was beginning to turn. Before the month was out, the Italians had been pushed back behind the Albanian border, prompting Winston Churchill to remark that instead of saying that the Greeks fought like heroes, it should now be said that 'heroes fight like Greeks'. This welcome bit of hyperbole, harking back to Marathon and Thermopylae, lifted the Greek morale no end. Yet except for a brief burst of national frenzy over Mitralexis and his feat (which prompted dozens of often-fanciful illustrations in the magazines, and was reproduced even on a postage stamp), the RHAF fought its battles out of the limelight.

In the meantime the fall of General Visconti Prasca had been sudden and unexpected. The elimination of the Julia division was just one of a series of blunders that the highly mobile Greeks had taken immediate advantage of. Visconti Prasca pooh-poohed the reverses, insisting that Ioannina would be in Italian hands within three days. Pricolo, the air force chief, told Mussolini to his face that he believed Visconti Prasca had taken leave of his senses. On or about 10 November, therefore, General Ubaldo Soddu, the deputy Army chief of staff, arrived in Albania to take over. (By year's end, Visconti Prasca would be on 'indefinite leave,' his military career over.)

Soddu's appointment as commander of the Italian forces attacking Greece made little, if any, difference. It wasn't a question of who was in command but of a seriously flawed strategy from the outset. The ablest general in the world couldn't have extricated the Italian Army from the administrative and tactical quagmire it had blundered into. Here may lie an answer as to why Pricolo was so apparently neglectful of air strategy. There was certainly no love lost between him and Visconti Prasca, and it's hard to avoid speculating that he may well have secretly hoped the bumptious general would fail. After witnessing appalling disorganization on the front lines, Pricolo had flown back to Grottaglie on the evening of 2 November in a depressed mood.[5]

Whatever Pricolo was feeling, he must have kept it from his senior officers and aircrews. He may have disgreed strongly with the vague and unfocused missions ordered by Visconti Prasca, but there is nothing to indicate that he tried to change them. His bombers continued to drone over Greece's cities and convenient close targets such as Corfu, taking a steady toll of non-combatants. There seemed to be little strategic purpose to the raids except to give the bomber crews something to do. Their ostensible purpose was to keep Greece's fighters occupied over home territory. But that didn't take into account the RHAF's bomber force, which in retaliation hit back at Albanian bases. On 11 November, 32 Mira suffered its first loss when Flight Lieutenant Yannis Kapsambelis's Blenheim was downed by a fighter over Gjirokaster. Faced with a stalemate on the ground, the Italians beefed up their Albania-based squadrons by about 250 aircraft. As a result RHAF bomber losses began to mount, though a lucky air gunner might down an Italian fighter or two.

In the middle of November the war on the ground took its decisive turn. The Greek Army consolidated its attacking front and began to push the Italians back, well into Albania. The Regia Aeronautica, however, remained stronger in the air. The Italian base at Korce became a key Greek target, to be eliminated or captured as soon as possible to ease the air raid pressure on Greek towns. On 14 November the Blenheims of 32 Mira and Fairey Battles of 33 Mira, thirteen aircraft in all, hit Korce again, destroying five Italian planes on the ground. A second wave of two Blenheims and two Battles destroyed ten more enemy aircraft and damaged ten others. Papageorgiou's Blenheim was hit by flak and blew up in mid-air, killing him and his crew.

Warrant Officer Nikolaos Nikitidis, the gunner in Flight Lieutenant Sophocles Baltatzis's bomber, claimed two Fiats. Margaritis's Blenheim returned to base with its crew unhurt but the plane itself full of holes. A single persistent Fiat stuck on the tail of Flight Lieutenant Panayotis Orphanidis's Blenheim almost all the way home, firing intermittently, and diving and weaving to try and get a good aim on the faster bomber. Orphanidis's plane was crippled, but not fatally. Despite hits on the fuel and oil tanks, neither was leaking, though his gunner was nursing a bullet wound. Orphanidis knew the Italian would have his best chance to get him as he was making the final turn for landing at Kazaklar near Larissa. So instead of making the turn for Kazaklar he continued, setting course for Sedes. Somewhere over the sea south of Thessaloniki, the Fiat gave up the pursuit. At Sedes, fitters counted 165 holes in the Blenheim.

That same day six Battles of 33 Mira swept in at low level from Corfu, hugging the mountain tops, to plaster Gjirokaster airfield. 'Tracer was thick over Albania,' recalled Skatzikas, 'but either [the gunners] were clumsy or we were lucky. We topped a mountain and there was Gjirokaster airfield down below ... In my dive I must have topped five hundred miles an hour, as one of the upper gun parts flew off.' About a dozen Italian aircraft were destroyed on the ground. Pilot Officer Yannis Kipouros, exhilarated after the raid, wrote to his mother: 'I know that one day I might plunge to earth, yet I will die defending my beautiful country – what are the Italians defending? ... The joy I feel when completing a mission is indescribable.'[6]

The speed of the Greek ground counteroffensive caught the RHAF by surprise. The strategic objectives in the air were hastily altered to include that of providing air cover for the advancing Greek III Corps. Six PZL24s from each of the three pursuit *mirai* were quickly moved to Florina near the Albanian border – too quickly, in fact. The crews at Florina found themselves without billets or basic facilities and plagued by conflicting orders.[7] Above all, Florina had no anti-aircraft protection, and lay helpless against a lone Italian bomber that appeared overhead in the early afternoon of 14 November while the ground crews were feverishly servicing the PZLs for more sorties. The single bomb dropped went wide, and a perfunctory strafing of the airfield didn't do much damage. At about that time, three army cooperation Henschels bombed and machine-gunned to bits a retreating Italian column on the road to Pogradec inside Albania.[8] Pilot Officer Constantine Sarafis, an observer, took control of one Henschel when the pilot, Warrant Officer Dimitrios Yakas, was killed and brought it to a bumpy landing at base. The Greeks claimed eight Italian fighters downed with no loss of their own. That day was one of the busiest of the early campaign, with forty-two Greek sorties in the morning alone.

On 15 November the Regia Aeronautica hit back, striking heavily at dawn with a large force at Florina airfield, taking full advantage of the lack of defences which the previous day's Italian visitor had no doubt noted. Incredibly, little damage was done; not a single plane or fuel dump was hit. 'Were [the enemy] just unlucky, or inexperienced and hasty?' wondered Squadron Leader Grigorios Theodoropoulos, the 31 Mira CO. 'God stood by us once again.'

Later in the day 33 Mira was ordered to hit Italian Army units occupying Mount Morova and Mount Ivan in Albania. The two heights guarded the vital pass through which the Greeks could march on Korce. During the operation an enemy fighter poured bullets into Flying Officer George Hinaris's Battle, killing his gunner/observer, Warrant Officer Miltiades Kontidis – the first squadron member to die in the war – and forcing Hinaris to bale out. His flying overalls on fire, Hinaris was saved from immolation by fortuitously dropping into a mountain stream. He came to in a farmhouse, and after receiving first aid was sent to hospital, and captivity, in Tirana.[9] A Fiat CR42 of 363 Squadriglia shot down Sergeant Frangoulis Arnidis's Battle, killing him and his gunner/observer, Warrant Officer George Daravingidis. Flight Lieutenant Dimitrios Pitsikas's plane also took multiple hits. Pitsikas was able to nurse the plane to land at Ioannina, but on the way, his gunner/observer, Warrant Officer Aristophanes Pappas, bled to death. (The Battle's propeller was set up over Pappas's grave.)

Karnavias led three Potez 63s of 31 Mira to bomb enemy artillery positions on the Devoli river. Vladousis had bombed and just regained the Greek border when his cockpit canopy shattered with a loud bang, and the Potez burst into flame and lurched into a spin. He had been hit by his own side's anti-aircraft guns. Preparing to bale out he told his observer to do the same, but the observer was dead. Floating down, Vladousis found himself under fire from the Greeks on the ground as well as the Italians in the Fiats buzzing overhead. Approaching the ground, he took a letter from his mother from a pocket and waved it, yelling at the top of his voice: 'I'm Greek! Greeeeek, you fellows!'

Hitting the ground, Vladousis would have toppled into a ravine, but was pulled back just in time by an Army sergeant who recognized him as an old schoolmate. He was trying to relax and chat with the local Army colonel when a captain burst into the room, his face stricken. 'I never imagined the Greek air force had such fast planes!' the captain blurted. 'All I know are the Breguets. How should I know we had Potez 63s?'[10] He had commanded the anti-aircraft battery that had brought Vladousis down and killed his fellow crewman. Shortly after that episode Vladousis doffed his flying overalls to reveal a snappy dress uniform beneath. 'Are you going to war or a dinner dance?' the thunderstruck colonel said.

'It's war, colonel,' the airman replied with the insouciance that some pilots cultivated as a defence mechanism, 'but since we never know if we're going to come back, we figure we ought to dress properly.'

On 18 November Sergeant Grigorios Valkanas of 23 Mira, trying to emulate Mitralexis, slammed his PZL into a Fiat CR42 of 160 Gruppo, but he wasn't as lucky. He and the Italian were killed. The day before, Valkanas's flight commander had chided him for not having scored any kills so far. That day was not a good one for the Greeks. As 31 Mira hit the Albanian aerodrome at Gjirokaster, the fighters of 22 and 23 Mirai were sorely tried. The Italians reported six Greek PZL24s destroyed in a single day, one of them being that of Flying Officer Constantine Yannikostas. The RHAF claimed fourteen enemy aircraft destroyed. Yet while the Regia Aeronautica was able to replace lost aircraft and pilots fairly easily, the RHAF enjoyed no such luxury. Metaxas, the prime minister, confided to a government associate that he was 'having nightmares' about the constant attrition of aircraft.

The efforts of 33 Mira over Mounts Morova and Ivan helped the Greek Army take Korce on 22 November. Duly heartened, all three of the RHAF's bomber squadrons sent their Blenheims, Potez 63s and Battles roaring over the retreating Italian lines in formations of up to fifteen aircraft. Pilot Officer Alexander Malakis's Blenheim of 32 Mira, sent to bomb Gjirokaster on 20 November, attacked Permet by mistake. When Greek troops entered Permet a few days later they found that the 'mistake' had destroyed a considerable amount of Italian munitions that had burned and exploded for three days. At least fifty Italians, mostly patients in a military hospital, were killed.

Malakis and his crew earned decorations. But Rome loudly accused the Greeks of violating the Geneva Convention by deliberately bombing a hospital. For a long time, the claim was dismissed as Axis propaganda. Kartalamakis, from the Greek side, asserts that the Italian ammunition dumps at Permet were purposely located mere yards from the hospital in order to protect them. On the other hand, the allegation in the official report that Malakis's bomber attacked Permet in error, as the town 'spectacularly resembled' the proper target of Gjirokaster, needs to be taken with a grain of salt. The memory of Italian aggression was still very fresh in everyone's mind, and there was no lack of Greek soldiers and airmen who had few scruples about what they hit and where.[11]

Flying Officer Yannis Kyriazis was leading a flight of PZL24s over Korce when a couple of CR42s hove into sight. Kyriazis had given the order to engage when a stream of bullets slammed into his plane, wounding him in the left leg. One attacking Fiat banked steeply and returned with another salvo, peppering the wings. Bleeding and stunned, Kyriazis wheeled round to meet the Fiat head-on, fully intending to ram it and damn the consequences. In this deadly game of aerial chicken the Italian blinked first and pulled away. Back at base at Florina, Kyriazis made 'the best landing of [his] life'.

As the Greek Army closed in on Korce, in a panicky attempt to leave the air base before it was captured, an Italian SM79 collided with three CR42s and had to be abandoned. Once repaired by the Greeks, the bomber was promptly redecorated with blue and white RHAF roundels – the only Italian-built plane to see service with Greece before the jet age.

The day Korce fell, four Fairey Battles of 33 Mira took off to hit the Italian columns exiting the city. Flight Lieutenant Pelopidas Frangos was preparing to roar down on them when his observer, Flight Sergeant Christos Christidis, yelled: 'Port behind and above, sir – enemy fighters!'

'How many?' Frangos said.

'Nine. They just came out of the clouds. They're coming at us—' The clatter of Christidis's guns drowned out the rest of his words. At that moment the Battle took multiple hits, smashing the instrument panel and seriously wounding Christidis. Reflexively, Frangos released his bombs to lighten the Battle, pulling it into a tight 180-degree turn and climbing to face his attackers. Six of the Fiats roared over him, and he aimed the plane at the remaining three, firing as he did so. Looking behind him he saw that five of the other six Fiats had turned and were on his tail – the sixth was falling and trailing smoke, a victim of Christidis's first burst. But the gunner wasn't firing any more ...

Frangos and the eight Fiats stalked one another, the Italians waiting for him to crash and breaking off only when he regained the airspace over the

Greek lines. Then came Christidis's weak voice, asking him to lose height. 'Why?' Frangos asked. 'Are you lightly dressed?'

'No sir, I'm hit.'

'Where?'

'In the legs, sir.'

'Are you bleeding? Should we land somewhere?'

Christidis's voice gained a bit of strength. 'Take me to base, sir. I'll hold out.'

The Battle's landing gear had been damaged, but Frangos managed to land in one piece. Christidis, by now unconscious, was lifted out of the blood-filled cockpit with eight bullet wounds in the legs. The Fairey Battle, too, was wounded, with more than two hundred holes in it, and the contents of the fuel and oil tanks had long since leaked away.[12]

Chapter 6

With a Little Help from our Friends

Almost as soon as hostilities broke out, Britain came through with its pledge to help its Greek ally in the air. But conditions now were very different from the time the pledge was given in April 1939. The RAF could spare precious little from its Middle East force, hard-pressed as it was to confront the Italian drive across North Africa. Nonetheless, Air Chief Marshal Sir Arthur Longmore, the RAF commander-in-chief in the Middle East, cobbled together something. All that could be initially spared, in fact, were the Gladiators of 30 Squadron plus eight Blenheim I bombers, which flew to Eleusis airbase on 3 November under Air Commodore John D'Albiac, DSO, earning Churchill's thanks. Four Bristol Bombay transports of 211 Squadron followed with ground crews and spares.

Over the next three days four more RAF Blenheim Is and four Vickers Wellingtons of 70 Squadron joined the force at Eleusis to carry out familiarization flights over the Greek landscape before starting operations. 30 Squadron got its baptism of fire on 6 November when three of its Blenheims bombed Italian supply ships in the Albanian port of Sarande, moving on to attack airfields at Tepeleni, Gjirokaster and Vlore. No Italian fighters rose to meet them, so the Blenheims dropped to rooftop height to give the gunners something to do. When the gunners had a go at some enemy vehicles a trio of Fiat CR42s jumped out of nowhere and raked the bombers with machine gun fire, killing a gunner, Sergeant John Merifield, and wounding a few other aircrew.

The news of Merifield's death stunned the Greeks, who a few days before had welcomed the RAF with delirious joy. The British boys in blue were feted as latter-day versions of Lord Byron, the poet who died fighting for Greek independence in the 1820s. They were cheered in the streets and liberally treated in bars and cafes. Now one of them was the first young Englishman to die for Greece in the Second World War, and the emotional tribute reached the highest levels. Merifield was buried in Athens with full honours, in the presence of Metaxas and high government officials, including a representative of the king. His coffin was draped with the Union Flag and the blue and white flag of Greece. The funeral was filmed by Pathe News and shown in cinemas throughout Britain and the Commonwealth.

D'Albiac had weightier matters to think of as well. Almost from the moment he set foot in Greece he came under strong pressure from the Greek General Staff to use his aircraft as the RHAF had done – as mere aerial adjuncts to ground operations. This was not D'Albiac's idea of how to employ an air force, and he said so. While he was arguing the case, at dawn on 7 November six Wellingtons of 70 Squadron attacked the port and airfield at Vlore. Pouncing on them was a flight of Fiat CR42s of 349 Squadriglia. Sergeant G.N. Brooks's Wellington blew up in mid-air, killing all the crew. Another went down in flames. The remaining planes managed to bomb, but the lesson had been a hard one. Daylight raids with Wellingtons on a well-defended target such as Vlore were little short of suicide. The next Wellington operation against Albania took place at night, starting from a base in Egypt. On 11 November fuel dumps and port facilities at Durres and Vlore were heavily bombed, the fires visible eighty kilometres away.

Four days before the fall of Korce to the Greeks, ten Gloster Gladiators of 80 Squadron arrived at Tatoi, with a promise of ten more on the way. Metaxas fretted that they might not be enough to stem the attrition of the RHAF's dwindling number of airworthy combat aircraft. D'Albiac was feeling the pressure, but could do little about it. Greece's aerodromes were mostly rudimentary affairs, lacking bitumen runways and other basic facilities. The RAF continued to have its hands full in North Africa. Nonetheless, Longmore responded to Metaxas's appeal by sending over the additional Gladiators plus some Blenheim I bombers of 211 Squadron on 23 November.

The 80 Squadron CO, Squadron Leader William Hickey, had plenty of experience against the Regia Aeronautica in the skies of Libya. As for 211 Squadron, barely did it have time to enjoy a welcoming party at the Tatoi mess when it was called into action. A flight of Gladiators led by Flight Lieutenant Marmaduke 'Pat' Pattle, a South African-born Battle of Britain ace based now at Ioannina, ranged over southern Albania in the company of the PZLs of 21 Mira. Meeting a formation of Fiat CR42s and G50 monoplane fighters, Pattle gave the accompanying Greeks a lesson in how to fight in the air and scattered the enemy formation. News of the encounter triggered a fresh burst of national admiration for the RAF, exceeded only by joyous bell-ringing on 22 November when it was announced that Korce was in Greek hands.

Pogradec, next on the Greek list, fell soon afterwards. But by now the snow was thick on the ground and the Greek advance was slowing down. Metaxas, continually anxious, wrote in his diary on 1 December: 'Cold and snow – how I feel for my boys in the Army! How I wish I could be there with them!' Four days before, a 32 Mira Blenheim had been shot down over Albania, killing Malakis and his crew, the ones who had flattened the military hospital at Permet. Italian bombers in return hit the Greek airbases at Kozani and Florina, the home of 2 and 4 Observation Mirai, knocking out at least four observation planes on the ground. Florina was abandoned as it was too near the front for comfort.

The RAF's contribution to the war on the Albanian front gave the RHAF valuable breathing space. British Wellingtons and Blenheim Is hammered away at Albanian port facilities almost nightly, seriously disrupting the Italians' supply chain. Yet the Regia Aeronautica regularly brushed by the Greeks' defences to bomb towns and forward bases. The skies above Epiros were a superhighway for opposing bombers going in opposite directions, the Regia Aeronautica by day and the RAF and RHAF by night. By this time the Italian bomber squadrons had become expert in drawing Greek fighters away from the front. Two formations of G50s and CR42s led by Captain Edoardo Molinari of 364 Squadriglia staged a surprise attack on Kozani aerodrome, the home of 1 Mira. The fighters were followed by nine SM81 bombers that blasted what was left of the squadron's Breguet XIXs. One base pilot officer and three aircraftmen died in the raid.

Not surprisingly, in the face of such destruction some officers argued for more aggressive strikes at the retreating Italians on the ground. But it wouldn't have made much difference: the Italian Army was undersupplied, undernourished and suffering from low morale. It was unlikely to stop retreating. Moreover, the more the Greeks advanced on the ground, the longer the distance the Greek aircraft had to fly and their range was limited. By the end of November the RHAF was even unable to prevent a raid on Corfu that killed at least two hundred civilians.

At the beginning of December the arrival of fourteen second-hand Gladiators from 112 Squadron in the Middle East cheered the Greeks. These planes went to 21 Mira to replace some of its battered PZL24s. The Greek pilots swore that residual desert sand in the engines and airframes stung their faces on the first familiarization flights. On 3 December 'Pat' Pattle lifted off from Ioannina in his Gladiator to see what he could bag. Coming across a lone Meridionali Ro37 reconnaissance plane, he downed it with a couple of bursts. In a second sortie later in the day he took out another Ro37. At about the same time, six PZLs under Squadron Leader Yannis Kellas took on three times that number of Fiat CR42s over Moschopolis; one PZL, flown by Pilot Officer Constantine Tsitsas, was lost. By now, rain and mud were making some of the Greek airfields more hazardous than the enemy. Hard landings wrote off about one plane a week.

The Regia Aeronautica poured new planes into their remaining Albanian and southern Italian bases. The dogfight in which Tsitsas was killed saw the debut in Greek skies of the new Macchi MC200 *Saetta* fighter, for which the PZL and Bloch MB151 – not to mention the obsolete Gladiator – were no match. Monoplane Fiat G50s were now beginning to replace the CR42 biplanes. Ever greater numbers of CantZ1007 and SM79 bombers were becoming available. The winter was now settling in for good, and by the middle of December 21 Mira at Trikala and 22 and 23 Mirai at Ptolemais were hemmed in by three feet of snow. At Ptolemais the oil in the PZLs' engines froze, threatening to rupture the oil lines. Mechanics warmed the oil with bonfires but still, the frozen engines refused to start.

One enterprising engineer officer obtained an old delouser from the Army and had it dragged to the airfield. The thing worked, and the scalding steam played over the radial cylinders and got the engines to work. But the snow was too deep for anyone to take off. For two weeks the pilots fretted as Italian formations droned overhead on their way to bomb Thessaloniki. The Italians, fortunately, didn't know what was beneath, as the Greeks had taken the precaution of camouflaging their PZLs with white sheets. But the enemy's unawareness of the Ptolemais base could not be taken for granted, and so Wing Commander Emmanuel Kelaidis, the RHAF's fighter chief, thought up a daring solution.

If the planes could not be flown out of Ptolemais, he reasoned, they would have to leave by other means. After a reluctant nod by his superiors, Kelaidis had all twenty-two PZLs dismantled, sent overland to Sedes 150 kilometres away, and put together again in all of five days. Fitters were handed screwdrivers and pliers and put to work through the night in freezing conditions. When the men's fingers got too numb they would warm them over a brazier for a few minutes and then crawl back over the planes. The big job was detaching the struts and removing the wings. Once the wings were off, each fuselage was towed, tail first, behind a lorry. Ahead of the convoy a tractor cleared the way through three feet of snow. Squadron enlisted men followed on foot, keeping a hand on the planes to prevent them being blown over and a wary eye on the wolf-ridden hills on either side of the road.

Twenty-six kilometres later, bucking a blizzard all the way, the strange procession arrived at Amyntaion railway station where the planes were loaded onto flatbed wagons and the trucks sent back for a second batch of PZLs, and then a third. Once at Sedes, the planes were reassembled at top speed, and flying again within days. The feat entered RHAF legend as the 'Engineers' Epic'. The heroic ground crews got a well-deserved laugh a few days later when the Italian radio Greek service reported that Ptolemais airfield had been 'mercilessly bombed'.[1]

Rome's radio may have exuded confidence, but General Soddu, the commander on the Albanian front, was far from happy. Persistent and well-organized counterattacks by superior Greek forces had forced him to consider calling off hostilities and asking Greece for a ceasefire. Soddu's men were hungry, ragged and literally dying of cold. It wasn't unheard-of for soldiers to crack open the skulls of dying pack mules to warm their freezing hands in the steaming brains within. Mussolini, enraged, refused to believe the bad news; a ceasefire was out of the question.

And what of the Regia Aeronautica? It was, no doubt, the best equipped and strongest of the Duce's armed services. But was it being employed properly? General Mario Vercellino, the commander of the Italian Ninth Army, had strong views on the subject. 'The air force is a bluff,' Vercellino bluntly told his corps commanders early in December. 'It ought to provide more support for our troops instead of concerning itself with faraway targets.' He might have added that it sometimes made grievous mistakes. On 20 December a squadron of bombers mistakenly hit an Italian column, killing some forty soldiers.[2]

By now the RAF's Gladiators were bearing the brunt of the air battle over Albania, challenging the Italian pilots to what they called a *carosello infernale* (hellish carousel).[3] On 20 December six SM79 bombers were about to bomb the advancing Greek lines when they were jumped by fifteen Gladiators. The bombers' gunners managed to keep the RAF at bay, though one Gladiator – its pilot apparently dead – flew into one SM79 before crashing; the bomber limped to a landing at Tirana.

The following day, Hickey and Pattle took up ten Gladiators to meet an incoming bomber formation over Gjirokaster, to find the bombers covered by no fewer than fifty-four fighters led by fighter ace Molinari. In a twenty-five-minute dogfight the RAF scored eight confirmed kills – three by Pilot Officer William Vale – and three probables. But Hickey and one other pilot didn't come back. When Hickey's Gladiator was hit (probably by Molinari) he baled out, but he was machine-gunned to death as he floated down. He was due to return to his native Australia in a few weeks as a flying instructor, and reunite with his wife and children. Molinari was wounded in the same encounter and made an emergency landing at Tepelene.

21 Mira and its Gladiators relocated to Ioannina, where on 29 December they disrupted a twenty-eight-plane Italian bomber formation. To remedy a parlous shortage of observation and army cooperation aircraft, 13 Naval Cooperation Mira at Eleusis near Athens removed the floats from ten Dornier Do22 seaplanes and sent the results to the front to act as observation bombers, but they didn't do very much.

Greece's naval cooperation squadrons had not been inactive. They had enough to do protecting merchant convoys and troop-laden transports sailing from the islands to Thessaloniki, locating minefields, and inspecting and identifying individual ships. Some dropped a few token bombs on Italian naval and air bases on the Dodecanese islands, but that was a minor sideshow compared with the action on the Albanian front. The naval cooperation *mirai* could take justifiable pride in that between October 1940 and April 1941 not a single merchantman or troopship was lost to enemy action as long as the Greek Ansons, Fairey IIIs and Dornier D22s droned above them.[4]

Before the enemy could retreat too far into Albania, 31 Mira was ordered to carry out reconnaissance over Berat. Three Potez 63s led by Karnavias, the squadron CO, refuelled at Ioannina for the trip. Taking off from Ioannina, Karnavias circled the town. At least one eyewitness had the impression he was saying goodbye, and indeed he was, as it was the last anyone saw or heard from him or his observer, Squadron Leader Yannis Papadakis. They were most likely shot down by Lieutenant Livio Bassi in a Fiat G50, known to be patrolling the area at the time.[5] Just before Christmas two Blenheim Is of 84 Squadron RAF were shot down over the Berat oilfield and five others were seriously damaged.

On Christmas Day D'Albiac decided to cheer the children of Corfu by dropping toys and sweets for them. In the packets was a message from D'Albiac thanking the people of Corfu for taking care of Squadron Leader Gordon Finlayson who had landed there in his crippled Blenheim. Later that day, however, Italian aircraft dropped their own, very different, Christmas presents on the island – high-explosive bombs that killed eighteen civilians in the port area, including some having their Christmas dinner in a shelter. 'The bastards!' Metaxas fumed in his diary that night. An incensed D'Albiac ordered an immediate retaliatory air strike. Five crews of 211 Squadron, all that could be cobbled together on Christmas Day, took off from Tatoi and flew through solid cloud all the way to Vlore. Pilot Officer Eric Bevington-Smith, a bomb aimer/observer on one plane, recalled roaring over the port at 500 feet after dropping the bombs, as his gunners raked the decks of two Italian warships just entering port – all before the Italian flak gunners realized what was happening.[6]

The new year is a traditional time of gift-giving in Greece, and so on 30 December Orphanidis of 32 Mira took off from Larissa in his Blenheim IV to deliver some explosive holiday cheer to the enemy. Orphanidis was the last of a formation of three to take off. Barely had the wheels cleared the ground when the bomber blew up, immolating him and his crew. Hadjioannou, circling overhead, was so shaken by the spectacle that he turned back, his bombs still on board, for a hasty and perilous landing.

The Blenheim's engines were still running as he ran ashen-faced into the dispensary, overcome by nausea. But almost at once he was ashamed of his loss of nerve and let Potamianos, his CO, talk him back into the air. It was his last mission. After bombing targets at Berat he was bounced by a flight of Fiat CR42s of 363 Squadriglia under Captain Maurizio de Robilant, one of Italy's top fliers, and his wingman, Sergeant Enrico Michelli. Hadjioannou and his crew died in the hail of fire. No parachutes came out as the burning plane plunged to earth.

A bright spot in that dark day was the successful raid without loss by 33 Mira on retreating Italian columns.[7] On New Year's Eve Kellas led nine Gladiators of 21 Mira from Ioannina to attack Italian columns, but had to turn back because of low-lying cloud.

In sixty-five days of war so far, the RHAF had lost thirty-one officers killed and seven wounded, and four NCOs killed and five wounded. Its front-line strength was down to twenty-eight fighters and a mere seven battleworthy bombers. It was becoming clear that despite the Greek victories on the ground, the battle in the air was not going at all well. D'Albiac wanted to base a stronger RAF force at Thessaloniki. But Metaxas vetoed the idea. His sombre and realistic gaze was already looking north – to Nazi Germany, which could not be expected to stand idly by while its Italian ally was being trounced. A token British military presence in northern Greece, he feared, would provoke an attack from Hitler.

Over the years complaints have been heard that in Greece's supreme hour of peril Britain sent inadequate or even defective aircraft. In the case of the Gladiators and Blenheim Is there appears to have been some justification for the grumbling. One Greek historian goes so far as to say that 'the help that the RHAF ultimately received was not of the level, in quantity and quality, that it expected in order to reverse the air balance against the Italians.'[8] Such a view presumes that as the Italian ground forces retreated into Albania, the Regia Aeronautica would have eventually found itself at a tactical disadvantage and hence a more determined RAF push would have put it on the defensive.

Such a judgement is easy to make in hindsight. True, the Italian Army was on the run, but how far could it be expected to run? There was always the possibility that at some point it would dig in and counterattack, which in fact it did in March 1941. To pour more of the RAF into the fight presumed a coherent strategic aim that the Greeks lacked. How much of Albania could be occupied, and for how long? The Duce's military machine was far from knocked out. The RHAF, of course, was committed to fighting as long as there was a foe in the field menacing its homeland. For the RAF it was a different story. In November and December 1940 the Battle of Britain was far from over; the Blitz on Britain's cities was in full spate. In the Middle East the Suez Canal and as much of Egypt as possible had to be held at all costs. Greece was, and could not be anything but, a sideshow, a favour to a valued ally, but nothing more. To fritter away top-of-the-line aircraft in that theatre, no matter how deserving the Greek cause was, would have been a strategic error for Britain of the first magnitude.

Yet, that said, it is undeniable that the RAF's help, though it ultimately failed to ward off Greece's defeat at the hands of the Axis, nonetheless kept the RHAF flying and fighting long after it could reasonably have hoped to do so unaided. And few Greek airmen have ever expressed anything but admiration for Britain for helping out in those crucial days.

Chapter 7

'God Help Us'

'What a year 1940 has been!' Metaxas wrote in his diary on the last day of the year. 'War, victory, glory. How many times, in despair and in tears, have I appealed to God, and now I call on Him again ... Thy will be done ... Dangers and fears rumble still ... God help us!'[1]

The Greek leader would need all the divine help he could get. The year 1941 opened with the disturbing news that German forces were massing in Romania. The Nazi threat to Yugoslavia and Greece was becoming more distinct by the day. 'Is the end near?' Metaxas mused. On 4 January he presided over a war council. Now the Greek commanders began to see the logic of D'Albiac's insistence that attacks on Italian ports and supply sources in Albania be stepped up as independent air operations. On the ground, meanwhile, the Italian Army had halted its retreat and was showing signs of stiffening. Soddu had proved to be an indecisive commander, and had been replaced by General Ugo Cavallero, an intelligent but erratic and over-confident officer who appeared to have as little knowledge of air strategy as his predecessors had. Count Ciano, Mussolini's foreign minister, personally flew an SM79 to Albania to give pep talks to the exhausted troops. Severe winter weather stalled the Greek counterattack on the Pogradec-Himare line. In the air, the appearance of the Regia Aeronautica's new Macchi MC200s presaged a yet more difficult phase of the air war for the Greeks.

British victories in rolling back the Italian forces in North Africa enabled the RAF to send two more squadrons to Greece, one of fighters and one of bombers. New waves of Blenheims and Wellingtons hammered the port of Vlore to soften it up for the expected Greek advance. On the ground both sides suffered high casualties in the snow and ice. 23 Mira was moved to the base at Korce, while 21 and 22 Mirai transferred to Ioannina. On their outbound flights D'Albiac's RAF bombers had to take the warmer coastal route to prevent severe icing, thus increasing flight time and the chances of opposition.

During the fight for Vlore, on 6 January a Henschel observation plane was shot down, killing its pilot, Flight Lieutenant Spyros Nanopoulos, and the observer, Squadron Leader Dimitrios Paliatseas. Exactly seventy days before, Nanopoulos had been one of the first to fly into combat on the first day of hostilities, landing with an aircraft full of holes. In the following days the Gladiators of 21 Mira and the PZLs of 22 Mira joined up to attack a formation of enemy bombers, which declined the challenge and fled. The toughest job was to drop to under 300 feet over the mountain roads, in the fog and flak, to get at the Italian columns. By now the Greek fighter pilots had accumulated enough experience to be able to carry it off. Flight Lieutenant Andreas Antoniou of 22 Mira shot down a CantZ1007 that had just bombed oil tanks and railway sidings in Thessaloniki, starting his career as the nearest thing to an ace the RHAF could boast during the war.

From the middle of January the RHAF (beefed up by the RAF) and the Regia Aeronautica battled for control of the skies of Albania. Bad weather still held up the Greek advance on Vlore. The bombers of 31 and 33 Mirai were sent in on 21 January. Visibility was poor over the Clissura pass, but Kipouros in his Fairey Battle located a thick column of vehicles and infantry. After dropping a 100-pound bomb he came under tracer fire from one of the vehicles and was hit in the starboard fuel tank. 'I nearly drowned in petrol,' Kipouros wrote to his brother, 'and my eyes stung like they had alcohol in them.' Before the fuel could leak away, Kipouros turned to bomb the column again no fewer than seven times, landing with an empty tank behind the Greek lines.[2]

Skatzikas's Battle was also hit but he landed safely at Ioannina. Skatzikas, however, didn't feel like hanging around Ioannina until his Battle was repaired and took Kipouros's plane – the less seriously damaged – to try and return to base with it. He mistakenly believed he could fly the 200 or so miles to Nea Anchialos on a single operational fuel tank. The fuel lasted as far as Patras, where he had to make a hasty landing in a field, demolishing an olive tree and one wing in the process.[3]

Sometime in January a curious figure appeared in the halls of the Air Staff, resplendent in an old squadron leader's uniform. It was veteran aviator Dimitrios Kamberos, who had a flying record going back to May 1912 and whose name was a household word.[4] Caught up the general patriotic enthusiasm, he was offering his services as head of flying training at the EKI in Argos. Major General Ekonomakos, the deputy air minister, bluntly reminded him that he was fifty-seven years old, hadn't taken to the air in many years, and was not conversant with the newer aircraft and flying training methods. 'You're already an icon in the air force, Mr Kamberos,' the general added, sweetening the pill. 'I don't think you need more laurels. You've already rendered great services to your country.'

Leaving Ekonomakos's office in a huff, Kamberos tried another tack. He contacted Wing Commander Vilos, the former commandant of the Icarus School, who had just taken a group of flight cadets to train at the RAF base at Habbaniya in Iraq. Vilos, a compassionate man, agreed to have Kamberos there; at the very least he would be an inspiring presence, if nothing more. But Ekonomakos vetoed the move. Kamberos, unable to endure forced retirement while his country was fighting for its life, fell into a depression. About a year later, in the bitter winter of 1942, the veteran aviator was found dead in the kitchen of his home in Piraeus. He had apparently been brewing his bedtime tea when the water boiled over, extinguishing the gas flame but leaving the gas on. Was it suicide? To this day, no one knows.[5]

The full force of 23 Mira was scrambled to meet an Italian bomber force heading for Thessaloniki on 25 January, while 21 Mira under Kellas shot down two Breda Br88 bombers over Albania. Theodoropoulos, the CO of 23 Mira, found he had to deal with two raids coming from different directions at 20,000 feet. This was at the very limit of the PZLs' operational ceiling, though the Blochs of 24 Mira could fly higher. At serious risk to himself, Theodoropoulos tore off his oxygen mask, which was obstructing his vision. In the confused encounter that followed, and trying not to get hit by his own side's flak, Theodoropoulos confirmed one enemy bomber destroyed. (He landed with a colossal headache from the lack of oxygen and was barely able to move.) Flight Lieutenant Michalis Savellos, the CO of 24 Mira, claimed a kill before the .303 Hispano machine guns of his Bloch MB151 jammed.

Yet the clouds were darkening over Greece, and not just because the RHAF was steadily being ground down in numbers and pilots. Metaxas was keenly aware of the deteriorating wider situation. A pragmatic man and expert strategist, he fretted that the British did not perceive the threat to the Balkans keenly enough. Winston Churchill was pressing for a British expeditionary force to be allowed to land at Thessaloniki to deploy in northern Greece. The British leader was thinking in terms of 1918, when the Allied Macedonian front had helped win the First World War. To Metaxas, though, to repeat that move this time would be folly. The Germany of 1941 was far stronger than the Germany of late 1918. All Hitler needed was an excuse in the Balkans, and he could unleash a *blitzkrieg* on the whole region in short order. Churchill had hopes of widening the front by luring neutral Turkey into the Allied fold, but the Turks proved too wily for that. At any rate, the Italians were retreating in North Africa, and no more British forces could conceivably be spared for Greece.

The spokesman for Churchill's demand was Field Marshal Archibald Wavell, who tried to talk Metaxas into compliance during a meeting in

Athens on 13 January. Four days later Metaxas wrote in his diary: 'The British insist on entering Thessaloniki with a small force of artillery ... To the British I say: don't come with a small force unless the Germans cross the Danube ... Worked till late at night.' That was his last-ever diary entry. A few days afterwards he attended a staff meeting complaining of a sore throat. The malady developed into dangerous abscess. Medical treatment proved unable to prevent septicaemia. On 29 January the nation awoke to the news that Metaxas had died during the night, struck down at the very pinnacle of his wartime leadership.

The leader was suddenly gone, but the fight, of course, had to go on. 23 Mira was posted to an advanced base nestling deep inside a steep valley at Paramythia, already in use by the RAF, just short of the Albanian border. A spate of bad weather grounded all operations for nearly a couple of weeks. On 9 February nine Greek PZLs and six British Gladiators of 80 Squadron, patrolling the sky above Clissura, ran into about a dozen Fiats. Kellas, the 23 Mira CO, downed one of them, while Flight Lieutenant Ilias Dimitrakopoulos, Flying Officer Anastasios Bardavillias and Flight Sergeant Nikolaos Kostorrizos accounted for three more.

Joining the fight that same day was Antoniou's 22 Mira, as fifty Italian bombers escorted by thirty-six CR42s and G50s were intercepted on their way south. Mitralexis, the hero of 22 Mira, downed two fighters of 24 and 160 Gruppi and two probable bombers. Flight Sergeant Epaminondas Dangoulas claimed another, seven more going down under the guns of the RAF.

On 10 February almost the whole Greek fighter force was called out again. 21 and 22 Mirai, with just four Gladiators each, were assigned to escort Kellas's 23 Mira PZLs. At 14,000 feet over Clissura they encountered three enemy bombers and dived to attack them. This was the Greeks' first encounter with the classic entrapment tactic. At that moment fifteen Italian fighters pounced. Kellas's PZLs, though, had been flying 1,500 feet higher than the Gladiators and were able to take on the enemy fighters from above in a double entrapment. That day nine Italian aircraft were reported destroyed and three more damaged, with no loss to the Greeks, though several fighters were severely damaged and one pilot was wounded in the leg. That day the Italians reported nine kills, probably including two damaged Greek PZLs that broke up on landing back at base. Both were too badly damaged to be repaired, so their surviving parts were cannibalized to make up a new plane that was soon in action. Greek chroniclers proudly report that the British ground crews helping the RHAF assemble the fighter were 'speechless with admiration'.[6]

The depleted RHAF bomber force, on the contrary, wasn't enjoying comparable success. At about the time Kellas was staving off destruction above Clissura, 31 Mira was sent to bomb enemy artillery positions. Flying Officer George Stavraetos and Flying Officer Nikolaos Volonakis, in their Potez 63, climbed into the cloud layer in sub-zero temperatures. At 5,000 feet they glimpsed their target through a break in the clouds. 'Hold on,' Stavraetos said, and, throttling back, held the Potez poised like a hawk before the dive. After releasing a clutch of 500-pound bombs, he corkscrewed wildly away from the heavy flak – right into a formation of Macchi MC200s. Juddering violently from incessant hits, the Potez seemed about to disintegrate. The port engine caught fire. 'Jump, Niko, jump,' Stavraetos said. 'There's nothing more we can do.'

Volonakis baled out as the Potez entered a vertical dive, now completely aflame. He saw his skipper jump, too, and waited for the parachute to open ... It didn't. At that point Volonakis floated into a layer of cloud and saw nothing more until landing in deep snow. Greek ground troops found Stavraetos's body on a snowy ridge some hours later. His parachute was unopened and he had a gaping wound in the chest. Stavraetos (whose surname literally means eagle) had been one of the RHAF's best airmen. A former chief of cadets at the Icarus School, he had been widely respected as a stolid and courageous officer. His loss seemed to be a portent of grim times to come.

In mid-February Italian pilots bombing Thessaloniki reported tangling with 'Greek Hurricanes', which can only have been the Bloch MB151s of 24 Mira, similar in profile (at a distance) to the redoubtable British fighter. One CantZ1007 was shot down. At about that time an Avro Anson of 13 Naval Cooperation Mira flew into the Aegean Sea in low cloud while stalking Italian submarines. The crash killed two of its crew of three, Flight Lieutenants Pantelis Linos and Nikolaos Toumbakaris.

The indefatigable Mitralexis claimed part of the credit for downing three Fiat G50s that were escorting a bomber wave. On 11 February a mistaken report of an Italian bomber force heading for Ioannina without escorts issued by the Greek air defence command resulted in just two 21 Mira Gladiators being scrambled. Barely 1,000 feet off the ground they ran into a swarm of Macchis. Bardavillias was shot down in his Gladiator and killed. Kostorrizos in the other Gladiator was wounded and his plane badly shot up. Unmolested, the Italian formations bombed Ioannina, Preveza and the port of Piraeus.

However hard they might search among the snow-covered crags on the Greek-Albanian border, the Italians didn't discover Paramythia airfield, nestling inside a ten-mile-long valley formed by the meandering Acheron river – which the ancient Greeks believed was the entrance to Hades – and guarded by 6,000-foot peaks on either side. It was no easy field to operate from. Climbing out of Paramythia meant making a series of steep, tight circles to clear the huge heights. To a pilot of a larger aircraft such as a Blenheim or Wellington it seemed as if the gaps in the cliffs were barely as wide as his wingspan. Consequently, night operations by those bombers were unthinkable. The name Paramythia in Greek means 'fairy tales,' and that's how it was dubbed by the RAF – 'Fairy Tale Valley'. The great value of Paramythia, besides its seclusion, was that it was but a few minutes' flying time from Albania and the coast. It was put to considerable use by the Fairey Swordfish torpedo-bombers of 815 Squadron Fleet Air Arm. The Swordfish pilots, however, were under the strictest orders to avoid tangling with enemy fighters in case it should lead the Italians to discovering Fairy Tale Valley.[7]

By now the RAF had brought its Hawker Hurricanes to the Greek theatre of war. Towards the end of February they began to tangle with the CR42s, sounding the death-knell of the biplane in aerial combat. The aerial encounters over Albania and north-west Greece in the winter of 1940–41 had, in fact, been the last of the great biplane battles. The arrival of the Macchi MC200 and Hurricane changed the script. Yet one factor remained depressingly constant: while the Regia Aeronautica and, to a lesser extent the RAF, had little difficulty in replacing lost aircraft and crewmen, the RHAF – whose fight essentially this was – could hope for no such reprieve. All of the main types of aircraft the Greeks used – the PZL24, the Potez 63, the Blenheim IV, the Fairey Battle and the Bloch MB151 – were rapidly becoming obsolete, some more than others. The Gladiator, though it had more than proved its worth, was at the end of its admirable career. Would the RAF bear much of the RHAF's burden indefinitely? By February 1941 'the RHAF by all accounts should already have been decimated.'[8] How much of a chance of survival did it realistically expect to have?

D'Albiac, meanwhile, continued his administrative battle against the senior Greek commanders who insisted on using the RAF to support ground operations on the Albanian front. There was no Metaxas now to rein in his military men and the Greek government was rudderless without him. Only thanks to D'Albiac's insistence were the RAF's Blenheims and Wellingtons able to pound strategic targets such as the port at Vlore instead of operating as a mere adjunct to the Greek Army. But a note of hopelessness began to creep into the staff meetings. Victorious in Albania the Greek Army might be, but the shadow of an increasingly likely German intervention was fraying nerves in Athens.

The tension in the staff rooms inevitably leaked out. One foreign correspondent claimed (citing 'unofficial sources') that the British were deliberately leaving the most difficult aerial fighting to the Greeks in order to preserve British air strength for a bigger fight to come against the Germans in the Mediterranean. True or not, the last thing that Papagos, the Greek commander-in-chief, wanted was to give the Axis the impression that the Greeks and the British were bickering. He therefore asked D'Albiac to convey the Army's thanks to the RAF, whose raids on 13 February helped Greek ground forces 'meet all objectives'.[9]

A Potez 63 of 31 Mira was shot down over Mount Trebesina; its two crew members emerged unhurt from the wreckage. That same day, 32 Mira took delivery of six Blenheim Is from the RAF, to replace the squadron's lost Blenheim IVs. The earlier version of the Blenheim was a disappointment. It lacked the spacious nose section of the Blenheim IV, and consequently was nowhere near as easy to escape from in an emergency – the Greeks soon dubbed it the 'flying hearse'. Four days later 32 Mira received a new commanding officer in the person of Wing Commander Nikolaos Averof, a capable pilot but with a reputation for haughtiness and unapproachability. On his first raid, Averof led three of the squadron through thick cloud to bomb Italian positions on Mount Trebesina. The bombing completed, the Blenheims on their way back found themselves inside a great churning mass of cumulonimbus. Besides severe turbulence, such conditions carried a risk of engine failure caused by iced-up carburettors. As the bombers bounced about in the violent currents, Averof calmly ordered the formation to spread out for safety. He and Flight Lieutenant Haralambos Papatheou eventually landed safely at Sedes and Serres respectively; the third bomber crash-landed in a swamp near the Albanian border, its crew also unscathed except for a mud bath.

The remaining fighters of 21, 22, 23 and 24 Mirai, most of them now patched up but still – only just – airworthy, were scarcely given a rest. To raise morale Wing Commander Kelaidis, the senior RHAF fighter commander, did not hesitate to fly with his boys when he could. The average Greek squadron was now down to about half its pre-war strength. In terms of numbers, a typical day's action was that of 20 February, when out of eighty-one sorties, the RAF shot down eight Italian aircraft (plus one probable) and the RHAF accounted for three (plus one probable) – with no losses of their own.[10]

With Metaxas out of the picture, Churchill believed the way was now clear to send a British expeditionary force to northern Greece. The new Greek prime minister was Alexander Koryzis, who was the very antithesis of the tough, no-nonsense Metaxas – a mild-mannered banker wholly unsuited for the gigantic task of running a country under dire strategic threat. Yet Koryzis was not totally devoid of resolve. At a meeting in Athens in late

February with Anthony Eden, the British foreign secretary, General Wavell and King George II, Koryzis tried to hold out against the British demand for an expeditionary force. But as Eden pointed out, it was a bit late in the game to be standing on national pride now. Yugoslavia, to the north, was about to collapse. British advances in North Africa, he promised, would make available more forces for Greece. Besides, Eden argued, a German invasion was almost certain, any way one looked at it. Koryzis and the king caved in.

On 25 February a single Potez 63 of 31 Mira was sent on a photo-recce mission over Albania, escorted by fifteen PZLs and Gladiators of 21 and 23 Mirai. They joined up at 9,000 feet over Permet, to find formations of Fiats patrolling the airspace. 'Enemy to starboard and behind,' called Flight Lieutenant Dimitrios Skaltsoyannis, the CO of 21 Mira, who turned to starboard to meet the adversary head on.

Skaltsoyannis's sudden manoeuvre threw the Fiats into disarray. In the flurry of machine-gun fire from both sides, three Italian aircraft went down. Flying Officer Nikolaos Skourbelos of 23 Mira was killed by a burst. Flak came to add to the confusion in the air. Flight Sergeant Spyros Depountis's PZL took a flak hit, shattering the instrument panel and wounding him in several places. He managed to nurse his coughing plane to a landing behind Greek lines. A general ran up and gazed open-mouthed at the bullet-riddled monoplane. 'You mean you really fly that thing?' the general said slowly and incredulously, making the sign of the cross.

Flight Sergeant Constantine Chrizopoulos of 21 Mira had a particularly tragic end. Wounded and bleeding from the dogfight over Permet, he tried to find a piece of level ground to land his battered PZL on. There wasn't any, so he had no choice but to try his luck anywhere he could. Trying to land, his plane hit a boulder, turned over and caught fire. The few peasants who ran to the scene could get nowhere near the blazing pyre. Chrizopoulos, trapped in the cockpit and screaming for help, burned to death.

After that encounter Kelaidis, the fighter commander, recalled all fighters to their home bases for a short breather and refit. The RAF had now thrown its Hurricanes into the fight, and the Greeks felt they could briefly take some of the pressure off. On 26 February Eden, General Wavell and Air Chief Marshal Longmore flew into Fairy Tale Valley to observe what by now had become a wholly RAF operation out of Paramythia. On 28 February eighteen Gladiators of 80 and 112 Squadrons, followed closely by eight Hurricanes of 80 Squadron (now commanded by Pattle) and 33 Squadron, chased a gaggle of SM79s away from the coast opposite Corfu and turned to attack a formation of BR20s near Vlore. Pattle, after downing two Italian aircraft, was hit by a Fiat G50 and had to hurriedly land his Hurricane. Once down, he climbed into another and flew back into the fight. With something like a hundred aircraft wheeling and diving above the peaks, Pattle whacked another CR42 in between momentary blackouts caused by the sudden turns he had to keep making.

The results of the great air battle of 28 February were, according to the RAF, eight Italian bombers and nineteen fighters destroyed, six more fighters probably destroyed, and five bombers and one fighter damaged. The Regia Aeronautica, for its part, claimed seven British kills and three probables – almost certainly an exaggeration.

It was arguably the RAF's best day since the climax of the Battle of Britain on 15 September 1940. But the Greeks, to their great chagrin, could have no part in it.

That night, in the midst of the celebrations in RAF messes, a severe earthquake hit the city of Larissa, killing hundreds of people. Greek and British servicemen worked through the night to rescue people trapped in the rubble of their homes. A few days later, with the city and country still in shock, and rescue and recovery efforts still under way, Italian CantZs visited the luckless city, complementing the destruction. Two RAF Hurricanes and two Greek PZLs gave chase, downing two of the raiders whose crews baled out near Corfu.[11]

In February 1941 the Regia Aeronautica carried out 253 bomber sorties over Greek military and civilian targets, ranging as far as Maleme aerodrome in Crete, killing at least a hundred people. Yet on the ground the Italian Army had been pushed back to a line about halfway across Albania. Despite the efforts of General Cavallero, the demoralized and weary troops had proved unable to regain the lost ground.

According to Italian official records, nearly 5,800 officers and men had been killed in less than four months of campaigning. Therefore Mussolini himself decided to take matters in hand. On 2 March, resplendent in a field grey uniform under his flight overalls, he sat in the pilot's seat of an SM79 bomber and took off from Bari to fly to the Albanian front personally, escorted by two CantZ506 seaplanes and a dozen Macchi MC200s. With him was Pricolo, the air force chief.

The Duce didn't say much on the flight. Troubled by the low morale on the freezing front, he was no doubt wondering how he could salvage his own dented reputation. He had been delicately humiliated by Hitler during their meeting at Salzburg on 19 February, when the Fuehrer indicated that at any moment he could inundate Greece with German troops. To avoid such a loss of face, Mussolini wondered whether he might not be able to salvage the Greek campaign with a magnificent spring offensive, an *Offensiva di*

Primavera that would take advantage of the improving weather to hurl the advancing Greeks back.

Meeting him at Tirana, the Albanian capital, was General Ranza, the Italian air commander in Albania. Ranza radiated optimism, but not so his boss Pricolo, who accompanied the Duce on a tour of the front on 9 March. Mussolini gazed sombrely at the muddy roads and drawn, haggard faces of his soldiers. Yet the apparent absence of hostile air activity led him to believe that one strong, determined counter-attack would turn the tide of the campaign. If the purpose of the Duce's visit was to hearten his long-suffering soldiers, it to some extent succeeded. 'We want an attack!' some of the men shouted as Mussolini motored past. 'Duce, give us the order!' But Pricolo, for one, didn't quite trust the authenticity of some of the sentiments.[12]

As Mussolini watched, Ranza launched waves of bombers and escorts against the Greek positions, backed up by a massive artillery barrage, to mark the opening of the *Offensiva di Primavera*. Pricolo, observing, was not optimistic about the outcome. It was, admittedly, an odd attitude for an air force chief whose aircraft, unlike the ground troops, were yet undefeated. The initial artillery barrage shook but failed to seriously dent the Greek position. In the air, however, his Regia Aeronautica was in the process of speedily whittling down what remained of the RHAF. With the number of RHAF planes barely into the double digits, Pricolo could marshal 394 aircraft, of which the lion's share were CantZs, replacing the slower SM81s. The Macchi MC200 now shared with the RAF Hurricane the distinction of being the dominant fighter in the Greek and Albanian skies.[13]

On 11 March, as the bone-weary, hungry and frostbitten Italian troops were sent forward again, and savage fighting took place on the ground, 33 Mira received orders for a hit-and-run raid on the Italian lines along with the Blenheim Is of 32 Mira. Flying Officer Michalis Stratis's bomber lost a propeller in mid-operation, and he had to make an emergency landing. Flight Sergeant Evangelos Tzovlas's Blenheim was so seriously shot up as to be uncontrollable; Tzovlas jumped at the last minute – into Italian captivity. His two crew members were already dead.

33 Mira had a new CO, Wing Commander Menelaos Kinatos, who at the time was absent in Athens. Before the crews boarded the bus to the airfield, a newlywed flight sergeant asked for a special favour: as his wife had come to visit him for a few days, could he be excused from that particular operation? The deputy squadron commander, Squadron Leader Dimitrios Stathakos, said yes and prepared to fly in the flight sergeant's place. Technically, Stathakos was breaking the rules. A squadron commander and his deputy were not supposed to be away from the base at the same time. Waving away

the objections from the other crews, he took out his wallet and took off his watch. 'If I don't come back, give these to my sister,' he told the flight sergeant, and headed out to his Fairey Battle.

It was ten-tenths cloud all the way. Above southern Albania Flying Officer Sophocles Baltatzis pointed ahead. 'There they are,' he said. Like black dots in the sky, ten Italian fighters were waiting for them. Through a break in the clouds the squadron dropped its bombs haphazardly and turned for home. Stathakos and Pitsikas didn't come back.[14] On 29 March 33 Mira – now down to just four aircraft – successfully bombed an Italian ammunition store near Elbasan, streaking in before dawn and dive-bombing from 15,000 feet. Shortly afterwards, Kipouros disappeared on an operation and was never heard from again.[15]

For all its smoke and flame and propaganda, the Italian *Offensiva di Primavera* petered out within a week. Hurling themselves against the immovable Greek lines with desperate courage, in less than a week the Italians had sustained casualties exceeding 10,000. The Duce's last brief hope of subjugating Greece died along with his poorly led soldiers. He flew back to Rome on 21 March 'sickened', as he confided to the faithful Pricolo, by the incompetence of his ground commanders. The Duce's discomfiture was made worse by the realization that Hitler would now almost certainly step in and succeed where he had failed.

The next day the Regia Aeronautica finally discovered Fairy Tale Valley amid the melting snow. Some thirty Macchis zoomed down on Paramythia from 3,000 feet. The easiest targets were the Wellingtons (dubbed 'sows' by the Greeks for their dumpy shape), three of which were destroyed on the ground along with one Gladiator. Thick smoke filled the narrow valley. Three of the attackers were shot down. In another action over Albania, Italian ace Molinari was killed while trying aerobatics in a CR42. He had just returned to flying service after a three-month convalescence.

Regular British military forces began arriving in Greece on 2 March, unloading their equipment at the port of Piraeus under the noses of German consular officials. By 21 March 62,000 men had arrived, including mechanized units. Wavell had ordered the Britons to 'give your blood for Greece just as you would fight for Britain'.[16] The brave words were all very well, but all they amounted to was a false mask for the fate of Greece, which was now sealed. Much had changed since Metaxas's untimely death. The German threat cast its shadow over everything. The RAF in Greece had altered its organization accordingly; it was now split into an eastern and western section, the former to brace for the expected German attack from Yugoslavia and Bulgaria, and the latter to keep the Italians at bay in Albania.

Little is known and less has been written about the contribution of the Hellenic Aerial Transport Company (EEES), Greece's civil airline, to the national war effort. Set up in 1930, by the beginning of the war it was operating regular services from Athens to Thessaloniki, Ioannina and Heraklion in Crete. At the outbreak of hostilities, according to the terms of its original contract with the Greek state, the EEES's four sixteen-seat Junkers G24s and three twenty-seat Junkers Ju52s, as well as their crews, were requisitioned for war service. The latter examples had been delivered in 1938 and were pretty much the latest thing Europe could boast in air transport.

By an Air Ministry order on 2 November 1940 the EEES became the Regular Transport Mira directly under the control of the General Staff. For the next 130 days, until the Germans took Dekeleia aerodrome near Tatoi, the squadron carried out 149 flights for both military and civil purposes – one of those was the Ju52 inadvertently shot at by 21 Mira over Trikala and forced down onto a river bank on 2 November – over more than 520 flying hours, without a single fatality.

Some of the unsung feats of the Regular Transport Mira were in dropping supplies to the Greek front-line units in Albania, delivering the all-important mail and evacuating wounded men. When Greek forces overran the Italian bases at Korce elsewhere, the first thing the squadron did was set up communications centres. On 12 December the squadron's work was acknowledged by a medal of merit awarded to sixteen executives and pilots by Papagos, the commander-in-chief.[17]

Chapter 8

Thermopylae Revisited

The Greeks celebrated 25 March, their national independence day, in a grim mood. Many were quite prepared to believe that it would be their last national day celebrated as an independent nation for some time, and they were right. Three weeks before, German units had moved into neighbouring Bulgaria. The contrast with mid-November 1940 could hardly be greater. Then, the church bells had rung almost daily with the news of fresh victories on the Albanian front. Now, however, the bells and the people were silent. Any village idiot now realized that the Germans would pounce on their country, and soon.

Day by day there were reports of 'unidentified' aircraft overflying parts of northern Greece, though it was common knowledge that they were Luftwaffe. The Regia Aeronautica continued its raids. Two CantZs and three SM79s of 35 Stormo were downed at the end of March by a mixed force of RAF Hurricanes and RHAF PZLs. The RHAF could claim to have played its part with outstanding valour. The subsequent Greek claim that the RHAF 'never allowed the Italian air force to achieve air supremacy' may be technically correct.[1] But supremacy is not the same thing as superiority, and if the Regia Aeronautica came out of the Greek campaign in better shape than the RHAF, it was because it was simply stronger. The six months of aerial combat, however, had also worn down the Italian air force to the point at which Ranza, its commanding officer in Albania, warned Cavallero that he was down to seventy fighter pilots.

At dawn on 6 April the German ambassador in Athens, Prince Victor zu Erbach-Schoenberg, called on Koryzis, the prime minister, to read him a long, rambling and hypocritical list of 'complaints' that the Third Reich had stored up against Greece, culminating in the arrival of British forces. Thus, the envoy concluded, Germany had no choice but to intervene in Greece, 'to chase the British intruders from Greece and render a decisive service to the Greek people and the European community.' The text, of course, fooled no one, especially Koryzis, who despite his mild demeanour and lack of experience in political hardball responded with a Churchillian defiance in the name of the king. 'We shall win!' the royal proclamation declared. 'With the help of God and the Virgin Mary we shall win! The history of nations will write once again that the country of Marathon and of Salamis does not bend, does not submit, does not surrender.'[2]

Even as Erbach-Schoenberg was speaking, the Luftwaffe was sending Henschel Hs126 observation planes into Greek airspace. One of them was downed by Antoniou, now the CO of 22 Mira, in a PZL over Kilkis. A Dornier Do17 reconnaissance bomber was destroyed by Flying Officer Panayotis Ekonomopoulos of 24 Mira in a Bloch MB151. Later that day Hurricanes of 33 Squadron tangled with Bf109s in the first British-German air encounter over Greece. For a few minutes it was the Battle of Britain all over again as the Hurricanes shot down five Messerschmitts and damaged three others for no loss of their own.

Surprised at this initial discomfiture, the Luftwaffe launched twenty Junkers Ju88 bombers from bases in Sicily to hit the port of Piraeus. A formation of Heinkel He111s was scheduled to follow, to lay mines outside the port, which was crammed with all manner of supply ships, some laden with explosives and ammunition. The stage was set for a holocaust. Strong turbulence on the way over caused several Luftwaffe crews to jettison their mines. But the main bomber force, arriving over Piraeus at nightfall, dived onto the massed ships from 3,000 feet. One bomb hit the SS *Clan Fraser*, its holds packed with 250 tons of explosives. The British naval attaché, arriving on the infernal scene, ordered the ship towed out of port. The attaché's aide, Commander John Buckler, RN, had just jumped into an adjacent barge to do the towing when the *Clan Fraser* went up in a monstrous explosion. The entire seafront of Piraeus was levelled, with serious loss of life. In the centre of Athens, nine miles away, people were thrown out of bed and windows shattered. The explosion was heard for 150 miles.

Ground operations in Albania continued when they could. A Greek counterattack on 7 April resulted in the capture of an entire Italian battalion, and so the advance might have resumed had not the Yugoslav resistance precipitately collapsed, leaving the Greek front lines in Albania out on a dangerous limb. On the following day the Greek General Staff called a halt to offensive operations in Albania.

Attention was now fixed on the Yugoslav and Macedonian front, where the gloves were now off. Blenheims of 11 Squadron RAF escorted by eleven Hurricanes bombed German columns heading south. On the return trip Pattle, now a squadron leader, bagged a lone Dornier Do17 beetling along at low level. At the same hour the Luftwaffe sent some reconnaissance aircraft high over Thessaloniki. Flight Sergeant Eleftherios Smyrniotopoulos of

24 Mira scrambled in his Bloch to meet them. He managed to get above and behind one Do17, getting in a couple of bursts. The Dornier began weaving and Smyrniotopoulos found it hard to keep up. He ended up emptying his twin 7.5mm machine guns into the raider's tail, but received a few bullets in return, which smashed the Bloch's oil lines and blackened the windscreen. Smyrniotopoulos made it back to Sedes with some difficulty, while the Do17 made an emergency landing near the Evros river on the Turkish border. Despite the inaction on the ground, the RAF and RHAF cooperated in raids on Italian positions in Albania. Kellas's 21 Mira escorted a bombing raid on the strategic road connecting Lin and Elbasan; the Fairey Battles of 33 Mira were given pride of place on this one – their last operation.

On 11 April Pattle and his 33 Squadron jumped a formation of Luftwaffe Ju88s laying mines in the sea south of Thessaloniki, despatching two of them. On the following day Pattle continued his run of kills, bringing down a Dornier Do215 reconnaissance plane east of Thessaloniki, an Italian SM79 near Larissa and a Bf109 somewhere in between. That was the day when more than 800 Luftwaffe aircraft and 300 of the Regia Aeronautica accompanied the panzer columns that burst through Greece's defensive Metaxas Line along the Yugoslav and Bulgarian borders. Facing this juggernaut were about eighty RAF and forty RHAF battleworthy aircraft.

The Greek Army's planned defence along the Aliakmon River, north of Mount Olympus, crumbled through a misunderstanding with the British that has never been adequately explained. Probably a creeping defeatism was already infecting the Greek military and the political establishment on which it depended. If there was such defeatism, the much-diminished RHAF certainly didn't share it. On 13 April 21 and 23 Mirai patrolled the Albanian skies 'more to raise the morale of the troops on the ground' than anything else, in the words of the squadron records.[3]

The German occupation of Thessaloniki deprived the Greek defenders of their key anti-aircraft defences in northern Greece, with the result that the Luftwaffe could now roam at will over the airfields at Larissa, Kazaklar and Trikala in the centre of the country. On 14 April Theodoropoulos, the 21 Mira CO, on his own initiative sent up small batches of PZLs to intercept the Luftwaffe, but they were too slow to be of much use. However, Flight Sergeants Constantine Sioris and Pericles Koutroumbas chased a German Henschel He126 into a ravine in the shadow of Olympus. Koutroumbas claimed the credit for shooting it into the sea east of the mountain. That day also, Bf109s of II/Jagdgeschwader 27 and Italian Macchi MC200s claimed credit for destroying a Greek Gladiator over Florina, while 21 Mira claimed a Ju87 Stuka, the most feared aircraft in the Balkans at that time.

As German panzer units were attempting to outflank Olympus to the east, where it abuts the Aegean Sea, the defenders needed to keep close tabs on what was happening in that sector. The fast and manoeuvrable Potez 63 was considered the best aircraft for the risky job, and so 31 Mira was assigned what would be its final operation. Flight Lieutenant George Pangalos flew a lone Potez through the ravines of Olympus, to emerge into flak of an intensity he had never experienced on the Albanian front. Breathless with shock, Pangalos somehow kept out of the way of the swarms of Bf109s filling the sky and managed to photograph the German positions. But it was all to no avail. On the following day Bf109s shot up all the remaining Potez 63s at Larissa, and that, to all intents and purposes, was the end of 31 Bombing Mira.

Not much has been said so far about the RHAF's naval cooperation *mirai*, as they played only a very marginal part in the war. Their missions were confined to tedious patrols of the Aegean Sea and fruitless submarine chasing, punctuated by the occasional bombing of Italian targets in the Dodecanese islands. They never managed to get a sub, but neither had they suffered any combat losses. One real chance at a blow at the enemy had come on 19 November 1940, when two Avro Ansons of 13 Naval Cooperation Mira took off at night to bomb the Italian naval station on the island of Leros. The Italians were smart and kept all the lights off. The Ansons turned for home without having bombed.

Just before the approach to Tatoi, Flight Sergeant Spyros Papadopoulos was about to jettison his bombs in the sea when Flight Sergeant Constantine Paleologou, his wireless operator, said he had lost contact with the base. The greater Athens area was blacked out and, moreover, was under thick cloud. Papadopoulos glimpsed a group of lights where he figured Tatoi ought to be and aimed the Anson at them. The lights turned out to belong to some unrelated building on the slopes of Mount Pendeli, which he avoided at the last minute. He switched on his headlamp and looked for a suitable landing space, but he knew there was hilly country beneath, and wasn't too confident about it.

'Anyone want to bale out?' he asked.

Paleologou got ready to jump, but as soon as he got to the door the rushing, menacing darkness gave him second thoughts and he preferred to stick with the plane. At length, Papadopoulos thought he saw a very faint light ahead, but the Anson's headlight picked out nothing but pine woods. Fuel was now at vanishing point and the Anson's engines were sputtering. Papadopoulos decided to put the plane into a gentle stall and land on the tree tops. He had forgotten that his landing gear was already down, but that may have saved him, as they helped break his landing on the trees.

The crew jumped out and ran clear. Midshipman Dimitrios Diamantopoulos, the naval navigator/observer, ran back to salvage the code books and flare pistol, which he fired, hoping to attract some attention. Soon a group of villagers approached speaking an unknown tongue and looking distinctly hostile. Paleologou recognized the language as Arvanitic – a variation of Albanian spoken by groups of ethnic Albanians who had been migrating into Greece for a few hundred years, many of whom continued to use the old language, even in the Athens area. Paleologou, himself of Arvanitic descent, addressed them in their tongue: 'Look, people, we're Greek and we've run out of fuel. Is there a policeman around? Can you help us?'

'Don't give us that crap,' came the brusque reply from the shadows. 'You're Italians and you've come here for some mischief, to attack the aerodrome!'

The circle of villagers around the three crew members widened. Some of them lit lamps, and the pickaxes in their hands became visible. There were also a few policemen with their rifles levelled. Eventually, thanks to Paleologou's patient translating, the truth was accepted. The airmen were taken to the nearby village of Liatani, where a telephone call was made to Tatoi. Three hours later Flying Officer Spyros Diamantopoulos showed up in a staff car with orders to 'collect the bodies'.

When the party went to the downed Anson, they found Papadopoulos's unjettisoned bombs still on board. Just as disturbing, daylight showed the plane poised perilously close to the edge of a 1,000-foot-deep ravine. That height, not far from Tanagra airbase, was called Aghios (Saint) Thomas Hill. Papadopoulos was convinced that the saint saved him and his mates.[4]

The squadron had to wait three months to get a piece of the action again. On 9 February it was ordered on a convoy protection mission. That month, heightened Italian submarine activity had been noted in the sea lanes between mainland Greece and Crete. Toumbakaris and Flight Lieutenant Argyris Kouyoufas wrestled their bomb-laden Ansons through stiff northerly winds driving masses of thick, low cloud over the foaming sea. An hour's bumpy flight brought them into view of the convoy plunging through the waves, with Royal Navy cruisers in front and destroyers in the rear. Perhaps the last thing the sailors were expecting was friendly aircraft overhead. A burst of anti-aircraft fire jerked Toumbakaris and Kouyoufas out of their complacency. The fire stopped after the two planes separated and fired their recognition flares. The wind worsened as the two aircraft made their inspection passes, one on each side of the convoy. Kouyoufas's plane was tossed about so violently he feared it would break up. Twenty minutes later, he exited the worst of the weather and tried to locate Toumbakaris, but couldn't see him anywhere.

At about that time Greek Navy headquarters received a distress signal from Toumbakaris who claimed to be lost in the storm and was asking to be vectored home. Toumbakaris reported his position as off the southern coast of Crete. What happened next is unknown. An error in transmission could have given him the opposite course to what he should have taken, which is why he ended up south of Crete. Whatever the truth, Toumbakaris's fuel ran dry and he seems to have decided to make an emergency landing in the Messara Plain in Crete. First, though, he had to jettison his bombs. Before he had a chance to do so, at wave-top height he caught his lowered undercarriage on a mountainous swell and overturned. The impact set off the bombs, which were fused. Linos, the navigator, was already dead on impact. The wireless operator, Warrant Officer Tingas, somehow survived.[5]

On 18 March 13 Mira finally scored a kill. Sergeant Christos Spentzos, escorting a convoy out of Piraeus, spotted an enemy submarine outside the port, in a perfect position to torpedo the convoy. While Diamantopoulos, the navigator/observer in this mission, kept an eye on the sub, Spentzos gunned the Anson's engines and put it into a dive, releasing the bombs at the same time. They were accurate. As the crew whooped with joy, Diamantopoulos signalled the victory to base. Spentzos, opening his log book to record the action, found he wasn't wearing his watch, and so in the time column he wrote simply 'Now' (*Tora*). It became 13 Mira's motto for months afterwards. Another Anson attacked an enemy sub on 1 April, but the result was uncertain.

It wasn't until the German invasion that the naval cooperation *mirai* were really called on to fight for the Aegean Sea and islands. As the Luftwaffe was hammering aerodromes on the mainland, a Fairey III seaplane of 11 Naval Cooperation Mira came across four Ju88s flying south over the sea. The observer thought the planes were friendly – until they banked and he saw the black crosses on the wings. As the Ju88s opened fire, Flight Lieutenant Yannis Ekonomou jinked his lumbering biplane back and forth to throw the German gunners off their aim. Then the seaplane's Lewis guns jammed. Just as the rocky island of Skyros was coming into view below, a well-timed burst raked the Fairey from stem to stern and knocked out the engine.

Unknown to the Germans, the Fairey III was on another mission as well – that of ferrying thirty chickens and a thousand eggs as an Easter present to the squadron from Navy headquarters. As the plane began its violent avoidance manoeuvres the chickens broke loose and the cockpit became a pandemonium of flying feathers and straw. The flight engineer, Flight Sergeant Spyros Barbas, had a full-time job vainly trying to calm the squawking hens.

The seaplane was on fire by the time it glided onto the surface of the sea. Ekonomou was the first to jump overboard, followed by his observer. Barbas hesitated as he couldn't swim, but the rain of bullets smacking into the sea, as the Ju88s made repeated strafing sweeps, changed the engineer's mind. Skyros was about a mile away. A bullet grazed Barbas's forehead, stunning him. As he reflexively ducked his head under water, two more bullets grazed his left arm. The three airmen eventually crawled ashore on Skyros, as the clatter of exploding ammunition from the still-burning plane echoed off the rocks. (The ultimate fate of the hapless chickens is not recorded.)

It took Ekonomou and the others more than three hours of hiking over rocky hill and dale until they came across the hut of a hermit-shepherd who gave them their fill of milk and fresh island *feta* cheese. Meanwhile, a search for the missing crew was underway. Dodging the Luftwaffe that seemed to be everywhere in the clear spring sky, a 12 Mira Dornier Do22 scoured the sea around Skyros, found nothing, and landed in the main port. Hardly had the crew time to step ashore than a Ju88 roared overhead strafing the seaplane, repeating the attack eight times. By some miracle the Do22's engine was untouched, but one float was holed. After laborious repairs, the seaplane managed to make it to the main Greek Navy base at Salamis – which fell to the Germans a few days later.[6]

At nine o'clock in the morning of 15 April the pilots of 23 Mira noticed a single Luftwaffe Henschel Hs126 nosing towards Mount Olympus. Koutroumbas, a relatively new boy in the squadron and fired up from his kill of the previous day, offered to fly one of the two PZLs warming up to intercept the Henschel. He and Sioris took off to chase it, but it shook them off. Sioris had engine trouble and broke off the pursuit. Koutroumbas seems to have got in a shot at the Henschel, which is reported to have gone down. Perhaps overly complacent at his second kill in twenty-four hours, he turned and flew at low height and low speed towards Sedes. The Henschel was probably a trap, as without warning three Bf109s bounced him, killing him with the first machine gun burst.

About forty miles to the south-west, the ageing Blochs of 24 Mira rose to meet the Luftwaffe waves over Trikala. It was Holy Week in the Greek Orthodox calendar, and the Greeks were very much aware that their own crucifixion as a nation was just a matter of days away. Twelve fighters – six PZLs, three Blochs and three Gladiators, all that remained of the mainland RHAF – rose wearily to tangle with the invaders 9,000 feet up. As two Ju87 Stukas detached themselves to dive-bomb, two PZLs dived on them in turn, destroying one of them. A Gladiator of Kellas's 21 Mira bagged another Stuka. As if from nowhere, a fleet of Bf109s appeared from the clouds. The fight was grossly unequal – four to one in the Germans' favour. Several Bf109s took on Sergeant George Mokkas's Bloch, which quickly went down, trailing thick smoke. Mokkas was the last Greek airman to die in the mainland fight against the Axis.

Flight Sergeant Leonidas Katsarellis in his PZL struggled mightily to get at least one Messerschmitt in his sights as he manoeuvred wildly to get out of their line of fire. Finally he locked on one, and managed to get in a shot that damaged it. But moments later the mainspar on the starboard wing was shot away. Katsarellis, if he had any hope of landing at all, had to handle his winged plane gingerly, but this made him a sitting duck. More bullets holed his fuel and oil tanks. From the intense fumes filling the cockpit, Katsarellis lost consciousness and let his PZL fall into a dive.

Luckily for him, his Luftwaffe pursuers apparently thought they had written him off and turned to seek other prey. Katsarellis regained consciousness to find himself perilously close to the ground. He yanked back the stick savagely to pull out; fortunately, the PZL's damaged wing held, but flames were now licking back from the twin exhausts under the cowling. He shut down his engine, pushed back the canopy and loosened his harness, to be able to jump out as soon as he landed. Though the engine was off, the fire continued to burn, blocking Katsarellis's vision. When he found a level spot, the PZL bounced and turned over, throwing the pilot clear. He lived, but his right leg was badly burned.

Kellas, the 21 Mira CO, was wounded in the same dogfight. He was in a Gladiator pitted against the Bf109s, and there really was no contest. After a quarter of an hour in the air dodging two Messerschmitts almost at rooftop height, bullets smashed his elevators and ailerons. He managed a smooth landing, but rolled a bit too far down the runway, hitting a clump of bushes. The impact snapped Kellas's harness and hurled him out of the Gladiator's cockpit and into a newly-planted wheat field, injuring his right leg and left eye. The stricken biplane careered on for another hundred yards or so before burning up. Kellas's squadron mates, intent on their own fights, at first thought he was dead. But his service to his homeland was by no means over.

After 15 April the RHAF as a fighting force virtually ceased to exist. Though the RAF squadrons in Greece fought bravely on for a few more days, the Luftwaffe was unstoppable. Its bombers blasted twenty-two aircraft on the ground at Niamata, including all those of 113 Squadron, then moved on to Larissa to destroy nineteen more, including the remaining few Greek Potez 63s. In a simultaneous assault, Luftwaffe and Regia Aeronautica bombers made short work of Paramythia aerodrome. Fairy Tale Valley was no more.

The prevailing mood was summed up by Theodoropoulos, the 23 Mira CO, in his diary: 'For the first time, we're falling back ... Our combat capability is reduced to zero.' Resting a while at Amfikleia to the south, Theodoropoulos received orders to send his enlisted ground crews on two months' leave to slim down the squadron for greater mobility. Calling the crews together, he read them the order, to be greeted by a flat collective refusal. He promised that in two months the squadron would have new aircraft and be reorganized as already the Greek government was planning to continue the war in Crete. The enlisted men would have none of it. 'Every one of them asked to stay here with their weapons and fight with the ground troops.'[7] Shortly afterwards the Luftwaffe shot up the planes at Amfikleia except for four PZLs of 22 Mira that managed to escape to Argos, south of Athens.

With central Greece now gone, Papagos, the Greek commander-in-chief, and Major General Henry 'Jumbo' Wilson, the commander of the British forces, ordered a fallback to the famous defensive position at Thermopylai, where in 480 BC Leonidas and his Three Hundred had held off many times their number of Persians before dying to a man. But the Greek command of AD 1941 was in no shape for such heroics. The hitherto victorious Greek Army in Albania was completely isolated. With no more forward aerodromes available, there was no longer any possibility of covering the Army from the air. It was a bitter pill for the Greeks to swallow. The Regia Aeronautica now flew unchallenged over northern Greek skies.

King George II and Papagos, uncomfortably aware that British boys were fighting and dying in the defence of Greece, ordered the Army in Albania to set its own example and stand firm, but it was too late. Morale at the front had already crumbled. Papagos himself didn't think much could be done at Thermopylae against Germany's modern weapons of war. Wilson, on the contrary, believed it could be done, but the majority of the Greek government agreed with Papagos. The agony had gone on long enough.

Early in the morning of 19 April about fifteen Bf109s attacked Tanagra aerodrome, destroying eight of 23 Mira's nine Gladiators in two strafing runs. Kellas, whose 21 Mira was based at Amfikleia not far away, had predicted the attack, as an enemy reconaissance plane had droned over the area the previous afternoon. But by this time what was left of the RHAF lacked anything resembling a coordinated information and communications network. As a result, Theodoropoulos's Gladiators, neatly lined up on the runway, were a duck shoot for the Germans. Oddly enough, his half dozen or so PZLs remained unscathed.[8] With these he was ordered to move to Eleusis, nearer Athens.

Kellas, also ordered to Eleusis, arranged for his sole remaining Gladiator to be repaired. His mechanics, salvaging what equipment they could, and under the constant threat of Luftwaffe attacks, fixed up the Gladiator on the rainy evening before Easter Day. Flight Lieutenant Yannis Papadimitriou took 'the last free Greek aeroplane'[9] through a hailstorm from Amfikleia down to Eleusis.

That was the time the officers of 32 Mira were ordered to report to headquarters in Athens. Thinking they were about to be demobilized from the air force, the pilots were heartened to be asked to supply provisions to Greek troops isolated on the Albanian front. Three Blenheims were duly loaded with bread, tea and sugar. The planes got through, but the packages were dropped rather clumsily, breaking apart on the rocks and scattering their contents over a wide area. Successful or not, it was 32 Mira's last mission. When the Blenheims landed, some pilots and engineer officers approached Group Captain Averof, now the bomber force commander, with a suggestion that the Blenheims be flown to Crete or North Africa to carry on the war.

'But Greek units are still fighting here,' Averof replied. 'If you leave you'll be charged with desertion and face a court martial.' Averof was soon to change his mind, but encountered opposition from the General Staff. Had he been listened to, more RHAF aircraft would have survived to serve in another theatre of war.

As 20 April, Easter Day, dawned, 32 Mira was ordered to Eleusis, its old pre-war base. As soon as the Blenheims landed, a swarm of Messerschmitts appeared overhead. By the end of the day, 32 Mira's Blenheims were no more. As Eleusis was being hammered, thick columns of oily smoke were seen curling up from Hellenikon aerodrome; the Greek authorities were burning fuel stocks to prevent them falling into German hands. Wing Commander George Tzanetakis, the RHAF's chief liaison officer with the RAF, was struck by the defeatism of the move. It was the RAF that was now bearing the full brunt of the losing battle against the Luftwaffe, and the overt signs of growing panic in the Greek government were not helping morale.

Athens was now at the invaders' mercy. In the afternoon Bf109s of III/Jagdgeschwader 77 and II/Jagdgeschwader 26 destroyed the remaining aircraft on the ground at Tatoi and Eleusis. Attempting to defend the city by air were a mere sixteen RAF Hurricanes of 33 Squadron. 'Pat' Pattle hadn't been flying much recently; growing battle fatigue had morphed into a high fever. That morning had found him wrapped in his blanket, shivering with ague. In the afternoon the air-raid sirens sounded, heralding a Luftwaffe dive-bombing raid on Piraeus. 33 Squadron took off without him, but when the last Hurricane left the ground, Pattle hauled himself out of bed and went to join the fight. As the bullets of a Messerschmitt Me110 heavy fighter thudded into the hardstanding around him, Pattle slammed the throttle forward, climbing fast, accompanied by Flying Officer Vernon Woodward. Within minutes he was over Piraeus. About 1,000 feet beneath him were Me110s escorting a fleet of Ju87s unleashing death and destruction on the port.

Pattle threw his plane at a formation of Me110s. Woodward got one that had latched onto Pattle's tail, followed by another Me110 and a Ju88. He last saw his ailing CO surrounded by a cloud of Ju88s, before concentrating on attacking as many of the enemy as he could. He hit three more Me110s, ran out of ammunition and turned for home. It was an epic fight. T.H. Wisdom, the RAF's chronicler, mourned the many friends 'shot down fighting eight miles above the Acropolis'.[10] Pattle had just shot down three enemy aircraft when a concerted attack by two Me110s blew him up in mid-air and he plunged into the Bay of Eleusis, where he and his aircraft still rest. Already an ace when he arrived in Greece, he had chalked up twenty-three more kills in the Greek campaign and at least as many possibles. With at least forty official victories to his credit (and perhaps ten more unrecognized ones), 'Pat' Pattle has a legitimate claim to be the highest-scoring British and Commonwealth pilot of the Second World War.

The three remaining Fairey Battles of 33 Mira had meanwhile moved to Tanagra. While they were there a Messerschmitt Bf109 of III/JG 27 buzzed the airfield and shot up Skatzikas's plane before it was itself downed by anti-aircraft fire. A few days afterwards the squadron (or what was left of it) moved south to Tatoi, where the Germans caught up with it and destroyed the few Battles left. Several airmen, including Skatzikas, escaped on foot through the woods to Athens.[11]

The last act of the RHAF in embattled Greece, however, had yet to be played out.

During the six months of hostilities so far, eight converted Dornier Do22 ex-seaplanes of 12 Naval Cooperation Mira had been waiting at Eleusis to replace lost bombers and observation aircraft. On 14 April two of them, now officially belonging to 2002 Special Observation Mira, finally took off from Ioannina. Their unfamiliar silhouettes drew the fire of Greek anti-aircraft batteries that pursued them as far as the frontier. The Dorniers were not built as fighting planes, and so when three enemy aircraft came into view they quickly dived out of range into the murky mountain mists. Flying Officer Constantine Exarhakos's plane suffered engine failure during the plunge and he was seconds from hitting the ground when the engine revived and the plane pulled out, giving the hitherto agnostic Exarhakos the conviction that Someone up there was watching out for him.

A week later Exarhakos was taxying at Agrinion, preparing to ferry his Dornier to Eleusis, when a *Staffel* of Bf109s strafed the airfield. He and his passenger, Army Major Epaminondas Tselos, jumped out and sheltered under some olive trees until the attack passed. He then took off, arriving over Eleusis as it was being hammered by waves of Stukas. Exarhakos waited until that raid, too, was over, then took off from Eleusis for Argos with Flying Officer Constantine Panagopoulos, intending to head for Crete. It was not to be. Soon after the Dornier landed at Argos, it was bombed to bits along with all the other aircraft there, though Exarhakos and Panagopoulos survived.

Pilot Officer George Kytariolos's Henschel Hs126 of 3 Mira was hit during its take-off run at Agrinion. Slewing off the runway, it collided with a parked RAF Hurricane and overturned, catching fire. His observer, Pilot Officer Dimitrios Voutsinas, reflexively jumped out of the burning plane, but seeing Kytariolos motionless in the pilot's seat, turned back to rescue him. On fire himself and ignoring the frantic cries of the ground crew to run and save himself, Voutsinas managed to pull the pilot out before collapsing. A brave medical officer carried both to safety, but Kytariolos died in hospital a few days later. He was the last Greek airman to die in the battle for Greece.[12]

With the Germans now at the approaches to Athens, Lieutenant General George Tsolakoglou, the former commander of the Greek Army III Corps and now commanding the West Macedonia Army Group, decided that his country had bled enough. At six o'clock on 20 April Tsolakoglou met the German advance columns in the mountains east of Ioannina and signed the initial protocol of Greece's surrender with Major General Sepp Dietrich, the commander of Hitler's SS bodyguard. The Fuehrer himself made no secret of his admiration for the tough Greeks who had discomfited the Duce's armies in Albania. He authorized permission for Greek officers to keep their sidearms – a rare mark of military respect for a defeated foe. Tsolakoglou had the presence of mind to make clear to Dietrich that Greece was surrendering to Germany only, and not to Italy, whose armies Greece had thrown back. Dietrich tended to agree. But Mussolini, when he heard about it, ranted to such a degree that Hitler decided to allow him some of the credit. Greece signed a formal ceasefire with Italy three days later.

The Greek government under Koryzis and King George II had already made arrangements to escape to Crete in 13 Mira's nine Avro Ansons, to be ready on 22 April. The prime minister wanted to keep the whole operation under wraps. Each Anson had room for two government ministers with basic baggage. Everything was ready when, for reasons never satisfactorily explained, the crew of a destroyer that was to take equipment by sea refused to sail. Koryzis, in a fit of despair, shot himself.

Finally on 23 April the king – now assuming duties as interim prime minister – and his government sailed for Souda Bay in Crete on a British warship. On board were the king's aide-de-camp, Wing Commander Potamianos, and eighteen RAF men. The British pullout began the following day, but not before forty Me110s plastered the airfield at Argos. Over five nights, to avoid attacks by the Luftwaffe, nearly 51,000 British, Commonwealth and Greek servicemen swarmed onto eleven transports and twenty-five Royal Navy warships in a Mediterranean version of Dunkirk. Two transports were sunk with heavy loss of life.

The sixteen executives and pilots of the Regular Transport Mira (the former EEES) never got to receive their medals of merit. Red tape thickets being what they are, especially in a crumbling country, the Germans marched in before the decree could be implemented. In the confused days before the German takeover, there seems to have been an order for the seven transports to fly to the Middle East. Such an order, if there was one, somehow didn't get through to its intended recipients, and so the Luftwaffe was handed a present of all seven Junkers transports, which it put to good use. The Germans employed a skeleton local staff of sixty-seven people to keep the planes in the air as a military-controlled civil airline, with its technical base at Tatoi. After the war the EEES was formally dissolved and its successor set up, to eventually develop into today's Olympic Airlines.

In the week-long German invasion, the RHAF shot down four Luftwaffe planes, with anti-aircraft fire accounting for twenty-five more. The air force's contribution to the fight against the Italians in particular has tended to become lost in the glare of the Greek Army's spectacular successes. Since then, Greek popular culture and the media have polished and re-polished the Albanian campaign into a gold-tinged page of national glory, right up there with Troy and Marathon. Yet not much has ever been said about the audacious raids of the RHAF bomber *mirai* behind Italian lines, especially during the Greek counter-offensive after mid-November, which did much to weaken the Italian position. Kartalamakis credits the RHAF with heartening the Greek ground troops by the mere sight of the blue and white roundels soaring above them.[13]

Unlike the pilots of the Battle of Britain, of whom they were fully the equals, Greece's airmen were denied the supreme reward of eventual victory over great odds. During the six-month Albanian campaign thirty-seven RHAF aircraft were lost to at least ninety-two of the Regia Aeronautica.

Twenty-eight of the latter were destroyed on the ground at Korce and elsewhere. Italian figures, on the other hand, speak of sixty-five of their aircraft lost and 495 damaged. In 2,710 combat flying hours, fifty-two Greek aircrew died. Twenty men of 33 Mira alone received decorations.[14]

The RHAF effort had been hampered by two major drawbacks that were never satisfactorily eliminated, one tactical and the other doctrinal. The tactical problem was the sheer diversity of aircraft in Greek service, from Blenheims and Potez 63s to PZL24s, Gladiators and Bloch MB151s, not to mention the equipment of the Naval Cooperation *mirai* and training schools. All these types had different flight characteristics and performances, resulting in a high degree of operational inefficiency. The preponderance of non-British aircraft types had resulted in severe parts shortages as France and Poland had fallen swiftly under the Nazi heel.

The other drawback was more serious, and involved the lingering concept of the air force as a mere aerial adjunct to the ground forces, with tactics dictated by ground warfare considerations. Theoretically, the Regia Aeronautica appears to have gone beyond that stage of thinking, though perhaps it was fortunate for the Greeks that its commander, the enigmatic General Pricolo, did not have the willpower to impose more modern aerial warfare doctrines over the outdated ideas of his superiors. Therefore his *squadriglie* arguably did far less damage than they could have. Moreover, as the ground war was fought largely over Greek-held territory, those Italian aircrew who survived being shot down were taken prisoner, while few, if any, Greek airmen fell into Italian hands.

There is no evidence that the RHAF senior leadership, either, had learned anything new from the months of slugging it out over the mountains of Greece and Albania. As with the Italians, it was very much the Army's show. Almost all the publicity and all the war correspondents' reports had emanated from the ground front. Now, in April 1941, all the glory was gone. As the goose-step sounded through Greece's occupied towns and villages the unbowed remnant of the RHAF, under strange skies and in stranger climes, was far from giving up the fight.

Chapter 9

The Flight to Egypt

As German forces occupied Athens and moved with lightning speed on southern Greece, the EKI at Argos had to move, and fast. On 16 April 1941 all remaining RHAF aircraft at Argos and elsewhere were ordered destroyed. It was an exceptionally cool-headed officer or NCO who could literally obey the order to take an axe to the faithful old Breguet XIXs that had been part of their service lives for as long as they could remember.[1]

No such fate awaited the ten Ansons of 13 Mira, the only active RHAF squadron left, stationed at Hellenikon on the Athenian seafront. The crews had no intention of smashing their planes up, orders or no. But they didn't want them falling into German hands, either. Moreover, the Anson was the only naval cooperation aircraft with a range enabling it to fly directly to Crete. After some hesitation the CO, Squadron Leader Spyros Dakopoulos, fixed the Ansons' departure for six o' clock in the morning of 23 April.

The planes were lined up and ready to go when a couple of flights of Bf109s zoomed out of nowhere and proceeded to thoroughly and repeatedly strafe what was left on the ground at Hellenikon. Five of the Ansons were shot up beyond repair. After the attackers left, four of the remaining five took off amid the columns of smoke rising from the shattered airfield. Papadopoulos and Flight Sergeant Dimitrios Galanakos flew the first two, followed by two more flown by Flight Sergeant Vasilios Kourdis and Sergeant Nikolaos Kavourinos. A fifth, though holed, was quickly patched up and flown off by Flying Officer Constantine Davakis. It was the last that 13 Mira would see of its homeland for three and a half years.

The trip to Crete was no cakewalk. They flew low over the sea to escape the attentions of the Bf109s and Ju87s milling around in the Aegean skies. The Anson's single dorsal gun would have not done very much against a determined attacker. The German pilots, however, were preoccupied with looking for and dive-bombing the multitude of vessels evacuating British troops from Greece's shores. Kourdis, looking down, described what he saw as 'a scene from Dante's Inferno'.

Somehow, the five Ansons made it to Heraklion, the main town of Crete. Dakopoulos wanted to keep them there, as the king and government were already on the island. But the constant air raids and tension determined the crews to fly on to Egypt at once. Dakopoulos had little choice but to agree, and the RAF helped him set course for Mersa Matruh on the Egyptian coast. Thirteen hours after leaving Athens, the Ansons of 13 Mira crossed the North African coast. Peering down through the desert haze, Kourdis picked out a few camouflaged Hurricanes, which meant a landing ground. After causing the RAF station a flurry of an alert, one by one the tired crews landed, to be treated by the RAF to tea, which Kourdis thought was the sweetest thing he had ever tasted.[2]

The official order to destroy all remaining RHAF aircraft in the face of the German onslaught has been criticized as unnecessarily defeatist. Kartalamakis argues that if cooler heads had prevailed the few Blenheims and Fairey Battles left could have been evacuated to Crete and thence to the Middle East, to continue the war.[3] Though it's debatable whether such types – not to mention the Dornier Do22 and the Fairey III – would have been able to accomplish much against the Axis air forces in North Africa, their presence at least would have sent a stronger signal to the British that some Greeks, at least, were not about to give up.

The commander of 11 Mira, Squadron Leader Christos Passialis, ignored the destruction order and flew his Fairey IIIs to Monemvasia, a Gibraltar-like rock on the southern tip of the Peloponnese, on the first leg of an escape to Crete. But the Luftwaffe caught them there and finished them off. A single Dornier Do22 of 12 Mira only just made it to Egypt in the hands of Flying Officer Dimitrios Dimitriadis. His engine cut out over Aboukir Bay but he managed a dicey landing at Alexandria.

As for the EKI at Argos, 136 trainees, instructors and staff boarded a transport at nearby Nafplion and sailed to Crete. Barely had their ship arrived at Souda Bay when a formation of Italian bombers attacked. By sheer luck no bombs killed any Greek airmen. But the shock of defeat at home was already having its devastating effect on morale. Insubordinate rumblings, mainly from communist sympathizers among the enlisted men, had already been heard at Argos. In the near-anarchic conditions of Crete those rumblings became louder.

Squadron Leader Xenophon Varvaressos, the head of training at the EKI, saw the danger and took steps to avert it. After the first chaotic night at Chania, to maintain some semblance of an *esprit de corps*, he led a squad of cadets on a ten-kilometre forced march to take their minds off the pervasive fear of the unknown. Like his famous ancient namesake, Xenophon the Athenian, who in 400 BC took command of the Ten Thousand at a critical juncture in the wilds of what is now Iraq, Varvaressos left his men no time to brood. 'Gentlemen,' he announced in his brusque and laconic manner, 'the college is in operation. We just haven't got any planes to fly.'

The EKI thus shakily got itself together again at Armeni, about five miles inland from Souda Bay, housed in a school, a church and few village huts. In these unpromising premises Varvaressos rode his cadets hard to stop them thinking too much. Varvaressos believed, according to one cadet, that 'now, in this dismal situation, with no control or supervision or country, [was] the time to show that we had discipline and will.'[4] At that time the total RHAF strength in Crete came to 54 officer pilots, 145 flying cadets, 7 staff officers, 1 medical officer, 85 ground NCOs, 81 sergeant pilots, 80 trainee bomb-aimers, 21 engineer officers, 141 engineer NCOs and 200 aircraft-men.[5] Varvaressos can take credit for preserving the morale of the RHAF as a fighting force when all seemed lost.

In May waves of German paratroopers descended on the north-west coast of Crete. Despite sustaining horrific losses from the British, Greek, Australian and New Zealand defenders, the Germans prevailed thanks to mistakes on the Allied side. The grounded Greek airmen could only look on helplessly as the Luftwaffe Junkers Ju52 transports disgorged hundreds of paratroopers while Bf109s, Me110s and Ju87 Stuka dive-bombers reduced Souda Bay and Chania to rubble. Some of the Greeks, though, couldn't help observing that the Stuka pilots couldn't bomb worth a damn. 'They seemed to be trainees in their baptism of fire,' one wrote later. 'Their squadron commanders at least should have been more experienced. Their failure was inexcusable.' With morale like that, the Greek air force couldn't be written off so easily.

As Crete was evacuated, the Greek airmen were assigned to board the SS *New Zealand*, an ocean liner requisitioned as a military transport. But the ship's crew panicked, and during a lull in the air attacks they attempted to sail out of Souda Bay before all of the Greeks were on board. Some cadets were heavily laden with their precious course textbooks, which they kept in their kitbags despite orders that they throw the books into the sea to lighten themselves. Some of those left ashore wandered around the Cretan villages. A few were caught by the Germans and herded into prisoner-of-war camps.

Among the former was Group Captain Philippas, the former fighter force commander, and Sergeant George Lambropoulos of the EKI's 1939 intake that had been hurriedly graduated two months before. In the company of a few other Greek servicemen they joined the Allies' gut-wrenching overland retreat to Sfakia on the south coast of Crete. Lambropoulos remembered walking behind one New Zealander who had a grisly collection of dead German paratroopers' ears strung over his shoulder. At Sfakia the few

British evacuation ships available gave priority to British and Commonwealth soldiers, leaving the Greeks to fend for themselves.

Philippas was torn between surrendering to the advancing Germans or splitting up and letting each man fend for himself. The latter seemed more palatable. While Philippas and his adjutant managed to find an evacuation boat, Lambropoulos and his dwindling group set out on foot for eastern Crete, living off lettuce and pumpkin leaves cadged from friendly farmers. At the coastal village of Plakia they found a boatman who said he could take them across to Alexandria for a considerable sum of money – in advance. At the rendezvous, the boat was there but the boatman wasn't. He never did show up.

The boat was eventually sold for half of what was paid for it. Lambropoulos and his group stayed briefly at a mountain monastery. When the monks warned them that the Germans were approaching, the group split up for each man to find his own way back to the north coast of Crete where there seemed to be a better chance of catching a boat back to Athens. With Allied ships now gone from southern Crete, escape to Egypt seemed an impossible dream.

Lambropoulos survived by getting work on a farm near Rethymnon. When word got around that he was a pilot, a search for a bride was immediately begun among the local farm girls. He escaped that fate by hearing of a German-requisitioned boat scheduled to sail to Heraklion to collect Italian ex-POWs and repatriate them to Italy. Pretending to have nautical experience, he got himself hired on the boat but was put off at Heraklion when a more experienced crew became available. After a few hungry and homeless days he got passage on an overloaded cargo boat for Piraeus and returned to his village in the Peloponnese.

The tiny remnant of the RHAF had just passed through the greatest physical threat in its history. But even before the *New Zealand* docked in Egypt, a subtler but equally serious hazard was at work – communist agitation in the ranks of the NCOs. The trouble appears to have started in the unlucky 1939 Icarus School intake whose interrupted course meant that they were denied commissioned rank. To some proud cadets, this was intolerable. Nourished by a suitable dose of communist egalitarianism, such sentiments boiled into open insubordination. At the first roll call in Egypt Vladousis called two of the more egregiously insubordinate NCOs onto the carpet, slapped them across the face and told them they would be shot forthwith. They weren't, thanks to the intervention of Varvaressos, who was present. But for the rest of his life Vladousis regretted not having carried out his threat; if he had, he wrote later, other and more serious communist-led mutinies would not have occurred to hamper the Allied war effort in the Mediterranean.

In the midst of this grim atmosphere the Greek airmen were left to linger a month without knowing where they would go next. Eventually, they were billeted at Qasasin in the desert, where at least they could have regular meals and sleep on beds, even if the beds were made out of crates. The insubordinates continued to grumble, trying the patience of Varvaressos. On one occasion a corporal cook mistakenly added petrol to the olive oil in which he was preparing lentil soup, a Greek favourite. At mealtime, as sounds of disgust and complaint erupted from the men, Varvaressos stepped in. Knowing that the agitators in their midst might well use the complaint to manufacture a full-blown crisis, he called for a full bowl of the soup and gulped it down, petrol and all, smiling beatifically.

Said one cadet later:

> If Varvaressos had not been at Qasasin, the School would have disintegrated [under the impact of] communist propaganda... Indoctrination was taking place in the large tents. Most of us were just simple young lads and didn't know any better.

Though chronically limping from a leg injury sustained from a crash during his training days at Tatoi, Varvaressos would walk miles across the scorching desert every day to liaise with the RAF on how to improve the food and ease his men's harsh living conditions. On one occasion his Homeric sense of honour bridled at an order that his men use wooden imitation rifles for drill practice. 'No, sir,' Varvaressos replied to the British officer who relayed the order, 'the Greeks drill only with real weapons.' Varvaressos 'protected us like we were his own children'.[6]

The EKI cadets and staff were not the only Greek airmen in the Middle East. In January twenty-one officers and nine NCOs of the EKI, headed by Wing Commander Vilos, had been sent to Habbaniya, Iraq, to continue their training at the RAF's Fourth Special Flying Training School. As the Germans were smashing into Greece nine more flight sergeants and five sergeants of the 1939 intake under Flight Sergeant Byron Germanos were sent to Habbaniya to join the other Greeks in advanced training, including night flying, on Hawker Audaxes and Airspeed Oxfords.

The initial Habbaniya group had expected to return to Greece. But with the German conquest it was re-routed to Gaza, which was becoming a general assembly point for RHAF personnel who had escaped the mainland by various means. The second group hadn't been at Habbaniya long before Rashid Ali, the pro-German ruler of Iraq, made a threatening demonstration against the British base with 7,000 men. Vilos agreed to lend some Greek crews for an RAF 'counter-demonstration' of 100 planes that flew in menacing formation for two hours above the Iraqi positions. To Vilos the flight was his students' 'first experience of proper modern aerial warfare'.

At dawn on 2 May the Iraqis got serious and raked the compound with artillery and machine gun fire. The RAF and RHAF took off to hit back. Pilots had to scramble from plane to plane dodging bullets and shell bursts. Margaritis, Flight Lieutenant Constantine Platsis and Pilot Officer Leonidas Drenas, flying Hawker Harts and Audaxes, dived almost vertically onto the enemy, with Flight Lieutenant George Markou following in an Airspeed Oxford.

On the ground, Flight Lieutenant Nikolaos Koskoros was just emerging from an all-nighter in the mess. Quite inebriated, and still clutching his whisky glass, he was helped to a dugout shelter where he calmly noted the positions of the Iraqi artillery muzzle flashes, plotting them on a chart so they could be later bombed accurately. He did the job so well that he was given the same job every night for the five days the battle of Habbaniya lasted. An apocryphal story tells how, one night after the Iraqi shelling had stopped, Koskoros remarked: 'It's finished again, boys.'

'What, sir?' someone asked. 'The alarm?'

'No, you idiot – the whisky!'[7]

Margaritis, a future chief of the air staff, himself flew forty-five sorties in the battle for Habbaniya, about one-third of the RHAF total. On one of them he bombed an Iraqi fuel dump containing a million gallons, turning a good part of the desert into a roiling fireball. He and Drenas smashed an Iraqi convoy on the Habbaniya-Falluja road, an operation credited with helping end the siege of the base. When King George II and the Greek government-in-exile landed in Egypt about that time, Wing Commander Vilos was deputed to meet the king in Cairo. After shaking the officer's hand the king gave a wry smile and deadpanned: 'So you're the one who declared war on Iraq!'[8] Shortly afterwards Vilos and his Greeks were put in an old Vickers Valentia transport and flown to Lydda, and from there to Gaza. There Vilos was promoted to group captain and given command of what was left of the RHAF, directly answering to the British Middle East command.

Was there an RHAF in real terms at all? With Greece defeated and under occupation, it could be argued that there was not. Greek air personnel were now enrolled as RAF personnel and assigned to RAF units. Yet one core refused to be assimilated thoroughly, and alone among the Greek-manned units, still proudly bore the blue and white roundels. This was 13 Mira, down to five Avro Ansons, the only squadron to escape Greece in any strength whatsoever. Other planes that made it out were Dimitriadis's Dornier Do22 of 12 Mira and four Avro 621 trainers from the EKI.

After a few days of enjoying the cosmopolitan delights of Alexandria, 13 Mira was moved to Heliopolis near Cairo.[9] The crews were handsomely put up in a Greek tycoon's mansion that was also the headquarters of the Greek Air Ministry-in-exile. Life in Cairo, though, proved too good to last. In the RAF's eyes 13 Mira's five Ansons were too valuable to be doing nothing. Within six weeks the unit was back at Dekheila as part of the Fleet Air Arm's 201 Group. Dakopoulos, the CO, got the unit into shape for its first mission, a series of mock bombing runs by a single Anson at about 18,000 feet to test radar reception and Hurricane pilot reflexes. The Greeks were proud of their sleek Ansons that stood out against 201 Group's stringy and clumsy-looking Fairey Swordfishes and Supermarine Walruses.

Finding spare parts for the Ansons wasn't easy. Pilot Officer Adamantios Aidonopoulos, who had flown the mock bombing runs, took off to try and find some. The unit's single junior engineer officer, Pilot Officer Evanghelos Babas, was having to perform miracles of improvisation. At Abu Sueir, Aidonopoulos was lucky to come across an RAF Anson that had just been severely damaged in a crash-landing. Soon he was winging his way back to Dekheila laden with its valuable parts.

In the middle of 1941 Britain needed every scrap of Allied help it could get in the Mediterranean theatre. The German conquest of mainland Greece, Crete and the Aegean islands was the northern half of a giant pincer movement aimed at squeezing the British out of the Middle East. The southern half was spearheaded by General Erwin Rommel, whose hard-driving Afrika Korps had taken over from the faltering Italian effort in North Africa. At about the time Squadron Leader Pattle fell defending Athens, Rommel was besieging the strategic Libyan port of Tobruk that was vital for supplying any armed force in the area. Counteroffensives by the new British commander, General Wavell, failed to dent Rommel's positions and Egypt came under serious threat.

In late June 1941 13 Mira's operations began in earnest. Its task was to fly anti-submarine patrols over an area bounded by the Nile Delta, Cyprus, the Dodecanese islands and Crete. On a clear day the snowy peak of Crete's Mount Psiloritis would be visible, filling the crews with melancholy as they imagined the island suffering under the Nazi boot. The missions were long and fatiguing. For days not a single U-boat periscope would be seen, though one Anson claimed credit for sinking an Italian sub off Haifa. When the 201 Group brass asked the squadron what it wanted in return for the kill, the reply was a couple of orderlies for the officers' mess – to come from the captured Italian submarine crew![10] The favour was not granted.

As the months passed the venerable Ansons began to show their age. There was talk of replacing them with Bristol Blenheims, but the promised deliveries were constantly delayed. Therefore, two enterprising flying officers, Davakis and Panayotis Manavis, took to scouring aerial graveyards where they were lucky enough to find several Blenheim IVs rotting away. From those relics they managed to assemble no fewer than five airworthy Blenheims that were pressed into training service, easing the burden on the fatigued Ansons. The feat impressed the 201 Group brass enough to deliver the promised replacements in February 1942. The Ansons were honourably retired, and the squadron officially redesignated 13 Light Bombing Mira.

In Gaza the Greek air war effort took rather longer to organize. Fortunately, Group Captain Vilos knew many British officers from the days of his training in Britain. In his view, training took precedence over equipment. But there had to be somewhere to train first, and something to train on. There wasn't much to do at the cockroach-infested quarters in Gaza except ogle the Australian nurses sunning themselves on the adjacent beach. Then in the summer of 1941 three ex-EKI Avro 621 trainers arrived, reminding the Greeks that they were still an air force. Eventually, a few ancient Gloster Gauntlets ('clinically dead,' sneered one officer who viewed them) from Abyssinia and a single battered Gladiator joined the motley assemblage. Vilos got a promise of some Hurricane Mk Is from the RAF.

Yet trouble lurked beneath the surface. Nazi propagandists in Berlin and Greek communists in Moscow never ceased to broadcast that while the Greeks at home were starving, their airmen were 'running around in Cairo and Alexandria drinking whisky and enjoying beefsteaks and jam'.[11] Inevitably, some of this nonsense influenced the naive and idealistic among the enlisted men. Leftwing NCOs formed what was called the Greek Liberation League (EAS) with the aim of purging the Army, Navy and RHAF of remnants of the former Metaxas regime. Swelling the ranks of the dissidents was a steady stream of fugitives from occupied Greece, where an effective national resistance organization had not yet taken shape. Many, if not most, of these young men were genuine patriots with no political agenda. But the clandestine Greek Communist Party (KKE) was planting others that eventually would prove quite as dangerous as the enemy.

In seeking suitable training places Vilos learned from his British friends that the RAF operated training bases in Rhodesia (now Zimbabwe). His contacts in the RAF enabled him to cut through all manner of red tape, and soon 136 trainees – including some just escaped from Greece – were on their way south into the heart of Africa. If they thought, however, that

1. A naval cooperation Fairey IIIF seaplane, 1938. (*Hellenic War Museum*)

2. Avro Ansons of 13 Mira over Athens, autumn 1940. (*Hellenic War Museum*)

3. PZL24s of 22 Mira lined up at Sedes, 1940. (*Hellenic War Museum*)

4. A Bloch MB151 of 24 Mira just before delivery. (*Hellenic War Museum*)

5. A 32 Mira Bristol Blenheim IV being serviced between missions near the Albanian front, March 1941. (*Hellenic War Museum*)

6. Potez 63s of 31 Mira at a base near Larissa. (*G. Mermingas collection*)

7. Sqn Ldr Yannis Kellas in front of an Avro Tutor at Tatoi. (*Hellenic War Museum*)

8. The engraved wallet of Sqn Ldr Dimitrios Stathakos, given to a squadron mate for safe-keeping just before his last and fatal mission over Albania on 11 March 1941.
(*G. Mermingas collection*)

9. A 33 Mira Fairey Battle at Nea Anchialos.
(*G. Mermingas collection*)

10. A Dornier Do22, its floats removed and modified for land operations, at Eleusis airbase, 1940. (*G. Mermingas collection*)

11. Sqn Ldr Marmaduke St John 'Pat' Pattle. (*G. Mermingas collection*)

12. Luftwaffe reconnaissance photo of the eastern end of the Corinth Canal, probably from a Heinkel He111, April 1944. (*Hellenic War Museum*)

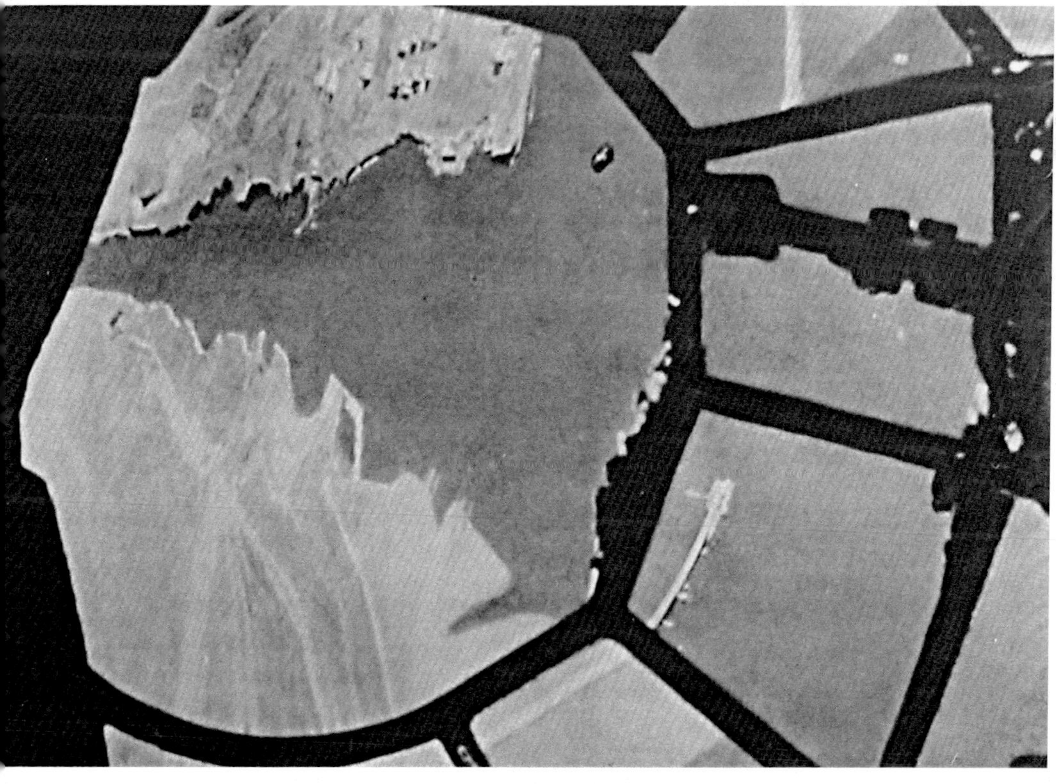

13. A North American T6 Harvard trainer over Rhodesia, with an unidentified Greek student pilot. (*G. Mermingas collection*)

14. Personnel of 336 Mira in front of a Hawker Hurricane in North Africa, 1942. Ilias Kartalamakis is standing on the far left. (*G. Mermingas collection*)

15. King George II (foreground, with hat and swagger stick) inspects the Bristol Blenheims of 13 Mira in North Africa. (*G. Mermingas collection*)

16. Flt Lt Sophocles Baltatzis with his Supermarine Spitfire Vb of 335 Mira, probably late 1943.
(G. Mermingas collection)

17. A 13 Mira Martin A20 Baltimore over an Italian port, probably Bari, September 1944.
(G. Mermingas collection)

18. 13 Mira's Baltimores line up at Biferno before starting the first leg of their flight home, October 1944. (*G. Mermingas collection*)

19. Retired Air Marshal Constantine Hatzilakos, aged eighty-seven, at home in Athens, 2007. (*Author's photograph*)

20. Marinos Mitralexis's widow, Anna, at home in Athens, with her husband's photo on the table, spring 2011. (*G. Mermingas*)

they would find the breezy informality of the EKI in their new home, they were mistaken. The RAF's Elementary Training School at Bulawayo was a classic spit-and-polish operation, a very different proposition from the loose existence in Palestine. The Greeks' irreverent attitudes in the air had their commander Platsis, now a wing commander, regularly on the station chief's mat.

Bulawayo provided only basic training. Specialized aircrew such as navigators, gunners, bomb-aimers and wireless operators needed to be instructed elsewhere. South Africa appeared to be the obvious safe place, far from the theatres of war. South Africa was where the Crown Prince Paul of Greece and his wife, Frederica, had taken refuge. Some of Greece's gold reserves, spirited away to South Africa just before the German conquest, helped pay for the Greeks' training.[12] Platsis travelled to South Africa to check out the possibilities. At a dinner arranged by Princess Frederica, General Jan Smuts agreed to provide training facilities for Greek airmen. There were plenty of places, Platsis was assured, for trainees in at least fifteen specializations. Platsis sent a message to Vilos in Cairo: 'This is a godsend for the Greek air force.'[13]

Chapter 10

The Air Force that Nearly Wasn't

The Germans may have lost a lot of men taking Crete, but once they had the island they turned it into a formidable Mediterranean fortress. In June 1941 the Luftwaffe's Aufklaerungsgruppe 123, a reconnaissance bomber squadron, took up its base at Tatoi with Junkers Ju88s, fast and powerful aircraft that could outfly most Allied fighters. The unit would later move to Kastello on the northern coast of Crete. II Gruppe/LG1 based itself at Heraklion along with its sister squadron II./KG1. These units, plus Heinkel He111s of II./KG26 out of Eleusis, wrought destruction on Allied convoys steaming south of Crete to such an extent that the Royal Navy dubbed the 100-mile width of sea between Crete and North Africa 'Bomb Alley'.

At the beginning of July 1941 General Sir Claude Auchinleck took over as British commander in the Middle East theatre. His single advantage against Rommel's strength was that he could only just hold on to Tobruk. Every ounce of extra air power was needed, therefore, to ensure that the convoys bearing troops, supplies and war materials got through 'Bomb Alley' safely and into Tobruk. The Ansons, and later the Blenheims, of 13 Mira were doing good work, but newly minted Greek fighter pilots were also coming on stream and needed to be used.

On 20 August 1941 the RAF Middle East command gave the green light for two Greek-manned fighter squadrons to be formed in the RAF. It wasn't until 1 November that the Greek Air Ministry-in-exile in Cairo authorized the creation of 335 (Greek) Squadron, or 335 Mira as the Greeks justifiably called it. The ministry secured a guarantee from the RAF that, though subject to RAF operational orders, the squadron would remain administratively and financially independent. Based at Aqir in Palestine and commanded by Squadron Leader Varvaressos, 335 Mira had a core of ten pilots trained at Habbaniya. At thirty-two, Varvaressos was considered ancient by some crews but everyone held him in reverence and some awe. To maintain national morale he insisted on hoisting the blue and white Greek flag over the camp every morning with the greatest ceremony.

Proudly bearing its new number and appropriate emblem – a phoenix rising from the ashes – 335 Mira took delivery of ten shiny new Hurricane Mk Is. They bore RAF roundels and code letters but sported blue and white spinners as a concession to the Greeks who were to fly them. Ten more followed over the next six weeks. On the last delivery, from Amman, Pilot Officer Theophanes Theophanopoulos got lost in the clouds swirling around Mount Hebron and flew into the mountainside – 335 Mira's first fatality. Eerily, while still a cadet two years before, Theophanopoulos had penned a poem that seemed to foretell his end:

> *We start out for the clouds,*
> *Swallows in flight,*
> *With danger our sport*
> *And death our delight.*[1]

Winter arrived at Aqir in the midst of a heavy night flying training schedule. As darkness fell on 10 December and cold winds screamed down from the Golan Heights, Pilot Officer Philip Plastiras tightened his harness and gunned his Hurricane down the runway, the propeller flinging sprays of rainwater into the slipstream. Moments after take-off, the ground crew observed the Hurricane's tail light describing an arc right into the ground. The countryside lit up with the flash of the explosion. Plastiras's squadron mate and best friend, Flying Officer Kartalamakis, stood rooted to the spot in horror until he saw a figure racing towards another Hurricane. It was Varvaressos. Tight-lipped and silent, the squadron commander climbed into the cockpit, tightened the harness and fired up the engine.

'We all realized what he was doing,' Kartalamakis wrote later. 'He was going to risk his life to save the morale of his pilots.' Kartalamakis went up to his commander and advised him to correct his altimeter, which was 500 feet in error. He was pretty sure it was a faulty altimeter that had caused Plastiras's crash. Varvaressos roared off down the wet runway and rose over the burning wreckage of Plastiras's plane. Many anxious pairs of eyes stayed glued to his tail light. After circling the airfield once, Varvaressos headed in to land, guided by a searchlight. But something seemed to be wrong – instead of aiming for the runway Varvaressos was on a collision course with the searchlight and the men around it! 'Oh, God, not another accident,' Kartalamakis found himself thinking. 'It'll be the end of the squadron.' The CO, buffeted by a stubborn crosswind, had come in too far left of the runway. He corrected just in time, touched down with a great thump, skidded and surged into the air again for another try, this time successful. His crews revered him even more after that.[2]

Christmas 1941 found the men of 335 Mira living the high life for a few precious hours in the Piccadilly Club on the slopes of Mount Carmel above Haifa. The unexpected star of the show was the squadron's medical officer, Pilot Officer George Dasios. Rakish in his fur-lined jacket and floor-sweeping scarf, a pipe seemingly glued to his mouth, Dasios would impress crowds of gullible clubbers with dramatic recreations of fictitious heroic stunts in the air, while the actual aircrews pretended to be engrossed and theatrically astonished. The revellers staggered back to their base at half past six in the morning to find a scramble order waiting for them. Italian bombers had just attacked a convoy including Greek ships off Cyprus. The bombers slipped under the radar to wave-top height and escaped. That night an enemy submarine slipped into Haifa harbour and set an Allied tanker aflame. The blaze turned the sky over Haifa into day.

The year 1942 opened with 335 Mira moving to Helwan near Cairo. A *frisson* of anticipation ran through the squadron at the prospect of rejoining the shooting war. After a few days at Helwan they received orders to proceed to El Daba on the Mediterranean coast. On the day of their departure an army of war correspondents and newsreel cameramen descended on Helwan to publicize to the world that some Greeks were still in the fight.

At El Daba 335 Mira was incorporated into 234 Wing of the Desert Air Force. Now came the Greeks' first real taste of desert flying conditions. The ubiquitous fine sand clogged engines and propellers and penetrated eyes and mouth. On most days the prevailing northerly breeze would keep El Daba free from the worst of the dust, but by the same token the January nights were damp and very cold. Shivering ground crews stayed through the night by the Hurricanes that had to be kept ready around the clock.

The squadron's task was to patrol the sea off El Daba, the southern sector of 'Bomb Alley', to protect the convoys sailing from Alexandria to Tobruk to reinforce the front in Libya. The battle for North Africa was getting into its stride. The Luftwaffe's Ju87s were hammering Tobruk and the transports almost daily. A typical German attack would begin with a solitary Crete-based Ju88 reconnaissance plane from Aufklaerungsgruppe 123 scouting the coast at a great height to detect convoys. The job of 335 Mira was to intercept the Ju88s and if possible keep them away from the convoys. Sometimes the reconnaissance planes were chased all the way back to Crete or the Dodecanese islands. They were faster than the Hurricanes, so they always got away.

Convoy protection and escort had to take place in all weathers. On the morning of 3 April 1942, for example, as a cold rain swept in from the sea under a low cloud base, the telephone in 335 Mira's headquarters rang unexpectedly with a scramble order. A convoy was sailing due north of El Daba and an enemy aircraft was detected nosing around it. The Germans apparently thought that the British wouldn't be scheduling patrols in this dirty weather. Two Hurricanes took off into the sheets of rain and roared over the wave tops. There was a lot to worry about on this type of mission. The worst fear was that of engine failure and ditching; if a Hurricane's Rolls-Royce Merlin cut out for any reason, the probable outcome would be a watery grave for the flier. Half an hour into this particular mission there was still nothing to see but black clouds and angry grey seas. There was also the very real danger that they might accidentally fly over the convoy, be mistaken for Germans and be blasted by the ships' defences. It took a second sortie in even worse weather to finally locate the Ju88 and chase it off.

The Hurricanes' Rolls-Royce Merlins were among the most reliable aircraft engines of the time. But the possibility that something could go wrong was, of course, always there. 'Merlins never fail,' the pilots of 335 Mira would tell themselves consolingly as a mental defence mechanism. But on 22 May one of them did. Warrant Officer Constantine Alexopoulos, the unlucky one, ditched and drowned in choppy seas. A jolt of fear ran through the squadron. Perhaps, as airmen, they had underestimated the power of the sea. They tried to mask their fears with black humour, animated discussions of 'safe' ditching procedures, and other defence mechanisms. But the squadron had finally been blooded. Future losses, as in all military units, would be taken more coolly, almost as routine. The first is always the worst.

Axis aircraft took advantage of moonlit nights to launch raids on El Daba and other airfields from bases in western Libya and Crete. Constantine Panagopoulos, now a flight lieutenant and flight commander in 335 Mira, demanded to be allowed to go up and meet them but Varvaressos vetoed the idea as too dangerous and tactically futile into the bargain. Eventually, in March 1942, permission for night interceptions came through from 201 Group. After a few days of night-fighting refresher training 335 Mira was ready. The debut proved a near-disaster.

The first full-moon scramble was to intercept fifty enemy aircraft on their way from Crete to attack El Daba. These Ju88s were very likely from a crack unit in I./KG1 known as the 'Hellbig Flyers', after its commander, Colonel Joachim Hellbig. As the first four Hurricanes took off into the night, squadron staff poured out of the messes and tents and huddled around the ops room wireless to monitor the operation's progress. There wasn't much of it. The Luftwaffe Ju88s got through to an adjacent RAF field and plastered it, damaging some Vickers Wellingtons. Deafened by the explosions, the Greeks on the base were 'like caged lions', while the Hurricane pilots above them tried vainly to get a bead on the raiders.[3] Flight Sergeant George

Papaioannou did manage to get the shape of a Ju88 in his sights about 1,000 feet above him, but as his orders were to stay at low level he couldn't do much. There was further confusion that night when the commander of an RAF squadron operating out of Malta mistook Panagopoulos's Hurricane for an enemy fighter and got onto his tail. Luckily the streams of tracer and bullets failed to hit.

The Greek pilots got the recall order without having intercepted a single enemy bomber. Then Papaioannou on his landing approach was ordered to turn around and climb back to meet another incoming enemy formation. The others followed him into the night sky. This raid, too, came and went with impunity. When Papaioannou finally was able to make his landing he ran out of fuel and had to put his plane down in the sand dunes. He was lucky to walk away unscathed. One lesson from this early frustrating experience was to increase the fighters' operational ceiling to at least 3,000 feet, to be able to get above the raiders.

One spring night Varvaressos and three of his pilots were lounging in the ops room on five minutes' readiness. As midnight approached, like thousands of other Allied and Axis servicemen at that hour, to keep their heavy eyelids open they tuned in to Radio Berlin for the nostalgic strains of 'Lili Marlene'. The telephone shrilled and the four airmen raced to their Hurricanes – Red One, Two, Three and Four – where they received orders to climb to 5,000 feet. Raiders were approaching El Daba from the sea. Already the western horizon was alight with bomb explosions and anti-aircraft flashes in neighbouring Mersa Matruh.

Kartalamakis in Red Two was frustrated because they weren't allowed out of their own sector. Coming in to land without having intercepted anything, he was startled by six explosions just ahead of him and to starboard. El Daba was being bombed. One bomb hit the runway about 200 feet in front of him. The shock wave battered Kartalamakis's Hurricane like a leaf in the wind. 'One second faster in my approach and I and my plane would have been blown to bits,' he recalled later.

His first reaction was to shove his throttle forward and take off after the unseen raider. In his eagerness he almost collided with Red One – Varvaressos – who was on his approach. Both of them manoeuvred smartly so that they both ended up flying in the same direction, line astern. But Kartalamakis had no idea his CO was in front, and when he spotted a suspicious shadow ahead he calmly cocked his Browning machine guns. The shadow then flew across the globe of the full moon, revealing it to be his commanding officer's plane.

'Imagine what a party that would have been, sir,' Kartalamakis told his CO over a hard-earned beer in the mess.

'At least we'd have had one night kill,' Varvaressos deadpanned in reply.

As spring wore into summer, 335 Mira's lack of kills was seriously getting on its crews' nerves. The Hurricane Mk Is, they complained, might be excellent gun platforms but they weren't fast or manoeuvrable enough for effective night interceptions. The occasional Hellbig's Flyer would even intrude in broad daylight over El Daba, knowing that by the time the Hurricanes got into the air he would be safely speeding back to Crete. Much valuable fuel and flying time was used up in futile attempts at interception. Friendly fire incidents were common, though fortunately they didn't result in any fatalities.[4]

One night Pilot Officer Evanghelos Karydis got lost in the dark. By some fluke his radio didn't work and he spent more than three hours flying around desperately trying to locate some shore light that might give him a fix. With fuel almost at zero, there seemed to be no choice but to make a forced landing anywhere and trust to fate. Switching on his headlight, he saw he was about to slide into the sea and hauled the stick back, setting a course south at 9,000 feet. Once he saw land lights he decided it was time to abandon ship.

'It's a moment,' Karydis said, 'when you've no thought or hope for anything except divine providence.' As the fuel-starved engine began to cough, he whispered a prayer. He slid back the cockpit and began to invert the plane in order to slip out into the inky blackness. The fierce slipstream tore him away from his plane before he was ready to let go, knocking him out. He came to just before hitting the ground, his parachute somehow open and weighed down by the dinghy. On landing, his back hurt atrociously. Exhausted, he wrapped himself in his parachute and tried to sleep.

'I awoke to the cries of a Bedouin who was standing over me with a rifle trained on me,' Karydis recalled. 'There was no way we could communicate. He shouted, "German?" and I answered "Greco".' The Bedouin appeared quite put out that Karydis's plane had almost fallen on top of his tent. Eventually, satisfied that the downed flier was from a friendly country, the Bedouin loaded him onto his camel and took him to the nearest railway station, about fourteen miles from El Daba.

Life at the El Daba base was spartan in the extreme. Well was it said in the Eighth Army that the worst scourges of the desert were the flies, the dust storms, thirst, heat, the scorpions, the Germans and the Italians – in that order. The flies were big, black and seemingly in the billions. They stuck into the skin like pins and fell into food and tea. Water was scarce and often reeked of petrol. The men of 335 Mira were lucky to get one container of water a day, mostly to make tea. They bathed and washed their clothes in the sea. Sandstorms covered food plates with fine dust that grated in the mouth.

Worst of all was the ordeal of stand-by in the overpowering heat, when pilots would spend perhaps hours belted into their cockpits, oxygen masks tight, waiting for the red flare that would signal take-off. In the upper air they could finally unbuckle their masks, slide back the canopy and let the blessedly cool wind play over their sweat-soaked heads.

The ground crews, of course, had no such relief to look forward to. They were obliged to crawl over the Hurricanes in the blazing desert sun. The metal was hot enough to fry an egg on. Fortunately, they were issued pith helmets, but even then men would often collapse on the job, prostrated by the heat. Every night deadly black scorpions crawled into bedding and flying boots, terrifying even hard-bitten pilots. After a particularly fierce rainstorm Flight Sergeant Byron Hadjioannou was raising his tent's main pole that had collapsed when he felt a sharp sting on his hand. A big black scorpion fell onto the ground and scuttled away. The wound began to bleed copiously.

Hadjioannou panicked. So did the medical officer, which rather convinced the pilot that he was about to become a non-combat fatality. A sting from a North African black scorpion, they had been warned, was invariably lethal. As Hadjioannou's hand swelled and he drifted into unconsciousness, a telephone call was made to 201 Group, which sent over a Hurricane with an antidote. Hadjioannou was lucky and recovered. The scar remained with him for the rest of his life.

Brief periods of leave in Alexandria and Cairo were naturally highly prized. The men marvelled at the clean sheets and downy pillows, the hot bath water and sumptuous food of the smart hotels. But something seemed to be lacking ... Flight Lieutenant Loukas Dakoronias, an engineer officer, discovered the rather eccentric solution. 'At the Metropole hotel in Alexandria the sheets were so clean I couldn't sleep a wink. So the next time I was in town I brought a little bag full of sand, spread a bit over the bed and floor, on the sheets and pillows, and slept like a little bird.'[5]

In April 1942 Flight Lieutenant Markou, an instructor at the Bulawayo field in Rhodesia, fell in love with a Rhodesian girl of good family and told Platsis, his training CO, that he wanted to marry her. Greek military rules forbade an officer marrying a foreigner. But Platsis said he would be quite prepared to wink at the rule and allow the wedding to take place, as long as it was done quietly. And there the matter would have ended had not Platsis suddenly been replaced as air training commander in Rhodesia by Group Captain Averof.

Averof, the erstwhile CO of 32 Mira on the Albanian front and RHAF bomber force chief, had brought his notoriously overbearing character and ways to Rhodesia. He was close to the Greek royal family and let everyone know it. A steely look from him, according to one engineer officer, 'was enough to make you break out in a cold sweat.' As one of his first acts Averof imperiously banned Markou's planned wedding. In doing so, little did he realize that he had set in motion a particularly controversial chapter in Greek air force history, a chapter that the meticulous Kartalamakis, writing a half century later, would describe as 'the blackest spot' on the service's record.[6] This was the infamous Rhodesia mutiny.

Decades afterwards, Averof was still at a loss to explain how the mutiny erupted.[7] True, his own irascible authoritarianism had made him widely disliked. But the truth lies deeper. Ever since the days of Thermopylae and Salamis in the fifth century BC the Greek military has never managed to shake off the germ of politics. To try to explain this tendency in terms of national character would be beyond the scope of this book. Suffice it to say that for most of the nineteenth and twentieth centuries many Greeks with officers' shoulder-straps felt the irresistible urge to strut taller on the national stage than their strictly military duties permitted. The 1930s had seen a raft of coups and attempted coups. A clique of liberal officers had staged one in 1935; its adherents, cashiered by the Metaxas regime, had recently been reinstated and were thirsting for revenge.

The old rivalry between the Army and Navy also left its bruises on the RHAF. By 1942, probably because they were actually the better men, Navy-derived air officers such as Vilos and Varvaressos filled most of the senior posts and squadron commands. Some of the Icarus School cadets felt elbowed aside in the promotions, and as representatives of the 'pure' air force nursed a grievance that they were being usurped by the older services. The fate of the Icarus School's 1939 intake, having to serve as NCOs rather than commissioned officers, added its own ingredient of bad feeling. Added to this was the simmering resentment at the sight of large numbers of senior Greek Army officers – many of them politically promoted and without the slightest intention of exposing themselves to danger – strolling the streets of Alexandria and Cairo and flooding their hotel bars. The controversy over Markou's planned wedding and Group Captain Averof's implacable stance set the potent mixture to boiling over.

It was a situation that Flight Lieutenant Theophanes (or Fanis) Metaxas (no relation to the late Greek leader) had been waiting for. Though a member of the Icarus School's very first graduating class in 1934, Metaxas had been given non-flying staff duties in Rhodesia. For some months now he had taken it upon himself to lead a curious kind of socialist revolution in the air force. In the middle of 1942 the idea of resistance had begun to take shape in occupied Greece and the first Resistance bands had taken to the mountains. News of these activities inevitably percolated down to the Greeks in the Middle East, and in doing so acquired a romantic tinge. Few, however, realized at the time that the Greek Resistance was slipping under the control of the Greek Communist Party (KKE) whose policy, directed by Stalin, was to sovietize Greece after the war. In the late 1930s the KKE had already infiltrated the junior officer corps of all three services. Now the dragons' teeth had grown.

On 28 April Platsis had just returned to his Bulawayo hotel after handing over command to Averof at an official reception when he heard a knock on his door. He opened to find five grim-faced instructor officers, including Metaxas, who without preamble told the thunderstruck Platsis: 'Get out of Rhodesia now, you and Averof. The time has come for the officers of the Icarus School to assume command of the service.' Platsis walked over to Averof's room and told him what was happening. Averof calmed him down and while he was trying to contact the British command another of the mutineers, Squadron Leader Gerasimos Pitsilis, flung down an ultimatum to his new CO: 'Resign and leave now, or as of tomorrow we stop training.'

Averof's response was to kick Pitsilis out of the room, slam the door and telephone the staff of the RAF command in Rhodesia. King's Regulations were at once enforced and the five soon found themselves behind bars and scheduled for a court martial in Cairo. Yet such was the number of sympathizers they had among the 130 or so cadets and staff at Bulawayo that the training programme had to be suspended. But forty loyal cadets under Flight Sergeant Stephanos Molyvadas refused to be swayed and telephoned their support to the CO.

With the immediate danger over, Crown Prince Paul ordered an investigation into the mutiny. In Cairo, Vilos, the Greek air commander, wanted to keep news of the Rhodesia mutiny away from the men of 13 and 335 Mirai, fearing its possible effect on morale. Vilos was acutely embarrassed by the whole affair and by the justifiably angry incomprehension of the British. It was, in truth, a sad come-down from the RHAF's glory days over the Albanian mountains. Vilos had no choice but to threaten with dishonourable discharge any airman accused of mutinous acts. That was the stick. The carrot came in the form of Averof's resignation as chief training commander in Rhodesia and his replacement by Group Captain Pelopidas Razelos, a staunch ex-Navy loyalist.

Vilos visited the jailed men at Guelo, urging them to sign statements of repentance, as a court martial might very well have them shot. They refused. They knew, as one of them admitted later, that the Greek officers who would try them were themselves mostly liberals who could be expected to lend a sympathetic ear to their claims. They also employed delaying tactics, with the result that the Greek government-in-exile, to end the whole messy affair, acquitted them by decree in October.

Was the Rhodesia mutiny, as Kartalamakis suggests, a communist attempt to gain control of the air force in preparation for a seizure of power in Greece after the war? The evidence is equivocal. Those inclined to sympathize with Fanis Metaxas say that far from being a political radical, he was simply a slightly unbalanced megalomaniac who believed he was wresting control of the air force back from the ex-Navy clique at its head to the hands of the Icarus School graduates, where he believed it rightly belonged. If that is the case, he certainly went about it in a completely counter-productive way. In 1942 the Greek air force was still only eleven years old. What Metaxas failed to realize was that the Icarus School intakes of 1931 to 1940 were simply not numerous enough to provide enough senior cadres in time of war. Ex-Navy and ex-Army officers, with their command experience, were still desperately needed.

That said, however, communist influence was very real. Evidence in plenty emerges from the activity of Metaxas's senior co-conspirator, Squadron Leader George Georgakopoulos. As a head of cadets at Tatoi he had boasted of putting hot chilli peppers up the anuses of leftwing cadets as a disciplinary measure. Then from a fascist bully, by his own admission, he turned into a communist bully and by 1942 was almost certainly a KKE agitator. His actions, and those of Metaxas, hobbled the Greek training effort and cast a shadow over the whole Greek air arm at precisely the time the whole Allied strength was needed to stop Rommel's advance on Egypt.[8]

After the German conquest of Greece in April 1941 the Royal Hellenic Air Force – with the symbolic exception of 13 Mira – had to all practical purposes ceased to exist. 335 Mira and the trainees in Rhodesia and South Africa were under formal RAF command, flying aircraft with RAF markings on them. There was no room in the RAF for any of the mutinous fun and games of the Greeks. But the whole embarrassing episode had set Vilos thinking. The Greek airmen at this stage were in the RAF Volunteer Reserve category, sharing the status of the Czechs and Poles who had their own ethnic squadrons in the RAF but not their own air forces. The Free French, by contrast, had their own planes with the French roundel and Cross of Lorraine on them. If the Greeks could enjoy a similar privilege, might some of the ill feeling be alleviated? In Cairo Vilos called on Air Chief Marshal Sir Arthur Tedder, the RAF Middle East C-in-C.

Tedder listened attentively as Vilos explained the situation, then waved a document under Vilos's nose. It was a memo from the Foreign Office suggesting that an independent Free Greek air force be set up.

'How do you think we should reply?' Tedder asked.

'I for one am not signing for Volunteer Reserve status,' Vilos said.

'What happens if the others don't sign as well?'

'That's a matter for your government,' Vilos replied diplomatically.

Tedder's reaction to that is not recorded, and the idea was put on hold. But Vilos had unwittingly opened up another contentious issue. Officially, the whole Greek training set-up in Rhodesia and South Africa had no legal basis at all. It was the result of purely informal contacts between Vilos and his upper-level RAF friends. Tellingly, the staff and trainees at Bulawayo had been offered full incorporation into the RAF, but they had declined, 'preferring to keep a Greek identity'.[9]

If there had been any hopes of setting up a Free Greek air force, the Rhodesia mutiny dashed them. The British were understandably unwilling to relinquish control over the Greeks who had proved unruly and politically suspect. Moreover, in March 1942 Emmanuel Tsouderos, the Greek prime minister-in-exile, had signed an agreement with Anthony Eden, the British foreign secretary, giving up the right to form an independent Greek air force. In July Vilos sent Platsis to London to get a fuller view of the picture.

Platsis put his socializing talents to work, getting himself invited to a society gala at the home of an air commodore. The gala was to cement a hoped-for marriage between exiled Prince Peter of Yugoslavia and Princess Alexandra, the Duke of Kent's daughter and a Greek by extraction. Platsis made his case with the air commodore who telephoned the Chief of the Air Staff, Marshal of the RAF Sir Charles Portal, for an appointment. Portal, however, was reportedly too busy to see the Greek officer for the next two weeks.

Platsis, not giving up, called on King George II at Claridge's Hotel. 'Your Majesty,' he said, 'I need to see Portal. I'm sure you meet him at society events. I'd like you to put in a few good words for me.'

'You're the first Greek,' replied the king, 'who has asked me for something I *can* do. Everybody else wants me to get them ships, planes and tanks. I'm due to see Portal tonight at the Queen Mother's reception.'

Platsis's meeting with Portal was brief and not totally discouraging. In reply to Platsis's request that the Greek air effort be placed on some official basis, Portal passed the buck to the Supreme Air Council, which, he warned, could be formidable to someone with a mere three stripes on his sleeve. As Platsis took his leave with a salute, Portal cracked a smile. 'If the King of England,' he said, 'had said about me what George said about you, I'd have to be the happiest person in the world. Your king believes you're the best officer in the Greek air force.'

With Portal's praise still ringing in his ears a few days later, Platsis sat down in front of an imposing weight of RAF braid, including Portal himself. Nothing less than the future of the RHAF was on trial. Platsis began by outlining the projected needs of the RHAF after the war – at least three fighter squadrons, one bomber squadron, one naval cooperation squadron and one transport squadron. The whole structure would have to start being set up at once.

'That's about three thousand men,' one member of the Air Council interjected. 'Where are you going to find them?'

Platsis replied that enough volunteers were escaping from occupied Greece and filtering through to Egypt to take care of that problem. Besides, there were plenty of Greek families that had been living in Egypt for decades and could provide manpower. Another officer asked where these men would be trained. Platsis at that point probably inadvertently spilled the beans about the training programmes in Rhodesia and South Africa. A stunned silence fell on the room. None of the brass, including Portal, had the slightest idea that Greek airmen were being trained at RAF bases in Africa! Platsis felt himself going red in the face. When the subject of the mutiny inevitably came up, Platsis explained it away as a service grievance that had got out of control, carefully avoiding any mention of communist agitation. Three hours after the close of the meeting, the Supreme Air Council issued its decision – the Royal Hellenic Air Force would again be recognized as a national military service. It was the greatest of personal triumphs for Wing Commander Platsis.[10]

One of those who picked up the pieces of the Greek training programme in Rhodesia was George Lambropoulos, now a flight sergeant. After his adventures in Crete he had spent a bored and frustrated year in his home village in the Peloponnese. In May 1942 he had escaped from occupied Greece in a caique (fishing boat) that took him to Turkey, from where he had made his way to the RAF in Syria and eventually to 335 Mira after training in South Africa and Rhodesia. Not for him were the false siren calls of the mutineers. To make up for lost time, and conscious that the RAF chiefs were breathing down the Greeks' necks, Lambropoulos overworked himself. The stress put him in hospital with temporary amnesia.

Veteran flyers from past RHAF units such as 31 Mira joined the instruction staff. But hasty training and lax flight discipline meant more accidents. Unsuitable pilots were kept in the programme both through political patronage and to beef up the Greek contingent; several were killed in crashes before the year was out. Another reason for the accidents was that men who had flown Potez 63s and Blenheims in battle conditions regarded the de Havilland DH82 Tiger Moth basic trainers and North American T6 Harvards as virtual toys and were often a tad careless with them. Flying Officer Alexander Nasopoulos, the chief basic training instructor, only just managed to pull out of a spin he had inadvertently caused. Fatigue was also an ever-present menace. Flight Sergeant Yannis Ekonomidis, another instructor, ignored his dizzy spells in the air and crashed in the midst of an aerobatic manoeuvre. Ekonomidis's pupil was not badly injured, but he himself was taken to Salisbury hospital presumed dead of severe head injuries. Thanks to his tough constitution and fanatic love of flying he was back in the air a year later flying Spitfires.

Flying Officer Kleiamakis, who had narrowly missed being shot down by his own flak over Tatoi on the morning of 28 October 1940, had another close shave after finishing a night-flying training mission over the jungle with his instructor, Flight Lieutenant Exarhakos. He was on the landing approach with Exarhakos at the controls when Kleiamakis in the back seat, according to procedure, opened the Harvard's cockpit instrument-training hood for visual contact with the runway. He should have kept it open, but the wind was too cold so, against regulations, he shut it again. As Exarhakos touched down flying blind a tremendous crash jolted the plane and flipped it upside down. The Harvard had smashed head-on into another that was landing from the opposite direction.

An investigation revealed that in the minutes between Exarhakos receiving landing clearance and the actual landing, the wind had veered 180 degrees. Had Kleiamakis kept the Harvard's hood open he would have seen the windsleeve and changed course. Luckily no one was killed, but Kleiamakis was hospitalized. A medical board decided that he'd cheated death long enough and grounded him.

Night-flying exercises over the Rhodesian jungle were an ordeal. Platsis rose to the occasion here, too, lightening the crews' anxious concentration on the instruments with periodic sightseeing tours of town lights. As with their brethren in Egypt, the biggest fear was of engine failure that in this case could cast them down into the black jungle where, for all they knew, they might never be found. Flight Sergeant Vlassis Dedes was coming in over the lights of Bulawayo, when his rear-seat pupil, Sergeant Andreas Dimakopoulos, asked him to do a roll over the city for a thrill. Dedes went into a shallow dive to gain speed and started the turn. It was when the Harvard was inverted that the city lights and instrument lights somehow 'all came together in a dizzying jumble,' as he wrote later.

With Dedes suddenly and totally disoriented, the Harvard nosed down and hurtled towards the jungle. Instinctively, he hauled back on the stick with all his strength. It seemed ages before the plane eventually flattened out, groaning and shaking in every rivet – and the altimeter showing *minus* 300 feet! The plane had actually dived into a 500-foot depression in the jungle floor, emerging with just feet to spare. (Dimakopoulos was killed in February 1943 when his trainer crashed on take-off.)

Other, less potentially serious, problems included language difficulties between the Greeks and their British instructors. These resulted in some hilarious, if hairy, moments, such as the time Flying Officer 'Fuzzy' Davis, RAF, was instructing Sergeant George Kounoupas in instrument flying. After the first bout of instruction Davis landed to change places with Kounoupas. Davis climbed out onto the wing to make way for his pupil to move into the front seat. Instead, Kounoupas slammed the plane's instrument-flying hood shut.

'Open the hood and get out!' Davis shouted, leaning into the empty front cockpit.

By way of reply, Kounoupas opened the throttles and thrust the Harvard forward, throwing Fuzzy off the wing. Picking himself up from the dust, the dazed RAF officer watched the plane take off like a rocket. As he returned to his home base at Cranborne, still not quite believing what had just happened and fearing the worst, a Harvard with Greek training code letters on it was seen making drunken manoeuvres above the runway, lurching up and down before making a clumsy landing. When the plane came to a halt, Davis's superior, a Squadron Leader Morris, sped up in a fire engine for a sharp word or two with the Greek trainee.

What emerged was the stuff of a slapstick war comedy. Kounoupas, it seemed, hadn't noticed his instructor getting out of the cockpit, as the hood had not been completely opened. He thought Davis was still in the plane. To him and his imperfect ear for English, Fuzzy's order to open the hood and get out sounded like open the throttle and take off. Which he duly did.

Morris reported the embarrassed Kounoupas as saying afterwards:

> I'm under the hood. My instructor, he says nothing. I open throttles, I climb and climb, but my teacher he says nothing. I think he is angry with me and does not speak. I'm still climbing and my feet get cold. I say, "Excuse me, sir. Excuse me, sir." But he says nothing. So I open the hood a bit and look in front. I see nothing. I open some more, again I see nothing. I think maybe teacher sitting low, with seat down, so I loosen harness and get better look at front seat. No teacher. He not there. Then I think teacher must be very angry and jumped with parachute ... I think, I must return to base.

The realization that he was alone, and that he had just taken off solo with a hood over the cockpit, hit Kounoupas at 10,000 feet. Among the awful thoughts in his head was that Davis could have dropped out of the plane during some roll. Diving into a cloud layer, he emerged at 2,500 feet, scattering a formation of three squadrons in training. He saw a railway line, which he decided to follow. Within ten minutes he recognized Cranborne aerodrome but wondered why there were hardly any aircraft on the ground. (They were in the air searching for his wreckage.) But landing a Harvard from the back seat was no small matter, and he had to abort a couple of approaches before he got up the nerve to make a successful one. His engine sputtered to a halt, out of fuel, just as he turned into a parking position. He was rewarded with a drink at the home of the admiring Squadron Leader Morris.[11]

Before a cadet at Cranborne could earn his wings he was required to carry out a solo flight at 8,000 feet of at least two hours. No one looked forward to this qualifying exercise. It was all too easy to get lost. The ever-present possibility of an in-flight emergency and forced landing in those vast tracts of jungle was unnerving. Instructors hammered home horror stories of pilots who had come down in the jungle to be consumed by wild animals or cannibals. The flight plan was to fly from the base for half an hour to an abandoned mine, change course for a third point – difficult to recognize – for forty-five minutes, and then return to base. There were, of course, the inevitable nervous jokes about ending up in cooking pots. But for Flight Sergeant Dimitrios Voutsas the jokes didn't fall far short of reality.

The sun blinded Voutsas after he took off for his graduating solo, and he tried to shade his eyes with a map. He was nervous at first, but the smooth drone of the Harvard's engine reassured him as the magnificent jungle spread out beneath him. Then he noticed that his radio had failed, but that didn't worry him too much as the sky was clear and he didn't have a problem navigating. He arrived over the abandoned mine and turned towards the third point. Keeping his eyes glued to the compass, he suddenly wished the whole thing was over and he was back in civilization with his mates. What was so damned important about flying solo over the jungle anyway? He wished his radio were working so that at least he could take some comfort from the familiar voices of the controller in the Cranborne tower and the other pilots.

Voutsas duly arrived over the third point at the correct time, and, hugely relieved, turned for the last leg home. Twenty minutes later he began to worry. By now the familiar landmarks near the aerodrome should have appeared. Instead, an unknown landscape was sliding below. He rose in his seat for a better view out of the cockpit, peered again at his compass, and had to come to the bitter conclusion that he was lost. But how could that be? He had followed to the letter all the navigational instructions. A simple radio call, of course, would have solved the problem. But the radio was broken. And he was getting low on fuel.

Voutsas was at the prayer stage when a familiar sight jolted him – the abandoned mine! Instead of taking the leg back to base he had somehow returned the way he had come. In his nervousness and wish to be rid of the whole experience he had made a basic navigation error. All he had to do now, he thought, was fly back to base along the first leg out. There was one snag – he had at most ten minutes of fuel for a thirty-minute flight! Breaking out in a cold sweat, he throttled back to reduce fuel consumption and began looking for a clearing to force-land. He wished he'd paid more attention to the RAF instructors when they'd lectured on what to do when making an emergency landing in the jungle. He saw a column of smoke rising on the horizon, figured that it signified a human presence, and set course for it.

He arrived over the smoke but saw no signs of humanity around it. Brushing the treetops, he aimed for a tiny clearing. On the verge of a stall, he cleared the tallest trees and slammed the Harvard's flaps down for a hectic landing. Luckily he didn't collide with anything. When the trainer lurched to a halt he sat in his seat dazed, overcome by the sudden awesome silence. Moments later, he heard voices. Amazingly, they were the voices of the Cranborne controller and fellow pilots ... The shock of the landing, it seems, had jolted the radio back into action!

The controller told him to sit tight and use the radio only in emergencies, to save the battery. It would take two days, the base said, for a rescue party to reach him, adding ominously and not very helpfully: 'Be careful, the area is full of cannibals and wild beasts.'

Voutsas had climbed out of the cockpit to stretch himself when he noticed some natives cowering behind the trees. He beckoned for them to approach. First the men crept forward, with poles in their hands, and then the women, all naked except for a ragged cloth around their loins. With verbal communication impossible, Voutsas handed the men a few cigarettes, which they puffed delightedly. Still, that was not necessarily a guarantee of friendliness, so in order to impress them with his power he fired into the air with his flare pistol. It was a mistake that almost cost him his life. The natives scattered in terror but the flare landed on some dry grass and set it aflame. The blaze spread with astonishing speed, directly threatening the Harvard and the natives' huts. By some fluke the wind changed direction before the fire could consume the plane and Voutsas's own chances of survival.

Shaken, the natives appeared in the clearing once more. One of them spoke some English. 'Sir,' he said, 'I want to help you out of here, but you must help me.'

'What can I do for you?' the Greek airman asked.

'Take me with you.'

The man, it turned out, had once worked for the British in a canteen. He stayed close to Voutsas, acting as his interpreter. The women invited the pilot to sleep in one of their treetop huts. He declined graciously, citing his orders to stay with his plane. For supper he was given a foul-smelling boiled chicken with all the innards and half the feathers still on it. There was no way he could eat that, so he explained to the interpreter that as he wasn't hungry he would eat it later But he was thirsty, so he went to drink from a nearby stream where a herd of orang-utans were gathered. Unused to the sight of a white man, the apes backed away suspiciously.

Wrapping his parachute around him against the cold, Voutsas slept in the Harvard's cockpit. He thought he heard lions nosing up to the plane in the night. When morning came there was no sign of the interpreter. The natives tried to tell him something. He was trying to figure out what when the blessed sound of an Airspeed Oxford echoed among the treetops. The twin-engined plane circled a few times and dropped some cigarettes and an encouraging note from his chief instructor, which told him that food and blankets would come soon. (He kept the note for the rest of his life.) Relieved once more, Voutsas shared the new cigarettes with the happy natives. Another plane duly arrived on time and dropped food, blankets and fruit juice, which he also shared out.

He spent the second night as he had the first, wrapped up in his cockpit. About noon on the third day the search party numbering about a hundred men arrived to take him home. Before leaving the two Britons at the head of the party solemnly placed a sign on the Harvard: 'PROPERTY OF THE R.A.F. TO BE COLLECTED.'

In wartime all aircraft were valuable. The interpreter was never seen again. For two days and nights Voutsas hiked with the rescue team through the jungle, staying the nights in friendly native villages. Food and drink consumption was kept to a minimum. On the third day they came to a road, where Voutsas was turned over to the care of a British sergeant who drove him the three-hour trip to Cranborne. His fellow-Greeks, of course, loudly celebrated his 'escape from the cooking pot'.

Chapter 11

Back into the Fight: El Alamein

In May 1942 335 Mira was moved west to Karaola airfield near Mersa Matruh. Karaola was even more hellish than El Daba, but the squadron was not to stay very long. Rommel and his Afrika Korps were pressing hard in Libya. On 21 June Rommel took Tobruk. Soon afterwards the British had to abandon Mersa Matruh and fall back to a position sixty miles west of Alexandria – a front between the sea and the great Qattara Depression called El Alamein.

Before the withdrawal the Greeks at Karaola had an unexpected visitor. He was Air Vice-Marshal Keith Park, the former commander of 11 Group RAF and main architect of victory in the Battle of Britain. In his new appointment as AOC Egypt, Park was tasked with protecting the Mediterranean from Sicily and Malta to Palestine, including the precious convoys steaming back and forth. Park's personal Spitfire had engine trouble over the desert and had to land at Karaola. Squadron Leader Varvaressos presented his pilots one by one to the fabled airman but if they sought some sympathy from him they were disappointed. Rather brusquely, one imagines, the sharp and no-nonsense Park asked the Greeks what he could do for them.

'Give us Spitfires and send us to the front,' they replied. They were getting tired of the monotonous and apparently ineffectual convoy protection duties in their Hurricanes.

Park shook his head. 'Your aircraft are fine for the Stukas and Ju88s,' he said with an ironic smile. The Greeks were nonplussed. Any oaf knew that a Ju88 could outrun a Hurricane any day. Park's haughty and crisp manner put them off, especially when he asked Varvaressos how many German planes his squadron had shot down.

'The Germans we've seen so far have managed to get away,' the Greek commander replied testily. 'Give us better planes so we can shoot some down.'

Kartalamakis reports that Park gave a sarcastic little laugh. Varvaressos may not have been aware that with Tobruk gone, Malta was now in great danger, and that the RAF in the Mediterranean would soon have to throw all its strength into the island's defence. Park undoubtedly had cogent reasons for refusing to divert any of his precious Spitfires from that all-important task. But the Greeks needn't have worried. Their time to enter genuine combat would soon come.[1]

On 13 June, a week before the fall of Tobruk, four Hurricanes of 335 Mira and two Free French fighters were sent up to guard a massive sixty-ship convoy sailing from Alexandria to Malta, led by a battle cruiser bristling with guns and radar. Seen from 6,000 feet, the convoy stretched from horizon to horizon. The sun was about to set and soon the planes would be called back to base. Then Kartalamakis, in Blue Two, was told that an enemy formation was approaching from the north. 'All fighters continue patrol,' came the strident voice from the cruiser controller through his earphones.

Orders were orders, even with fuel running low and night falling. There wasn't much time to think about it as Blue Section was vectored onto the attacking formation. The Germans were doing their job well, attacking when they knew the Hurricanes would be low on fuel and unable to fight. Visibility rapidly deteriorated to near-zero in the gathering murk, and Flight Lieutenant Drenas, the mission leader, requested permission to return to base.

The reply from the cruiser was peremptory: 'All fighters continue patrol. Enemy approaching from the north.'

Kartalamakis's wingman, Katsaros, wanted to continue, but it was obvious to everyone else that the mission could not credibly go on. Reluctantly, the Hurricanes turned for home, the frantic calls of the controller on the cruiser ringing in their headphones. Barely had the pilots time to grab a drink in the mess than the air raid siren went off. Huddling in the shelters, the men of 335 Mira heard the first bombs falling on the hapless convoy and cursed their luck.

Within days the squadron was ordered back to El Daba, Rommel's Afrika Korps hard on its heels. Some of its Hurricanes were already holed by bullets from Luftwaffe Bf109s. The Free French Escadrille d'Alsace, sharing the same base, suffered two fatal losses in one heroic engagement. Kartalamis from his cockpit could see the vast dust cloud raised by the advancing Afrika Korps panzers.

Kartalamis wrote in his diary on 28 June:

> Will the Germans go as far as India? I see stores burning in the port of Mersa Matruh and explosions of munitions. We are seized with despair, and only one thing keeps us going: the desire to do our job till the last ... Our squadron – I can't tell whether by accident or design – has remained to play the part of rear-guard.

335 Mira soon had to move again, to Edku on the outskirts of Alexandria. The night for the move arrived, with the tents struck and everything packed, and various insulting messages scrawled on the walls for the Italians and Germans to find. The squadron waited by their Hurricanes, wrapped up against the freezing desert night. Edku, a tiny airstrip, would be devilishly hard to find in the blackness. It was dawn before the order to move finally came. One by one the eighteen Hurricanes took off. Dakoronias, the last man out, imagined he could hear the panzers' treads hard on his tailwheel.

As the crews were resting in their tents at Edku, a skinny Fieseler Storch monoplane droned in, and out stepped none other than Air Vice-Marshal Park. He had been using the captured Luftwaffe light plane as a personal hack. As the tired and unshaven Greeks surged around the strange aircraft, the first to greet Park was not Varvaressos but Emmanuel Xydis, a flight sergeant. Enraged at what he perceived – probably correctly – to be a protocol snub, Park turned on his heel and got back into his Storch. In Cairo he formally requested Vilos to dismiss Varvaressos as commander of 335 Mira, even if it meant replacing him with an NCO! Platsis went to see Park to see if he would change his mind, but the New Zealander was still simmering. 'I'm Air Vice-Marshal Park,' Platsis quoted him as saying. 'I won the Battle of Britain and know something about fighters. My decision is that [335] Squadron be given to that flight sergeant [Xydis] with immediate promotion to squadron leader. No one else is good enough.'

Platsis, who had earned the plaudits of his king and no less a personage than Portal himself, was not to be intimidated. 'I am a graduate of the Central Flying School,' he replied stiffly. 'I have the DFC, and as a Greek aviator, I know best the mind and character of the Greeks. Such a proposal cannot be accepted by the Greeks or the RHAF.'

'Then what do you suggest?' Park snapped.

'Keep Varvaressos in command of 335 Mira, sir, and everything will be all right.'

Park appeared to relent. But his continuing personal dislike of Varvaressos probably played a part in the Greek officer's replacement as squadron commander within the month. Others say Varvaressos was in declining health.[2] The new commander was Flight Lieutenant Kellas, the popular and highly regarded veteran of the Albania campaign and fight against the German invasion. The squadron continued its patrols over Alexandria and the coast. Still Rommel advanced. Arrangements were made to evacuate Cairo at two hours' notice. Public opinion in Egypt began to take a dangerously pro-Axis turn. The indefatigable Platsis was ordered to prepare for the Greeks' evacuation, probably to join 13 Mira in Gaza. Crown Prince Paul and

Panayotis Kanellopoulos, the air minister-in-exile, made morale-boosting visits to the squadron.

In August Montgomery took command of the Eighth Army, with Tedder in charge of the Allied air forces, and carefully built up a strong position at El Alamein. Now it was Rommel's turn to worry. The Afrika Korps' long thrust eastwards along the North African coast had dangerously stretched his supply lines. That same month 335 Mira was moved to better quarters at Dekheila, which had bitumen runways, and began an intensive schedule of combat training to prepare for the big showdown sure to come.

With the training came accidents, fortunately none of them fatal. Depountis's engine failed over the sea; levelling his Hurricane at wave-top height, he skimmed the waves until it beached. Volonakis, who had baled out of his stricken Potez 63 bomber over north-west Greece in February 1941, now had his second close call. On 29 September, flying as Kellas's wingman, Volonakis collided with his CO. Pieces flew off Volonakis's Hurricane as it continued inverted, leaving a thick plume of oily smoke behind it. As Kartalamakis flew alongside he saw Volonakis abandon the aircraft and parachute onto the shore, badly bruising himself as the wind dragged the chute along the rocks. Kellas nursed his own stricken plane to a forced landing, to find himself surrounded by a Greek Army contingent that happened to be in the area. One curious soldier climbed into the cockpit and fiddled with the Hurricane's gun button, with the result that two others standing in front of the wing fell to the ground, their legs riddled with Browning bullets. They survived.

Kellas drove his men hard. He was able to because of his glowing record in the Albanian campaign and a reputation of fearlessness. What the strait-laced RAF called the 'noisy Greeks' soon found fellow-spirits in the newly arrived Americans whose bumptiousness and disregard for rules equalled their own. One day when dust storms reduced visibility to nearly nil, Lord Trenchard, the legendary founder of the Royal Air Force, paid a visit to 335 Mira. Unlike the curmudgeonly Park, Trenchard was full of praise for the Greeks. 'The only good Hun is a dead one,' Trenchard declared, cheering the Greeks no end. This was more like their way of thinking. Next to call on them was Tedder, who, tieless and with pipe in mouth, wished them good luck and reminded them to be a bit more careful with their aircraft – five Hurricanes written off in accidents was five too many. On 23 October the squadron was moved to an advanced airstrip.[3]

El Alamein had a religious significance for the Greeks. Since about AD400 it had been a shrine for Menas, a local saint martyred by pagans. Legend has it that when the executioners threw Menas's mutilated body into the fire, a part of it didn't burn. His followers took away the part on a camel, which stopped at El Alamein – which is Arabic for 'place of Menas' – and buried it there. Well might the Greek airmen pray to Saint Menas now as Montgomery marshalled them among the 250,000 men of all services waiting for Rommel.

The great Battle of El Alamein opened on 23 October. Montgomery outwitted the 'Desert Fox' by attacking on the northern sector of the front where Rommel least expected. Keeping the Germans fully occupied there, Montgomery launched another assault on the Italian lines in the south. By 4 November the Axis forced had been decisively beaten; the hunter had now become the hunted.

On the eve of the opening of the battle, twelve fighters of 335 Mira – now a part of the Seventh South Africa Wing – and twelve of 80 Squadron RAF (the late 'Pat' Pattle's unit) patrolled the skies above El Alamein. The patrols continued through the opening days of the battle. Then on the evening of 27 October, when 335 Mira's pilots were leaving the mess and heading for bed, came the telephone call that Kellas had been hoping for. 'At last,' he shouted, waving the message in his hand, 'we've got authorization to hit the Italian headquarters!'

A burst of wild cheering drowned out his words. Now, after two years, they would have their chance to get back at the Italians. He held up his hand. 'Boys,' he cautioned, 'it's going to be difficult tomorrow. We could have serious losses.' But who could think of losses when the Italians were again in their sights? Tedder had known precisely when to send the message. The following day would be 28 October, the second anniversary of Mussolini's attack on Greece and a date that rankled in Greek minds above all others. 'Everyone wanted to go on that raid,' Kartalamakis recalled many decades later. 'We wanted to catch the Italians napping, like they'd caught us.'[4]

Then, like a thunderclap, came the voice of a dissenter. 'I think the whole idea is stupid,' snapped Flight Lieutenant Constantine Hondros, 335's deputy commander, in front of all the squadron.[5] Hondros had not been heard from before. As a flight commander in 335 Mira he had done his job as well as anyone else. But he wasn't turning out to be a team player and fancied he had tactical talents above his rank. He simply didn't think that the psychological boost of hitting the Italian headquarters was worth the risk involved.

Kellas pointedly ignored him. 'So who'll join me as volunteers?' he called. The mess echoed with loud cries. Kellas picked Kyriakos Panagopoulos's B Flight to do the job, leaving Hondros's A Flight (but not its commander) dejected. A map was brought out, and heads huddled over it to find the target. Kartalamakis, one of those picked for the operation, couldn't sleep for excitement and apprehension. Few could, in fact. A God-fearing man, he nonetheless fought a constant inner battle with insidious fear. As a non-smoker, he couldn't even allow himself the comfort of chain-smoking through the long night like the others.

The mission briefing was held at dawn. Going with 335 Mira would be 274 Squadron RAF to bomb adjacent targets. Then, as they were being briefed, the bombshell hit: there was a change of plan. Instead of roaring in at low level, as the original plan had stipulated, 335 Mira would dive onto the target from 12,000 feet; the low-level attack would be the privilege of the South Africans instead. The squadron was stunned. Losing the element of surprise, besides depriving the Greeks of slaking their thirst for revenge, would make the operation yet more dangerous. Grumbling and disheartened, 335 Mira took off and set a course west at 12,000 feet, followed by 274 Squadron.

Heavy flak met them in the target area but they flew through it unscathed. Ignoring four Bf109s on the north-western horizon, the Greeks screamed down almost vertically on the Italian headquarters, twelve dozen Browning machine guns blazing. Down the Hurricanes plunged, past 4,000 feet, sending torrents of bullets through the Italian tents. The Duce's soldiers raced for the dugout shelters. Kartalamakis drew a bead on a flak battery which, he noted with rueful admiration, was firing coolly and steadily. He could make out each member of the flak crew at his post. At 1,000 feet, with fierce revenge for October 1940 burning in him, he pressed the button.

'The Italian soldiers, blasted to bits, jerked and fell by their guns, drowned in their own blood,' he recalled. 'It was a tragic sight. I could see clearly their expressions of agony and their blood staining the desert.'

The next minute there was a loud bang behind him and the cockpit began to fill with smoke. A 37mm shell had exploded behind the armoured seat back. The smoke cleared but control was gone. As the rest of the squadron shot up the Italian headquarters at barely twenty feet, Kartalamakis fought to keep his Hurricane aloft. Then the engine cut out and he radioed Kellas that he was about to crash-land behind enemy lines. By now he could see the great tank battle of El Alamein unfolding beneath him. Flak continued to stalk him through the sky: scores of tracer bullets slammed against his fuselage. At least twenty miles from Allied lines, and with all hell breaking loose around and below him, he looked for a place to land, resigned to – at best – spending some time in a prisoner-of-war camp.

Gliding over a flat stretch, he tried to avoid a minefield and a lagoon but couldn't keep the Hurricane in the air any longer and crash-landed on a pile of earth. There was a loud explosion followed by a thick cloud of dust that dissolved to allow him to look in his mirror. Blood was pouring from a gash over his right eye, down his face and over his flying overall. Gingerly he climbed out of what was left of his Hurricane. The impact had sheared off the engine and thrown it fifty feet. The entire tail section was folded under the shattered wings. After his relief at not being killed, he was even more relieved to find he hadn't landed behind enemy lines after all. Some Australian soldiers took him to their tent.

An operation to stitch up Kartalamakis's wounds took five hours, during which he deliriously regaled medics and nurses with ingenious curses on the Germans and Italians. As soon as he could stand, he insisted on being allowed to return to his squadron. After some hesitation his request was approved. Kartalamakis arrived back at base with his head bandaged and his flying overall still stained with blood. When Kellas, the CO, came out of his tent he stood stock still. With tears in his eyes, the otherwise granite-nerved commander raised his arms to thank God for not losing anyone in the recent attack. The squadron had not been gently handled. In addition to Kartalamakis's crash, Panagopoulos had taken two flak hits and only just managed to return to base. Two others belly-landed in the desert. The only unscathed Hurricane was that of Hadjioannou who was in genuine despair that his plane hadn't received a scratch to prove that it, too, had been in combat!

Kellas had reason to be moved. After the operation, and with Kartalamakis missing, he had come under fire from the naysayers, especially Hondros. From the first, they'd labelled it as a suicide mission. But they were a distinct minority in 335 Mira, which, despite the hammering it received, could finally rest satisfied that it had got in a long-awaited blow at the enemy. The pilots also got in a good belly-laugh that night when they learned over Italian radio that the insolent Greek squadron had lost eleven out of its twelve planes!

The next day the eleven Hurricanes of 335 Mira took off as escort for 274 Squadron. Pilot Officer Yannis Anagnostopoulos spotted four Bf109s and with his wingman turned to intercept the nearest one. The Messerschmitt got in two cannon bursts that missed. Lining up about 150 feet behind the German and slightly below, Anagnostopoulos sent a long machine burst into the Bf109, which stalled and spun down, disappearing into the cloud layer. Returning to base a quarter of an hour later, Anagnostopoulos breathlessly gave his report. The cloud layer had prevented him from seeing what happened to the German, but he was fairly sure it was a kill. Confirmation came a few hours later from Army observers who reported seeing a German plane crash in flames. It was the Greeks' first confirmed kill since April 1941.

On 2 November Hondros, the A Flight commander, was leading an escort patrol at 12,000 feet when he noticed a couple of German fighters about to pounce on 274 Squadron. The Greeks forced the Germans to break off the attack. Flight Sergeant Dimitrios Soufrilas dived to 4,000 feet, got on the tail of one of the Bf109s and squeezed his gun-button. Pieces flew off the Messerschmitt. Soufrilas changed position slightly to get another burst when the German pilot baled out. It was another kill for 335 Mira.

By now Rommel was in full retreat. 335 Mira was given the job of following up ground attacks by 274 Squadron, strafing the German columns. The enemy flak, though, was fierce, along with the rest of the German resistance. On the second sortie of 3 November, flak hit Anagnostopoulos's engine on the climb-out from a strafing attack and he had to ditch at sea a few yards from the shore. The plane's tail section stuck out of the water but the cockpit was submerged. Anagnostopoulos, fortunately a good swimmer, managed to free himself from his harness and rise to the surface. Staggering onto the beach he found he was in an enemy-held zone, so he slipped back into the water, intending to swim east to the Allied line. But German machine-gunners saw him and opened up on him, and he thought it prudent to give himself up.

Italian soldiers escorted him at gunpoint to the nearest German flak battery, where the NCO in charge treated him with surprising chivalry. From his temporary confinement in a captured trailer, Anagnostopoulos observed the German retreat close-up: 'There were thousands of vehicles crowding on the only narrow road leading west [he noted in his diary]. They were tightly massed on Halfaya [Pass], offering the ideal strafing target for fighters ... But I didn't see any good use being made by the air force.'

Well might Anagnostopoulos wonder why the Allied planes weren't upon the retreating Germans day and night, even though it would entail some personal danger to himself. Montgomery, in fact, has been blamed for missing chances to follow up the victory at El Alamein. For two days the Greek pilot was driven along in the retreating columns, vainly searching the sky for Allied aircraft. He ended up in a prisoner-of-war camp in Italy.

335 Mira got the recognition it deserved. Air Chief Marshal Tedder telegraphed King George II that he was 'proud to have [the Greeks] with us'. As Montgomery's Eighth Army began its advance to retake North Africa, 335 Mira was assigned a new airstrip, Landing Ground 13. Before the Hurricanes could land there, an RAF Spitfire touched down and promptly blew up in a fireball. A staff car rushing to the scene blew up as well. The retreating Germans had sown LG13 with land mines. The Greeks, before they could come to similar grief, were reassigned to neighbouring LG12.

The Greeks of 335 Mira may have acquitted themselves well at El Alamein, but all was not well in the leadership. Squadron Leader Kellas was a brave and capable officer, but hampered by a lack of proficiency in English. In a unit directly under RAF control, that was a failing that could have disastrous consequences in combat. During the El Alamein operations Kellas had depended on Hondros, his second-in-command, to communicate with his controllers from the cockpit. Group Captain Vilos had known this when he appointed Kellas to replace Varvaressos as squadron CO, but had gambled that Kellas's undoubted fighting qualities might overcome the language barrier.

Kellas's linguistic inadequacy probably reinforced Hondros's display of aggressive independence in the squadron. It may well have confirmed his prejudice in favour of graduates of the Icarus School, which he represented, against the 'outsiders' in senior positions. Kellas himself was an ex-Army man. Here could lie an answer to why 335 Mira was switched at the last minute from its assignment to strafe the Italian headquarters at low level on 28 October. The indications are that the Seventh South African Wing, to which 335 Mira belonged, had got fed up of having to use Hondros as an interpreter in the air and insisted that Kellas be replaced, as the split-second coordination required for the mission could not be guaranteed. But there are experienced Greek airmen who are prepared to argue, if somewhat irrationally, that the switch was a British plot to keep the Greeks from stealing the RAF's thunder.[6]

After the Battle of El Alamein, with the pressure off, Kellas was replaced by his predecessor, Varvaressos, as an interim appointment. For a more permanent CO Vilos had in mind someone else – Flight Lieutenant Pangalos, who was completing advanced training at 71 Operational Training Unit in Sudan. When Pangalos arrived at Sidi Barrani to take over, Varvaressos took him up for a familiarization patrol, as the squadron was back to providing escort and protection for convoys. Just as boredom was beginning to set in, the radio crackled to life: 'Bogey approaching from north-east.' The 'bogey', it turned out, was an American A26 Marauder bomber. Pangalos felt a bit sheepish turning away. His guns had been aimed and cocked, and his thumb glued to the gun button. The Americans, he knew, were even less disciplined than the Greeks in doing their own thing and to hell with the consequences.

Ennui on patrol had its own insidious dangers. Pilot Officer George Pleionis kept a little poodle named Max as a mascot in his tent. One morning in February 1943, as Pleionis was preparing for another convoy escort, Max was unaccountably frantic, yelping and nipping at his master's flying overalls as if to pull him back.

'You'd better not fly today, sir,' a fitter said. 'Can't you see the dog?'

But superstition wasn't Pleionis's strong suit, and so he duly arrived over a convoy off Alexandria. At 7,000 feet he opened the cockpit canopy a crack to fire his recognition flare for the benefit of the ships below. He pulled the trigger twice, but the pistol didn't fire, so he asked his wingman to fire instead, stuffing his own pistol into the map case. Somehow the trigger got caught in the map case spring, and the next thing Pleionis knew a blinding red light filled the cockpit. The flare was twisting around at his feet like a live thing, spitting and throwing off its liquid fire. Opening the canopy, of course, made the fire worse. Inverting the Hurricane, he baled out in a hurry. The wingman, seeing Pleionis diving and aflame, assumed he'd been hit by friendly fire from the convoy.

Kept afloat only by his Mae West, Pleionis struggled to keep his head above the rough sea. A vessel sent out by the convoy couldn't locate him in the deep swells and turned back. After several more tries the ship found him, but by now the sea was so rough that it bounced him up higher than the rescue ship's rail. With great courage the ship's crew lowered a lifeboat that managed to pick up the Greek pilot, shivering and on the verge of unconsciousness. In a warm cabin, bundled up in blankets, and with several glasses of whisky inside him, Pleionis had plenty of time to reflect that Max hadn't been so wrong after all.

While 335 Mira was busy patrolling the seas and contributing to the victory at El Alamein, a second Greek *mira* was taking shape at 71 OTU (Operational Training Unit) in Sudan from the pilots newly trained in Rhodesia. Haste in getting the crews combat-ready could have contributed to the spate of accidents that accompanied the formation of 336 Mira. Barely had the squadron been formed than two pilots died when glycol coolant fumes, lethal when overheated and leaking, seeped into their cockpits.

Pilot Officer Constantine Valavanis was kept on as instructor of Greek aircrew at 71 OTU. It may be that Valavanis was too junior in rank to shoulder the weight of responsibility of an instructor charged with turning out combat pilots. It's a job that requires a substantial element of toughness, to weed out the unsuitable, sometimes the hard way. Just before Christmas 1942 Valavanis took off near Khartoum with two students, Flight Sergeants Panayotis Sklavos and Christos Ioannou, for gunnery practice. The two cadets' task was to exchange roles as air gunner and target. At 12,000 feet Valavanis made his practice shots at Sklavos, followed by Ioannou. Valavanis gained height to see if Ioannou would follow the procedure correctly. Breaking off from the mock attack, Ioannou's port wingtip hit Sklavos's fin. Both planes went into uncontrollable spins. Sklavos managed to bale out. Floating down, he watched in horror as Ioannou plunged straight down and no parachute appeared.

'Jump, Ioannou, jump!' Valavanis yelled into his mask. No one will ever know whether the hapless Ioannou heard.

Back at base, a shaken Valavanis reported the fatality to the flight supervisor, an RAF wing commander, who without any emotion whatsoever said:

'Okay, then we have lost one pilot,' and turned back to his paperwork. He might as well have lost a paper clip. To do the wing commander some justice, however, he and Valavanis had suspected for some time that Ioannou wouldn't make the grade. Valavanis realized too late that he should have grounded the trainee before he lost his life through clumsy flying. One way or another, the bad fliers had to be weeded out.

Chapter 12

Unlucky 13 Mira

The Greek 13 Light Bombing Mira had not been inactive in the run-up to and aftermath of El Alamein. It shared the same duties as 335 Mira – escorting and guarding Mediterranean convoys – and was subject to the same risks. In January 1943 the squadron received about thirty Bristol Blenheim Vs (a variant known as the Bisley) to replace its ageing Ansons. The crews appreciated the Bisley's enhanced armour plating and defensive firepower. One day in February Flying Officer Angelos Angelidis was at the controls of a Bisley off the Libyan coast when the observer, Army Captain George Koumanakos, expressed a desire to do a bit of sightseeing – namely the port of Tobruk, recently retaken by the British. After five hours' droning boredom in the air, it seemed a reasonable request. That brief excursion, though, consumed a fair amount of fuel, with the result that on the approach to base the plane ran dry, the twin engines cutting out just short of the runway. Angelidis gained a few more yards of flight by keeping the landing gear up, missed a rocky ridge by inches and flopped onto a sand dune.

There was a similar incident in May, when Warrant Officer Panayotis Frangoyannis completed a night anti-submarine patrol and found the home base hemmed in by a sandstorm. 335 Mira's base at Mersa Matruh was also unapproachable, so Frangoyannis, out of fuel, belly-landed in the desert. The crew of three huddled for warmth in the night, keeping a wary eye out for hostile tribesmen who were known to hold downed Allied airmen for ransom. At daylight, after destroying the IFF (Identification Friend or Foe) transmitter, the crew found that the Bisley's nose had broken through a barbed wire barrier into a minefield. The field extended along the whole left side of the plane, while a few yards to the right stood a reinforced concrete pillbox, and straight ahead yawned a chasm. 'All three of us fell to our knees and thanked God and the Virgin for saving us from certain death,' wrote Captain Andreas Tsimbos, the observer, in his diary. The date was 8 May, which the three men thereafter would celebrate as their 'second birthday.'

Extraordinary luck also accompanied Vladousis, who volunteered to ferry one of 13 Mira's decommissioned Blenheims to a breaking yard near Cairo. The old and creaky plane lifted off clumsily, right into a sandstorm. Vladousis lost his way and ran out of fuel somewhere over the Nile Delta. Rightly distrusting the treacherous wetlands directly beneath him, he glided the Blenheim to a forced landing near a dusty desert village. Fortunately, the local Bedouin were friendly and the RAF picked up Vladousis the following day. The worst part of the ordeal, he admitted later, were the fleas that drove him mad by feasting on every uncovered inch of his body through the night.

Meanwhile, by Decree 3145 of the Air Ministry-in-exile in Cairo, dated 23 February, 336 Pursuit Mira had come into being, consisting of twenty-nine officers and NCOs. Commanded by Flight Lieutenant Spyros Diamantopoulos, a veteran of the Albanian front, 336 Mira included several 335 Mira veterans. Among the pilots was ex-Icarus School cadet Hatzilakos, now a warrant officer just having earned his wings. Most of 336 Mira's aircrew, in fact, were NCOs of the 1940 Icarus School intake, the class that turned out to have the most casualties of the war. But that class also had another, more dubious, distinction – that of being most vulnerable to political agitation and mutinous impulses.

It would be a pleasant exercise for the chronicler of the wartime Greek air force to be able to describe its development in a continuum from the first gallant encounters over the mountains of Albania to a share in the ultimate Allied victory.

Unfortunately, the narrative is not so simple. By early 1943 the RHAF had to contend with an insidious foe far worse than anything the Regia Aeronautica or the Luftwaffe could throw at it. This was communist subversion, which for at least two years had never really ceased.

In the summer of 1942 the first organized resistance groups had taken shape on the German-occupied Greek mainland and in Crete. The mountainous terrain made it easy for such partisans to operate, and with British arms and gold parachuted in at night, the Greek Resistance began to grow into a formidable force. The biggest Resistance group was the National Liberation Front (EAM), which quickly came under full communist control. As a result, the EAM often seemed more intent on stamping out non-communist rivals than fighting the Germans.

Much of the success of EAM was a result of its clever identification with the patriotic sentiments of most Greeks suffering under Nazi misrule. The ruse took in thousands of otherwise sterling and brave young men. It was thus only a matter of time before communist KKE agitation, in the false guise of egalitarianism and human rights, infected Greece's fighting units in the Middle East. The harsh desert conditions, the stresses of operations, the worry among the men that they might never seen their homes or loved ones again, all created a vulnerability to the indoctrinators who infiltrated the ranks of all three services. Personal political rivalries also played a part. For example, republican officers cashiered after the 1935 liberal coup and since reinstated, actively undermined their compatriots who remained loyal to the king.

Churchill was well informed about what was going on, but in the midst of the task of regaining North Africa from the Axis, there wasn't much he could do. Moreover, the mandarins in Whitehall (with precious few exceptions) figured that if the EAM had the allegiance of the majority of Greeks, as was endlessly propagated, then Britain had little choice but to do business with them. In Cairo, King George was becoming very worried, but there was little, if anything, he could do without provoking leftwing charges of royalist intervention. The KKE did its work well. The new buzzword in the Greek ranks was 'democratization,' – a pretty word for a Soviet-inspired ploy to destroy discipline in the Greek military and soften it up for a planned communist seizure of power when the war was over. Short-sighted moves by the Greek government-in-exile ensured that the dissidents had support at the top, mainly in the person of Group Captain Yannis Dimakis, newly appointed as commander-in-chief of the RHAF in place of Vilos. Dimakis had an energetic confederate in Fanis Metaxas, now a squadron leader safe in an office in Cairo and responsible for personnel affairs.

Metaxas's rebellion in Rhodesia was nothing compared to what was soon to come. The subversives' first target was 13 Mira. A navigator, Squadron Leader Yannis Manias, who studied Russian and was seen conspicuously devouring Marxist literature while lounging in the easy chairs of the officers' mess, took it upon himself to become the squadron's unofficial *zampolit*, or mid-level political indoctrination officer on the Soviet model. Squadron Leader Renos Pongis, the 13 Mira CO, had been warned in time and bent over backwards to relax wartime discipline as far as he could to deprive Manias of the chance to fish in troubled waters. 'I am a new Saul,' Manias liked to say to anyone who asked why he had become such an obvious Marxist, referring rather incongruously to Paul's conversion on the road to Damascus. 'When I saw that the time of communism had come, I converted.'

Pongis had no intention of putting up with such nonsense, so he decided to fight it with a little masquerading of his own. Slipping another stripe on his shoulder, making him appear to be a wing commander, he stalked into Dimakis's office claiming to have been promoted. Dimakis coolly asked him by what order. Pongis rather disingenuously replied by saying that if other officers with political connections had the right to promote themselves to senior rank, so had he. For his wardrobe stunt Pongis was removed from command of 13 Mira, which may well have been his original intention.

Replacing him was Group Captain George Alexandris, who barely had time to settle behind his desk when an insubordinate warrant officer marched in to announce in haughty terms that he represented the 'democratic' squadron members. By way of reply, Alexandris threatened him with internment in a British stockade, 'where you won't represent anybody'. The chastened NCO backed off. But Alexandris had blotted his copybook with the dominant leftwing clique in Cairo and was summarily replaced by one of their own, Wing Commander Alexander Papatsoris.

In his initial address to the men, Papatsoris made no secret of his preference for the enlisted men over his fellow officers, ordering the latter to 'care for these boys who left their country to continue the fight'. On Easter Day 1943, while the more traditionalist officers looked on in disgust, Papatsoris held a rowdy binge drinking session with the enlisted men. 'It looked nothing like a military unit,' one of the onlookers said later. 'Dissolution was complete.'

In April about half a dozen traditionalist officers in 13 Mira, loyal to king and flag, openly refused to do any more flying unless led by an officer from the original Icarus School or EKI that succeeded it. To Papatsoris this was counter-revolution, and so he had them put on a charge and sent to Cairo under guard. They would have been jailed for insubordination had not calmer counsel prevailed in Cairo. Three of them were sent to Rhodesia as instructors and the others quietly resumed their squadron duties.

The traditionalist officers' move may not have been the wisest one, as it enabled the communist cadres to claim that a 'royalist junta' was blocking the planned 'democratization' of the Greek military. Kartalamakis, for one, had no illusions that what might have seemed a mutiny within a mutiny was a desperate attempt by some officers to maintain a modicum of discipline, combat capability and loyalty in the service they were proud of. The ranks of all three services were flooded with underground communist newspapers that lambasted anyone who believed in the traditional values of country and flag as 'fascist' – a term that included most of the officer corps. At some point Manias, the *zampolit*, seems to have stopped openly flaunting his communism and, like a well-trained agent, begun to pull his strings unseen.

In Cairo, however, the left-sympathizing Dimakis was beginning to have his doubts. 13 Mira had to be kept in shape to participate in the planned Allied invasion of Italy, and by all accounts squadron efficiency was plummetting. The RAF, for its part, was signalling ominously that if the communist-inspired mutinies continued, it might have to take the Greeks' aircraft away. Flight Lieutenant Kyriakos Panagopoulos was sent to discreetly investigate 13 Mira. What he found was a virtual 'people's republic under the total control of the Communist Central Committee in Cairo.' All semblance of operational order had vanished. Aircraft failed to make their convoy rendezvous on time or at all, and many remained grounded on the most ridiculous pretexts, such as flat tyres and batteries, and the fact that no one bothered to refuel the planes after missions. Ground crews and many aircrew slept in as long as they felt like it. Moreover, Papatsoris was not a pilot but a navigator/observer, and hence with a reduced professional claim to command a combat squadron.

Before he could reduce 13 Mira to total chaos, Papatsoris was relieved of command and replaced by Flight Lieutenant Stratis, a combat-experienced Blenheim pilot. Stratis wasted no time in restoring discipline and some basic organized functioning. Against all expectations he managed to turn the squadron around. By July the RAF liaison officer with 13 Mira, Squadron Leader Lord Duke, could report to 235 Wing headquarters that the squadron was about back to normal. Stratis had a valuable helper in Vladousis, 13 Mira's executive officer. Lord Duke confided to him at one point that the RAF had been a hair's breadth away from disbanding the squadron altogether. Vladousis remarked that it would help if the squadron received some new equipment, from aircraft to tents. New tents soon arrived, but new planes would have to wait until September, when the ageing Blenheims were finally retired.[1]

The creation of 336 Mira had a galvanizing effect on its older sister, 335 Mira, in the form of a spirited competition that took much of the edge off destructive political tensions. Before that, the relations between 335 Mira and 13 Mira had been of the usual fighter-bomber rivalry variety. The rivalry sometimes went a bit too far. On 19 March 1943 Flight Sergeant Christos Koliopoulos of 335 Mira was sent to pick up a Hurricane that had been damaged in a forced landing at Sidi Barrani, 13 Mira's base. Valavanis, 335's executive officer and a notorious practical joker, saw his chance for another laugh.

Valavanis told the young pilot that after picking up the Hurricane he should repeatedly buzz 13 Mira's base so as to 'leave no tent standing'. The part about the tents, Valavanis claimed after the resulting uproar had subsided, had been meant metaphorically rather than literally. Koliopoulos, himself a bit of a daredevil in the air, needed no urging. The fighter boys craved the chance to show off their supposedly superior airmanship to the staider bomber types. At breakfast in 13 Mira Koliopoulos boasted to the bomber boys that he would show off the Hurricane's stuff in a low-level pass over the airfield.

About noon, with the whole of 13 Mira watching, Koliopoulos roared in fast and low, intent on doing what in his own squadron would have had him up on a charge. Among the expectant watchers was Flight Sergeant Stephanos Papageorgopoulos, a senior fitter. He was standing outside his tent eating lunch, his plate in his hand. Koliopoulos wowed the onlookers with all manner of low passes and steep dives, pulling out at the very last second. His last dive was a bit too daring. On the pull-out, Koliopoulos's port wingtip caught on a tent.

'He skimmed by like a plate, or a pebble on water,' Papageorgopoulos recalled. Tent after tent was demolished in the plane's wake. 'It left behind first the engine, then each wing in turn, until like an enormous cigar it shot along the sand at two or three hundred kilometres an hour, stopping a few metres away from a Blenheim.' Papageorgopoulos, the nearest man, dropped his plate and ran to the scene. The Hurricane's nose and cockpit were buried in a sand dune. Sparks crackled from the ends of cut wires, fortunately away from the fuel tanks. The cockpit canopy had been ripped off. Papageorgopoulos dug into the sand with his hands, found the hapless pilot and lifted him out.

Saving Koliopoulos from death had been the Hurricane's sturdy windscreen, which had stayed in place throughout the mad ride. He was quite conscious, and like a latter-day Lazarus he looked dazedly around him and at the spot that had come close to being his sandy tomb. Realizing he was in one piece, his bravura deserted him and he made the sign of the cross over and over again, muttering the Lord's Prayer in Greek. After that, a more mundane problem occurred to him: 'What am I going to tell my squadron commander now?'

Chapter 13

The Other Battle of Crete

Soon after the formation of 336 Mira the order came down from 219 Wing RAF that all three Greek squadrons should upgrade to full operational status. This meant, among other things, that they had to be prepared to fly day and night, in all weathers, at a moment's notice. Diamantopoulos, the CO, found a way to combine business with pleasure by sending his pilots in pairs on a day's leave in Alexandria, to return to base by night flight. The pilots were delighted at the order, seeing a chance to show off to their friends and girl-friends in the city. The practice didn't last long. Voutsinas, now a flying officer, made a low pass over the lights of the Greek quarter and very nearly tangled himself in the barrage balloons guarding the port area. The RAF got wind of what was going on and put a stop to it. Night flying practice would now have to be done over the desert.

There was, of course, the inevitable grumbling, but 336 Mira threw itself into the night-flying programmes with gusto. In one month the squadron had earned the sobriquet of Desert Owls. Now it could look forward to being deployed on the Tunisian front, to reap its own glory to match 335 Mira's creditable record at El Alamein. Competition between the two Greek fighter squadrons reached new heights. The men of 13 Mira, stationed between the two fighter bases, would watch in amusement as 335 and 336 sent night formations droning over each others' airstrips. Sometimes on joint exercises a flight leader in one squadron would issue conflicting or absurd instructions in the air, to catch the other squadron out. The RAF put a stop to that, too, and for good reason, as the Greeks' accident rate was climbing worryingly.

Kartalamakis attributes the accidents to sheer boredom with the routine convoy-escort missions, and the resulting urge among the wilder fliers, when alone in the sky for any reason, like the mythical Icarus 'to leave their nests on the summits of Olympus' and test their limits. In May Flight Sergeant Yannis Gyzas of 336 Mira was ferrying a Hurricane to Mersa Matruh when he couldn't resist performing a few stunts for the benefit of the occupants of a Greek Army truck he saw below him. The stunts ended abruptly when a wingtip touched the ground and Gyzas perished in the fiery crash.[1]

Gyzas's best friend, Flight Sergeant Marios Skliris, was deputed to gather up the remains and take them for burial in Alexandria. Skliris numbly picked the pieces of his friend from the charred wreckage of the plane and wrapped them in a blanket. The drive to Alexandria was bumpy, and the body parts kept falling out of the blanket. The gruesome experience affected Skliris's mind. A few days later, as he was coming in from a night flight, he landed outside the runway and came to a clumsy halt, damaging his plane's undercarriage. Panagopoulos, his flight commander, confronted him, distraught and shaking.

'I saw him, sir, I saw him in front of me,' Skliris stammered when he could.

'Who did you see?' Panagopoulos said.

'I tell you, I saw him. It was Yannis Gyzas.' Half a century later, Skliris still vowed that he had seen his dead friend.[2]

None of this reflects on the ground crews who by all accounts – except for the short-lived 'people's republic' of 13 Mira under Papatsoris – did their jobs competently under very trying circumstances. Unexpected new threats abounded, as when water was found in the fuel. The first sign was a sharp rise in engine failures and forced landings in both the Greek and the RAF squadrons. Flight Sergeant Ilias Papageorgiou was escorting a convoy at 2,500 feet in rough weather when his engine began sputtering and missing beats. Switching off the engine, he put the Hurricane into a glide just above stalling speed and prepared to ditch. But he had forgotten to jettison the wing tanks, which hit the water first, jerking the plane nose-down and pitching the pilot into the towering waves. Bobbing up and down in his Mae West, Papageorgiou was slowly blown shorewards.

His boots filled with water and dragged him down, so he kicked them off. Sharp rocks offshore lacerated his bare feet. A few squadron mates, watching from the shore, tried to swim out to help him but were driven back. A strong undertow dragged him along the coast to a sandy beach where he was rescued. The incident shook him so much that he could never again climb into a Hurricane cockpit without trepidation. On his next operation an oil line broke and filled the windscreen and his face with oil. Then he witnessed a shocking mid-air collision during dogfight practice that killed two of 335 Mira's pilots, Pilot Officer Vasilis Ekonomakos and Flight Sergeant Theodore Gazis. That made up his mind – combat flying was not for him. He requested a transfer out of the squadron and spent the rest of the war first at a desk in Cairo and then as an EKI instructor in Rhodesia. (He would actually resume combat flying on the Nationalist side in the Greek Civil War of 1946–49.) No one ever figured out how water got in the fuel, though sabotage by local base workers cannot be ruled out. Ground crews corrected the problem by double-filtering the fuel before gassing up the planes.

The indefatigable Kartalamakis, now with 336 Mira, suspected that his fuel had been watered down when his Merlin began to act up over the sea one night. Engine failure at night over sea was a Hurricane pilot's worst nightmare. The standard RAF procedure in such cases was to keep going and make the most convenient forced landing possible, on land or water. Eyeing the blackness all round him and cold with fear, Kartalamakis decided to scrap procedures and act on instinct. While the engine was still going he began a 180-degree turn. In the RAF that just wasn't done, as there was a serious danger of the engine cutting out during the turn and throwing the plane into a fatal spin. Luckily land wasn't far away and within minutes he managed to belly-land onto a sand dune. When they picked him up he was having a cheerful chat with the local *fellaheen* (Arab tribesmen) who apparently didn't mind that he'd narrowly missed demolishing their huts.

On 13 May the remaining Axis forces in Tunisia surrendered. The Allied forces in North Africa were now poised to jump across into southern Europe. Italy had suddenly become vulnerable; Mussolini's days in power were numbered.

On 25 July King Vittorio Emanuele III of Italy pulled royal rank and deposed the Duce, handing over temporary political power to Marshal Badoglio, who after two years under a cloud and in depression found himself again at the centre of events. The Italian strongholds on the Dodecanese islands off the Turkish coast could be expected to follow Badoglio into the Allied camp – that is, before the Germans got to them. Developments in Italy dovetailed with Churchill's aim of clearing the Aegean Sea up to the Dardanelles straits to be able to aid the Russians via the Black Sea.

Greek Army and Navy units serving with the Allies in the Middle East began training for landings on Rhodes, the biggest Italian-held island. 1 and 2 Greek Army Brigades were slated to spearhead the main landing. But they didn't count on the master in Moscow. Stalin had very different plans for Greece and the Aegean region. A quick Allied liberation of Greece, he feared, might thwart his planned communist takeover of the country. Hence secret instructions went out to the communist cells in the Greek military to stall operations as long as possible. The secret party cadres in 1 and 2 Brigades had done their work well. Both units were on the point of mutinying when they were placed under direct British command and taken off the Rhodes landing schedule. It was just as well, as Lord Jellicoe's surprise assault on Rhodes smashed itself against the fanatic resistance of 6,000 Germans who had meanwhile arrived to replace the Italians.

After El Alamein, Montgomery's advance along the North African coast meant that the Hurricane patrols had to be longer. One day in June 1943 the order reached 336 Mira to send up a couple of Hurricanes for an immediate and unspecified 'special operation'. Pilot Officer Stratis Xydis was available but had no wingman, so Warrant Officer Haralambos Stavropoulos was pulled off the roadside outside the base where he'd been standing, spruce in freshly ironed tropical gear, his kitbag at his feet, waiting for transport for four days' leave in Alexandria. Stavropoulos wasn't even given time to change out of his shorts and short-sleeved shirt. He had already taken off when he realized that in his haste he hadn't connected the dinghy. For an over-water operation the dinghy would have been already connected to the back of the pilot's parachute, but on desert operations it was normal practice to leave it off. As Stavropoulos's Hurricane had just come off a desert mission, it was in this dinghy-less and alarmingly unprotected state that he tackled the skies over the menacing Mediterranean.

In the air they were vectored about 100 kilometres north-west over a large warship steaming at top speed through the Mediterranean without an escort. It was a British heavy cruiser heading for the Indian Ocean after shelling enemy positions on Pantelleria island and fending off Ju87 Stuka attacks. The two Greek planes were the ship's first escort. Stavropoulos was making his first circles over the cruiser at 2,500 feet when his Merlin coughed and gave up. Strict radio silence meant that he couldn't notify Xydis of his plight, and he decided to jump. Inverting the plane and pushing back the canopy in the usual baling manoeuvre, he fell out of the cockpit, hitting his leg in the process, and spun down about 1,000 feet before his parachute opened.

As the vast expanse of heaving sea spread out below, he had a horrible thought: for the first time in his life he realized he had never learned to swim! Frantically he began to blow into his Mae West. He threw off his new suede shoes and put his new gold watch in his mouth to keep it out of the brine. His dinghy wasn't connected to his harness. But that probably saved his life, as at about fifty feet he slipped the harness and let himself fall into the sea. At once a large wave swamped the dinghy and left him bobbing in the swell along with his Mae West and holiday apparel. No one aboard the cruiser seems to have seen Stavropoulos bale out, and of course Xydis had no idea what had happened. Eventually, noticing a large oil slick on the surface, Xydis dived for a closer look and saw his wingman. The ship was notified. Shivering on board the cruiser, Stavropoulos found himself feted, from the admiral on down, as the ship's first rescued airman. After the first rush of curiosity, the admiral took him into his cabin and learned that he was a Greek pilot who had been escorting the vessel. Amazed and moved almost to tears (by Kartalamakis's account), the admiral offered the soaked airman a drink.

'I don't want a drink,' Stavropoulos replied, 'just a dry uniform to change into.'

Royal Navy ships didn't normally carry spare air force uniforms, so Stavropoulos was soon transmogrified from an RAF warrant officer into a Royal Navy midshipman. Ensconced in his own cabin, he received visits from all the ship's officers while his clothes and banknotes worth forty-five Egyptian pounds went under the dryer and his gold watch was cleaned of its sea-salt deposits. The following day Midshipman Haralambos Stavropoulos, RN, disembarked at Port Said, caught an RAF flight to Alexandria and was finally able to enjoy his four-day leave – still in his naval uniform, which he kept as a souvenir.

For more than two years the Germans had been turning Crete into a near-impregnable Mediterranean fortress. Operating out of Cretan bases, the Luftwaffe reconaissance bombers of I./KG1, II./LG1 and Aufklaerungsgruppe 123 were a constant menace to Allied warships and convoys negotiating 'Bomb Alley'. Meanwhile, word had been seeping out from Crete about the atrocities the Germans were committing on the population in reprisal for the islanders' fierce guerrilla resistance. Air Chief Marshal Sir Sholto Douglas, the RAF C-in-C Middle East, thinking in terms of morale, thought it might be a good idea for the Greek squadrons to take part in aerial attacks on Crete's German strongholds. In preparation, Douglas and King George II visited 335 and 336 Mirai to gauge their resolve.

There wouldn't be room, though, for all the Greeks. As well as 335 and 336 Mirai, at least five other RAF squadrons would also be having a go at Crete, including 94 Squadron with mixed British and Serb crews, 213 Squadron with Spitfires and 252 Squadron with deadly swift ground-attack Bristol Beaufighters. So there was no choice for the Greeks but to draw lots for who would go. The lucky ones whose names were called 'jumped up and shouted out loud like children'. The rest were sunk in gloom. A few of the latter offered to buy their way onto the mission, but no one was selling.[3]

Morale among the Greek flyers was probably never so high as in the early morning of 23 July 1943, when on airfields from Alexandria to Tobruk they slammed their throttles forward to finally exact some revenge for the brutal occupation of their homeland. Pilot Officer Eleftherios Athanasakis of 336 Mira lost a wing tank on take-off but was damned if he was going to miss out on the big day. His wingman, Pilot Officer Constantine Kokkas, drew alongside and signalled to Athanasakis to turn back, but no way!

Leading the formation of 120 attacking aircraft in a Beaufighter was Wing Commander Max Aitken, the son of Britain's minister for aircraft production and media baron, Lord Beaverbrook. In the first stage, Aitken was to knock out the German radar station at Ierapetra on the south coast of Crete. The formation headed swiftly in at low level. Aitken, Athanasakis and Kokkas were in the wave that bombed the Ierapetra radar. Flying on, they found themselves over the Aghios Nikolaos plain in eastern Crete, where Athanasakis, having flown on only one wing tank, ran out of fuel and radioed that he would have to force-land.

Kokkas later recalled:

The flak was ferocious but we gave as good as we got. I saw a German flag fluttering in a building on my right and sent a machine gun burst into it. We were almost touching the windmills and the milk-white houses, while the Cretans were throwing their hats into the air and dancing with joy, waving their hands all the time.[4]

The Cretans were overjoyed to see the blue and white spinners on the Hurricanes. Near Heraklion the Greek pilots caught some Germans bathing at a beach and dyed the sea with German blood.

The sky over Heraklion was black with flak bursts. A shell hit Pilot Officer Sotirios Skatzikas, the brother of Sarandis Skatzikas, covering his Hurricane in oil. Kokkas, alongside, saw Skatzikas make a thumbs-down motion and that's the last he saw of him. When the formation turned to go, thirty planes had been either shot down or forced to land. Athanasakis paid the ultimate price for his valour, as he may well have expected to. After belly-landing he tried to elude a German a patrol chasing him; when he saw he was cornered he drew his pistol to defend himself and was shot dead.

Skatzikas survived his crash but was captured, ending up in Stalag Luft III at Sagan. When the March 1944 Great Escape was organized he eagerly joined, and was one of the first to break out of the famous tunnel. Fifty recaptured Allied airmen were executed by the Gestapo, and Skatzikas was one of them. He may have remembered in his last moments that the date – 25 March – was Greece's independence day.

The first Crete operation cost the Greeks four pilots. The fact that they were lost in defence of their homeland fired the others to fresh resolve. In November they got a second chance to strike a blow for Crete in another joint raid with the RAF. This was to support amphibious landings on the Dodecanese islands by shooting up German targets on the Cretan coast. Again, the crews were chosen by lot. Diamantopoulos, the CO of 336 Mira, personally picked the names out of his own hat. The ground crews got to work polishing the Hurricanes and writing encouraging messages to the Cretans on the jettisonable wing tanks.

Before dawn the Greek Hurricanes roared off with their canopies open, hugging the dark waves, the sea spray stinging the pilots' faces. They sped over Gavdos, the small island to the south of Crete, and into the mountains. Again, the Cretan peasants, glimpsing the blue and white spinners, erupted in joy. 'Midshipman' Stavropoulos, the incredulous hoots of his messmates still ringing in his ears after his inadvertent five-day naval career, had the satisfaction of shooting up German fuel tanks and weapons dumps. Diamantopoulos, ignoring intense machine-gun fire from the surrounding heights as his orders were to make one pass only, caught sight of a fuel tanker on fire and on its way to Heraklion aerodrome. Intent on hitting it, and constrained by the defile he was flying through, he exposed his starboard side to a flak burst, which smashed into his engine and blinded him with flying glass from his windscreen. Already perilously low, the Hurricane dropped a wing and crash-landed.

Diamantopoulos, seriously injured, was picked up by a German patrol. The Germans didn't think he would live, so they didn't bother to give him emergency medical treatment. It would be 'a waste of medicine', the German doctor told the officer who found him. The officer, a major, turned out to be a rather kinder soul, however, and that same night put Diamantopoulos on a transport to Athens. The Ju52 had barely started its engines at Heraklion when a flight of Beaufighters appeared above Heraklion, plunging the city and aerodrome into blackness. It occurred to Diamantopoulos that it would be ironic in the extreme if an RAF rocket killed him while the Germans were trying to save his life.

His sense of unreality increased when the Ju52 landed at Tatoi, the site of the former Icarus School, which had been turned into a German military hospital. When he was placed in the ward that had been his pre-war dormitory as a cadet, he was so moved he couldn't speak, until the curious German airmen in adjacent beds started a conversation by asking him what kind of planes the Greeks were flying in the Middle East. He was later moved to a civilian hospital north of Athens where he found some survivors of the Greek submarine *Katsonis*, which had been sunk about that time, and a few British prisoners captured in the Dodecanese landings. All were later piled onto a train for the long trip to POW camps in Germany.

Flak had also hit Stavropoulos as he was making his third pass at 150 feet. He looked nervously at his port wing, which was full of holes, hoping the fuel tank wasn't hit. It wasn't, so with his mission completed, he turned for home. Strict radio silence had been imposed on all returning pilots up to fifty miles from the Cretan coast. When that point was passed, and Stavropoulos's

Hurricane was at 1,000 feet, he called up his wingman, Soufrilas, who he had last seen pulling up out of a ravine. By way of reply, Soufrilas came up by his side. Then Stavropoulos thought he was going mad.

Peering ahead over his gunsight, he saw two eyes looking back at him. The eyes came nearer, followed by two tiny legs. A weird fear crept over him. What was this monstrous hallucination? The eyes became a tiny face that resembled a piglet with a moustache and a great long tail. It took some moments for him to realize that it was a giant brown desert rat that somehow had got into his plane at the base and had been his fellow aircrew-member on a combat mission! The engine noise and gun bursts had terrified the poor creature. Stavropoulos felt sorry for it, reflecting that the rodent could have been a mascot that saved his life. Back on the ground, he took the rat back to its desert home.

The loss of Diamantopoulos cast a pall over 336 Mira. Sarandis Skatzikas, the brother of prisoner-of-war Sotirios now in Stalag Luft III, and meanwhile promoted to flight lieutenant, was given temporary command. The following day a flight of 336 Mira was again ordered to shoot up the important road between Heraklion and Chania on the north coast of Crete. The flight took off from Tobruk in depressed spirits. Skliris was the last in line astern as the flight swept into Crete. In an unguarded moment, while he stooped to switch fuel tanks, he hit a couple of trees, damaging the propeller. There was no alternative but to turn around and ditch, but before doing so he thought he'd get in a couple of hits at the enemy flak, which he did. In the event, Skliris's battered propeller didn't give up and eventually got him back. Each of the three propeller blades was found to be missing about six inches of its length.

By the middle of 1943 the Allies had acquired complete effective radar coverage of the North African coast. The Luftwaffe, naturally, tried to counter this by low-level under-the-radar raids. In response to that, the RAF organized wave-top-height sweeps in approximate three-hour shifts covering the daylight hours, starting out from airfields from Beirut to Benghazi. Each sweep would cover about 150 miles. It was tedious work and dangerous as well, as the very low height left no room for baling out or ditching safely in case of emergency.

Both 335 and 336 Mirai had their share of the sweeps, which they had to do over and above their normal convoy escort duties. A typical escort mission would involve an hour or more of circling at 2,000 feet above a convoy, and that was it. Thousands of flying hours were racked up this way, and naturally most Greek pilots chafed under the boredom of it all. The attacks on Crete were a tantalizing taste of what they could accomplish in real combat. Death by drowning after an engine failure over the sea, or in a fireball while releasing some pent-up high spirits, was not the way most men of the RHAF wanted to fall in battle. Kartalamakis, for one, was beset by mental images of 'Death greedily prowling the Mediterranean, brandishing his scythe to cut down the first unlucky, absent-minded or novice pilot in the momentary absence of his protecting Saint.'

Pilot Officer George Xanthakos's Hurricane of 336 Mira caught fire over a convoy eighty miles north of the coast. As he parachuted into the sea a rescue amphibian flew to the scene, but as it touched down a great swell overturned it and it began to sink. The five-man flying boat crew now joined Xanthakos bobbing in the rough sea, while back at base, his squadron mates waited anxiously by the telephone. Towards morning it rang with the news that while a rescue ship had picked up the five British airmen, it had found no sign of Xanthakos. Grimly, as daylight was approaching, the squadron got ready for another escort mission.

For the next two days, when they had time, the Hurricanes swooped and dived over the spot where Xanthakos had last been seen. Worst of all was the thought that their squadron mate may well have been waving frantically at them, but – as happened all too often – all that could be seen from the cockpit were the endless, undulating grey and white flecks. A terse order arrived from 219 Wing headquarters that all searches be stopped and Pilot Officer Xanthakos be considered lost. The RAF allowed a maximum seventy-two hours for searches at sea. A week later a camel with a donkey tied behind it lumbered slowly out of the desert towards 336 Mira's base. A few pilots lounging outside the ops room idly watched them approach in the company of a band of *jellaba*-clad locals. Hatzilakos, now a pilot officer, saw a hand shoot up from among them. It was Xanthakos, weak, and suffering from burns, whom the Bedouin had picked up on the coast.

He had floundered in the heavy seas in his Mae West for three days, seeing all too clearly the planes sent out to look for him. He was tortured by hunger and thirst, sunburn by day and cold by night, and salt water stinging his burns. Eventually, the waves cast him up on the shore. For two days the Bedouin nursed him in their huts until he could walk. He was driven to a hospital in Alexandria, where he recovered enough to be back flying with 336 Mira above the same treacherous seas. When asked about how he felt, he would laugh it off, saying that the sea had made its peace with him now.[5]

Re-equipment, meanwhile, was in progress at 13 Light Bomber Mira, based at Gabut. Its ageing and increasingly cantankerous Bristol Blenheim IVs and Vs had reached the end of the line. One of them had just been serviced at a maintenance unit at Tobruk and Flying Officer Nikolaos Hartokolis was deputed to fly it back to the base with Sergeant Anastasios Bales, a fitter, as his passenger.

The Blenheim's engines had been problematic. Though the RAF maintenance men insisted they were all right after the service, an initial engine run-up had found the twin Bristol Mercury radials unsynchronized. Hartokolis had been warned about that, but seems to have made light of the problem as he set out to pick up the aircraft. Shortly afterwards, witnesses heard the sound of a Blenheim taking off – followed by the unmistakable discordant sound of engines out of synch, and an explosion. Men ran out to see the Blenheim crumpled on the ground, awash in blazing kerosene and its ammunition belts going off. The sick odour of burning flesh wafted over the sand.

The fire eventually was brought under control to reveal the blackened bodies of Hartokolis and Bales still strapped into their seats. Then three more bodies were brought out – those of RAF men who had, against regulations, gone along on the proving flight! Officially, the crash was caused by a faulty control cable connection to the elevators, pushing the plane down when it should have gone up. But what seems equally likely, according to an engineer of 13 Mira, is that one engine failed on take-off, causing a wing stall. When the pilot pitched the nose up to deal with the wing stall, the weight of the three unauthorized passengers could have kept the tail down, causing a full stall.[6]

It was just after that tragic loss that 13 Mira received its shiny new Martin A20 Baltimore twin-engined light bombers supplied by the RAF and paid for by wealthy Greeks in America.[7] Faster, tougher and much more powerful than the Blenheim, the Baltimore bristled with ten guns in the nose, dorsal turret and belly, and could carry nearly 2,000 pounds of bombs. The new attack bombers had their baptism of fire on 14 October 1943 with orders to hit the German fuel dumps on Gavdos, the small island south of Crete. A three-Baltimore formation led by Flight Lieutenant Stratis, the CO, roared in low over Gavdos under the radar. Stratis could see farm chickens scattering in panic. Just as he and his fellow-pilots, Angelidis and Flying Officer George Pattas, were turning away after bombing, a volcano of flak erupted around them. Pattas's plane, on the inside of the curve, took the most punishment. Miraculously, the crew were unhurt and nothing vital was hit. All three returned safely to base. The Baltimore was starting out with a good omen.

A couple of weeks later 13 Mira was ordered back onto the Crete run. This time the task was harder – to cross the width of the island and bomb Souda Bay near Chania, where German warships and supply ships were berthed. Stratis led eight bombers on this operation. The squadron was supposed to rendezvous with a South African and Australian squadron at about the same time. When 13 Mira arrived, though, the sky over Crete was already black with fighters and flak bursts – the other two squadrons had got there early. Gritting his teeth, Stratis gave the order: 'Turn to starboard, dive and bomb individually.' One by one, the Greek planes peeled off and unloaded their high explosives onto the German ships.

In the middle of his dive through the deafening flak, Pattas heard something metallic hit his plane. Unknown to him, it was an unexploded flak shell that had penetrated the fuselage between the wireless operator's seat and the British upper gunner's position, and was rolling back and forth on the floor as the plane bucked and weaved. It was supposed to be common knowledge that flak shells either exploded on impact or not at all, but the wireless operator kept a wary eye on it. Pattas, meanwhile, started his own bombing dive a bit steeply. When he pulled up sharply he blacked out for a few moments. He came to, finding himself still flying north, with several Messerschmitts on his tail, and so made a sharp about-turn over western Crete, shaking off the fighters. When the Baltimore made its belated landing the nervous wireless operator jumped out first. 'There's a shell in plane!' he yelled. That was the first Pattas knew of it. The projectile was soon neutralized.

Crete, bristling with German flak, was proving a tougher proposition than expected. To minimize losses the RAF Middle East command changed tactics. From now on, smaller formations of three aircraft each would attack Souda at low level from the seaward side. Stratis didn't think much of the idea. In his view, losses would rise rather than fall, as the bombers would be turning in over the sea in plain view of the defences instead of weaving through the Cretan hills. In fact, it would be bloody suicide. But when orders for the first operation with the new tactics came through, Stratis felt honour-bound to lead it as an example to his crews.

Pattas protested. 'It's my turn, sir, and anyway, you're married with children,' he told his commander.

As Stratis blinked back tears, wondering what to do, the RAF liaison officer present got in touch with 201 Wing headquarters to see what it thought. 'I haven't got the luxury,' Stratis told headquarters on the phone, 'to lose crews applying tactics I don't believe in.' 201 Wing agreed.

The Greeks enjoyed flying the Baltimore, especially when the rugged American attack bomber left the Luftwaffe's fighters panting behind. To be able to fly it well, the crews of 13 Mira had to take a short conversion course. One newly arrived officer, Squadron Leader Dimitrios Dritsas, a former seaplane pilot, felt he knew enough not to have to take the course. Accordingly, when he took the controls of a Baltimore at Derna and attempted to take off, the powerful plane slewed off the runway, shearing off the undercarriage and slamming into the sand. As the plane was fully bombed up, the three other crew members leapt out of the plane. One of them tried to pull out Dritsas who was fumbling with the unfamiliar harness while flames licked at the cockpit. At that moment an RAF fire engine sped up and the three crew members were ordered away. Dritsas, one of them recalled, lifted his arm feebly and tried to crawl out of the blazing aircraft. Then the bombs went off, pulverizing Dritsas and the Baltimore.

On 24 October Flying Officer Nikolaos Koskinas took off to bomb any enemy shipping caught off the southern coast of Crete, or failing that, unload the bombs on the German positions on Gavdos island. The only thing he found even vaguely resembling a hostile target were a couple of fishing boats at Gavdos that supplied the German garrison. Koskinas had just let his bombs go at low level when a barrage of flak hit his Baltimore and it had to ditch. The bomb-aimer and New Zealand wireless operator sank with the capsized bomber, while Koskinas managed to get the dinghy out and pull his wounded navigator-observer, Flying Officer Panos Tsirikoglou, into the dinghy with him.

The current dragged the dinghy south into the open sea, so Koskinas decided to swim to Gavdos, about three miles away, to seek help. He had swum about a mile when a German boat picked up both airmen. They were taken in stages to Chania, Athens and Thessaloniki. Koskinas made the gruelling trip barefoot, as he had shed his flying boots while exiting the downed plane. In Thessaloniki he finally got a pair of shoes and some food. He and Tsirikoglou were then put on a train to Stalag Luft I in Germany. The slow trip took two weeks, interrupted by bombing alerts and the activities of Tito's partisans in Yugoslavia.

Stratis, the 13 Mira CO, was well-liked by his men, even the left-wing faction that still haunted the squadron. But according to Kartalamakis, the 201 Wing command never forgave Stratis for his near-insubordination in refusing to waste his crews in what he considered would be suicide missions against the lethal German flak batteries in Crete. One day Nasopoulos, now a flight lieutenant and the squadron's second-in-command, was called to Alexandria where a couple of senior RAF officers told him crisply that Stratis was being relieved of command and that he, Nasopoulos, was being recommended to replace him. Nasopoulos flat out refused and went grimly back to base to tell his CO what had happened.

Stratis didn't appear to be surprised. In fact, he was already thinking of asking for a transfer from the squadron. Nasopoulos suspected the British were making Stratis's life difficult. In retrospect, the fault appears to have lain with the heavily left-leaning clique in the Greek Air Ministry-in-exile in

Cairo, where 'power-mad' Fanis Metaxas, the instigator of the Rhodesia mutiny, held the key to personnel promotions and transfers. Stratis's superiors in Cairo told him with straight faces that he was being replaced for not being 'democratic enough' with his men.

'I belong to my country,' Stratis retorted, 'and to no political party. As long as I wear this uniform I will not allow anyone to tell me what my politics must be, or demand to know what I believe.'[8]

Soon 13 Mira found itself in the hands of Squadron Leader Panayotis Papapanayotou, a highly regarded and respected officer. It's a moot point whether Stratis was the victim of British resentment of his independence or leftwing fear that he was becoming too popular in the squadron. Kartalamakis, our sole source for the above exchange, leans towards the latter theory.

None of this, of course, made it any easier over Crete, whose German defences were becoming notorious. The sheer strength of flak on the island made any bombing mission an ordeal. No matter how fast and low a Baltimore could come in over the danger zone of Souda Bay, the blue Cretan sky would turn into a grey-black hell of flak bursts in a matter of seconds. The shock waves from the explosions buffeted the planes about violently, with serious risk of mid-air collision. The tension during the bombing run and the seconds of level flight needed to take the aiming-point photo was such that Pilot Officer George Tsitsoglou, for one, would whoop and sing uncontrollably during the pull-out. As Tsitsoglou would have been the first to admit, however, much of the bombing was wildly off. And it was a rare Baltimore that turned for home without some damage.

Even then the danger wasn't over. Luftwaffe fighters usually prowled the coast for the unwary straggler, but the Baltimores almost always shook them off by diving for speed and hugging the waves. One of those that didn't dive, though, was that of Tsitsoglou, who after one raid was seized with battle fever and decided to test his mettle against the Luftwaffe. His dorsal gunner soon saw a pursuer. 'Tally-ho!'

'Where's the enemy?' Tsitsoglou said.

'Enemy aircraft behind and upper port,' the gunner said.

'Stand by for attack.'

The adversary was an Arado Ar240 heavy fighter, which Tsitsoglou turned to meet head on, shoving the throttles to maximum power. The Baltimore's nose guns blazed first, throwing the Arado off and possibly unnerving its pilot who promptly fled. Shaking and sweat-soaked with the excitement of the encounter, Tsitsoglou barrelled home at top speed, forgetting to throttle back, at 12,000 feet. Much later, he felt more than a tinge of regret at unnecessarily endangering the safety of his crew. 'I still wonder if that really happened or if it was some nightmare brought on by the hell of the flak over Souda,' he wrote.⁹

The two Greek Hurricane squadrons also shared the hazardous Crete operations. Towards midnight on 13 November Flight Sergeant George Mademlis of 336 Mira went to bed after being briefed for the following morning's mission: to attack a concentration of enemy shipping in Mirabello Bay in north-eastern Crete. He slept fitfully if at all, very conscious of the adjacent empty bed that belonged to his squadron mate who had disappeared over Crete the previous day. Early in the morning Mademlis joined three other bleary-eyed pilots for hot tea while the ground crews ran up the Merlins.

It took the four Hurricanes an hour to cross the miles of sea to Crete, flying at no more than thirty feet above the waves. On the south coast the formation spotted a German military column and dived to rake it with cannon fire. At the same time a flak gun opened up on a hillside. They were entering the notorious Ierapetra plain that narrows at its northern end where it enters the hills. This narrow point formed a funnel into which German flak could pour murderous fire. Flight Sergeant Dimitrios Sarsonis's plane took two hits, caught fire and dived straight into a farmhouse; Sarsonis was flung out on impact, aflame from head to toe. The crash also killed a fourteen-year-old Cretan girl visiting her newly married sister in the house. Flying Officer Constantine Psilolignos's plane was also hit but stayed in the air. Mademlis flew in close to take a look and saw Psilolignos slumped over the controls, dead. The unfortunate pilot's plane flew on a while and crashed in the hills.

Flak shrapnel holes appeared in both of Mademlis's wings. Karydis, the mission leader and now a flying officer, led the way to the designated target and the two remaining Hurricanes found themselves over the brilliant blue of Mirabello Bay – and flak that the pre-mission briefing had said wouldn't be there. Their attack was successful and they were turning to go when a flak shell exploded in Mademlis's oil tank. He radioed Karydis that he was going to force-land, to hear the mission leader say that he, too, was hit and going to do the same. Once on the ground, Mademlis limped to hide in a small country church, wounded in the leg. The following morning a German patrol flushed him out at gunpoint. Karydis managed to reach the south coast of Crete, where he ditched in the middle of a marine minefield and was captured in short order.

Crowds of Cretans attended the funeral of Sarsonis and Psilolignos, the two dead Greek airmen, at Ierapetra cemetery. The Germans buried them with full military honours. The local German commander delivered a remarkable graveside eulogy, indicating that the sense of honour in the German military had by no means been extinguished. The officer said:

> Yesterday, our uniforms and flags divided us. Today, though, we are called upon to honour the soldiers who fell for their country ... These soldiers, however, were enviably favoured: they fell on the soil of their beloved country, a favour that all fallen soldiers would wish for, *especially our own soldiers on the Eastern front, where the bodies of our dead are exposed to the cold and inhospitable snow.*[10]

Four losses by 336 Mira in a single mission was the most concentrated blow the Greek air force suffered while based in North Africa. Crete was turning out to be a Russian roulette. Souda Bay had earned notoriety as a suicide target. An Australian squadron had recently been devastated over it. The Allied strategy was to use the Souda raids to disorient the Germans and confuse them as to the intentions of the Allies in the eastern Mediterranean. Costly, yes, but the other side of the coin was that Greek pilots browned off by constant convoy duty often sought the Crete operations for some excitement, however dangerous.

Spyros Diamantopoulos, the 336 Mira CO who was shot down and captured, had no regrets about Crete. Convoy duty, he wrote long afterwards, was fatiguing and boring to the point of neurosis. But the Crete operations 'were a kind of escape, something different, something exciting, a chance to fire our machine guns at the enemy ... the Crete operations gave the exiled Greek air force a chance to prove itself the equal of the mighty RAF.'[11]

Deepening the gloom in 336 Mira was the creeping realization that the Greeks' Hurricanes were ageing, slow and vulnerable to the bristling defences in the Ierapetra plain and Souda Bay. Requests to the RAF for newer machines were routinely turned down with Air Vice-Marshal Park's excuse that convoy escorts didn't need anything better. The pilots may be excused for not seeing it that way. In both *mirai* they had to suffer the regular humiliation of being unable to pursue the Luftwaffe's faster Junkers Ju88 and Heinkel He111 reconnaissance bombers. And nothing, oddly enough, was said about the Hurricanes' Crete missions. Soon, though, the tables would turn.

Towards the end of 1943 a *frisson* of excitement ran through 335 and 336 Mirai. At last they would receive the coveted Supermarine Spitfire! For many months King George II and the RHAF leadership had been pestering London for a fighter that would finally be able to meet the Ju88s and He111s, not to mention the Messerschmitt Bf109s, on equal speed terms. However, though a halo of a reputation had surrounded the Spitfire from its fabled Battle of Britain days, there was some concern that it might overheat in desert conditions, and that its narrow wheelbase – about one-third smaller than that of a Hurricane – might make take-offs and landings on bumpy ground a questionable proposition.

But those concerns were swept aside when both fighter squadrons received their first Spitfire Mk IVs and Vbs. Each pilot was given a forty-five-minute familiarization flight. Of course, that was not nearly enough to establish combat-readiness on the type. A conversion course was required, and here the fabled Greek reckless independence asserted itself again. Margaritis, a veteran of the Albania campaign, now a squadron leader and the 336 Mira CO, was impatient to show the RAF what his Greeks could do with the best of British flying machines. Without waiting for a thorough check by the engineers and ground crews, he sent up some Spitfires on sea patrols. Vladousis, his executive officer, was appalled.

'Sir,' he told his CO, 'we're not even basically ready on the Spitfire. We need gunnery practice, we need to see how the plane behaves. I think everyone on the squadron agrees.'

Margaritis was not to be swayed. 'Look,' he replied, 'I want to show the British that as soon as they've given us the planes we're using them on missions.'

Vladousis knew the RAF rather better than his boss. 'Sir,' he said, 'the British are going to accuse us of being hasty. We're going to have accidents.' Faced with Margaritis's intransigence, he asked to be relieved of executive officer duties on the spot.

Vladousis was right. And ironically, he almost became the Spitfire's first accident victim. He and his wingman, Soufrilas, were making a final check before a practice flight. As Vladousis bent down in the cockpit to release the handbrake there was a deafening splintering and churning just behind his head. Soufrilas, a short man, had been unable to see past his Spitfire's long and high nose and had ploughed into Vladousis's plane, the propeller slicing up the metal like ham. If Vladousis hadn't stooped at just the right moment, he would have been beheaded. The unhappy little flight sergeant leaped onto his wing, distraught and ashen, muttering to himself over and over: 'I could have killed you, I could have killed you.'

The first real Spitfire fatality can perhaps be attributed to a love affair. Around Christmas 1943 Pilot Officer Sotirios Christakos of 336 Mira almost hit telephone wires coming in to land at Sidi Barrani. His cousin Constantine, serving in the same squadron, knew he was smitten with a girl in Alexandria and feared the sentiment might be affecting his flying.

On 29 December Christakos crashed and was killed in circumstances that remain unclear.[12]

The squadron's Hurricanes hadn't had their last word. One pilot who was increasingly worried about his Hurricane's increasingly erratic behaviour was Hatzilakos. The engineers couldn't figure out what was wrong with the fighter, so they grounded it except for short flight practice hops. Seeing it sitting there, Warrant Officer Dimitrios Spyridonos decided to take it up for a spin over Sidi Barrani. Not bothering to don flying suit and goggles, he took off in his tropical shirt and shorts. As the great desert spread out before him, Spyridonos succumbed to the temptation to race across the sand at dune height. He had flown many miles and was about to return when flames suddenly engulfed the cockpit.

The Hurricane was far too low for Spyridonos to be able to bale out safely, so with flames licking at his legs he belly-landed at the first level spot he saw, hurtling a couple of hundred feet across the dunes before coming to a stop. Burned on his legs, arms and face, he scrambled out of the cockpit just as the Hurricane was consumed in flames. Spyridonos staggered across the desert for hours, in agony from his burns and seared by the Libyan sun, until he came to the main Alexandria–Benghazi road. A jeep with Indians in it came along, and soon Spyridonos was in an Alexandria hospital with grim-faced doctors bending over him.

He eventually recovered thanks to a British doctor who'd had experience treating burned Battle of Britain pilots, and the Greek volunteer nurses who treated him as a special patient. After months of successive operations, Spyridonos was well enough to return to 336 Mira, to be promptly given twenty days' detention for flying without proper apparel and equipment, thus endangering his own life. The penalty left a bad taste in mouths of the other pilots, who had been fervently hoping for their comrade's recovery without thinking of rules.

Yet the punishment could be considered justified in a way, as the Greek pilots were particularly prone to breaking service rules. One was Flight Lieutenant Stamos Karathanasis, who after taking off bare-armed on 25 November saw flames coming from under the instrument panel. In less than a minute the fire had spread to the windscreen and the engine began to sputter. Karathanasis had no choice but to belly-land his Hurricane as best as he could. He switched off the fuel and braced for the impact, as the flames scorched his arms. The Hurricane's underwing tanks broke the plane's fall and snapped off. Then the fighter blew up. Hatzilakos, who had been watching, jumped into a squadron vehicle and raced to the burning plane. Karathanasis lived but was badly burned.

The new Spitfire boys soon got the chance to see some action. One morning Soufrilas, the little guy who had inadvertently sliced up Vladousis's fighter, was patrolling over a forty-ship convoy when he was vectored onto a Ju88 in the area. Soufrilas dived in to the attack, hammering away with his Browning guns. Smoke poured from the German plane's starboard engine, and the return fire from the German gunner abruptly stopped. Seconds after its engine burst into flames, the Ju88 blew up in mid-air. Soufrilas had more than made up for his near-tragic runway blunder. He shared the kill with his wingman, Flying Officer George Tsotsos. 336 Mira's Spitfires had finally drawn blood.

A few days later Soufrilas saw his chance to score again. He and Christakos were scrambled to meet an unidentified aircraft about fifty miles out to sea at 8,000 feet. Arriving in the area, neither pilot could see anything. 'You're very close,' came the warning from RAF ground control, 'look harder.' They did, and instead of the expected Ju88 or He111 they saw an untethered barrage balloon at about 12,000 feet and climbing. It was a convoy-protection device consisting of a balloon at one end, a bomb on the other, and a rope in the middle that had somehow come loose. The pilots stared at it, mystified, wondering if it was some new German weapon. Ground control told them what it was and ordered its destruction. It wasn't a kill, but it was better than nothing.

Vladousis's warnings about a lack of preparation on the Spitfires were prescient. In May 1944, when the German threat to the Mediterranean convoys was much reduced, 335 and 336 Mirai were put on an intensive air combat readiness training schedule. The deadline for readiness was the last day of May. On the previous day Kartalamakis took up twelve Spitfires for close-formation practice. At 4,000 feet, heading south, they found five-tenths cloud going up to 5,000 feet. Kartalamakis ordered the formation to make a coordinated 180-degree turn. Looking in his rear-view mirror after the manoeuvre was completed, he saw two Spitfires on fire and falling. From one of the Spitfires, cut almost in two and disintegrating, a parachute sprang.

Kartalamakis ordered the formation to return to base, telling Kokkas to stay and circle over the two plumes of smoke. Back at base a Miles Magister that the squadron used as a hack flew to pick up Christakos, who had baled out. Dazed as he was being taken to hospital, he told his flight commander: 'It's a good thing we were flying high, sir.' The fault appeared to lie with the less fortunate pilot who had been initially rejected as a poor flier but had been reinstated in the squadron through political influence. It was politics, in fact, that would very soon become a far greater menace to the wartime Greek air effort than any Axis enemy.

Chapter 14

Mutiny!

As 1943 wore into 1944, the western Allies prepared for a thrust into southern Europe from the Mediterranean. Though Churchill and Roosevelt agreed that this front should be opened, they disagreed over just where it should be. Churchill, correctly suspecting that Stalin plotted to take over Eastern Europe and the Balkans, wanted to concentrate on retaking Italy. The Germans had no fewer than twenty-three divisions defending the peninsula, and besides, northern Italy would provide a springboard for the liberation of Austria, placing considerable Allied forces in central Europe to thwart Stalin's designs on the east.

Roosevelt insisted on a simultaneous landing in southern France and a drive up the Rhone valley. Stalin, meeting with Roosevelt and Churchill in Tehran in November 1943, eagerly seconded the idea, and Churchill knew exactly why – it would conveniently keep a good portion of the Western armies safely in the west and away from the Balkans. Montgomery also argued fiercely against it.[1] But the Americans, whose sheer industrial and military power were now vital to winning the war against Germany and Japan, prevailed.

Stalin had certainly not been idle in the meantime. About the middle of 1942, when the first resistance groups had taken shape in the mountains of mainland Greece and Crete, he had manoeuvred the Greek Communist Party (KKE) into running the show. One of the aims of the KKE was to provoke savage German reprisals on the Greek population, such as the frightful massacres at Distomo and Kalavryta, which naturally boosted partisan recruitment. A romanticized version of the Resistance activities filtered down to the men of the Greek squadrons in the Middle East and made some of them wonder whether they really were being useful by merely patrolling convoys.

Morale in the Greek squadrons was not high. 13 Mira might have the privilege of attacking German targets in Crete, but the privilege was costly. Training accidents, also, were taking their toll. On the night of 13 January 1944 Pilot Officer Yannis Georgopoulos died in a collision with an RAF

Baltimore in a close-order flying exercise. Exactly one month later two of 13 Mira's Baltimores touched wingtips 9,000 feet over Payne Field, a USAAF base in Libya. Flight Sergeant Efthymios Tzamtzis, flying right behind them, had to swerve hard to port and yank back on the stick to avoid the flying wreckage. Of the six men in both planes, only Flying Officer Anastasios Marmaras survived.[2]

Such events, it may be argued, are the inevitable concomitants of war and need not by themselves lead to low unit morale. Yet the Greeks taking part in the desert air war didn't have the ordinary privileges of most soldiers. Unlike their British or German counterparts, they didn't have the luxury of being able to write or receive letters or parcels from home. They had no way of communicating with their families in occupied Greece, of even knowing whether they were still alive. Who could tell how long the war had yet to run, or how it would end? Would anyone ever get to see their loved ones again?

Naturally, these sentiments were strongest among the enlisted men. And their anger would mount when they walked the streets of Cairo and Alexandria on their few periods of leave from the desert, and saw the posh hotels and bars bursting with Greek senior officers of all stripes, many of them appointed by some corrupt politician or other, strutting and showing off without having been a single hour in real danger.

It wasn't long before subversive leaflets and manifestoes began appearing among the Greeks of all three services. This was the work of organized KKE cells in Cairo, overseen by the Soviet Russian embassy, which cleverly played on the enlisted men's grievances. On the wider stage, Italy was next on the Allied invasion schedule, and Stalin wanted to weaken the Italian operation as much as possible, if not stall it altogether. As a part of this grand scheme to keep the Western Allies away from Central Europe, the Greek contingent had to be knocked out of the Italy campaign. Thus from Moscow's viewpoint subversion became a matter of the utmost urgency. It wouldn't be long now, the Greek government-in-exile said, before all three Greek *mirai* would be transferring to Italy. The KKE redoubled its efforts to stop them and the other Greek services from going. 'The Army has no business in Italy!' the propaganda leaflets shouted. 'Fascist officers will use it to fasten [King] George on our necks again!'

So pervasive was the KKE propaganda that it swayed even higher-ranking officers. On 31 March 1944 twelve officers, including six from the air force and headed by Wing Commander Tzanetakis, the former RHAF liaision officer with the RAF and now on the air staff in Cairo, formally demanded that the Greek armed forces in the Middle East join EAM, the communist-controlled Resistance organization, in a general 'liberation' effort.[3] After delivering their portentously worded petition to the Greek government-in-exile, they sent copies to the British, American and Soviet Russian embassies in Cairo.

The Greek government's response to this manoeuvre, which clearly exceeded the mandate of any member of the military, was to order the arrest of the twelve. King George II in London heard of the movement while dining with Churchill that same night, and left for Cairo at once. But the king was too late to halt events, and anyway, his presence in Cairo only fanned the flames of subversion. The unrest quickly worsened. The British authorities cancelled plans to deliver a much-needed destroyer to the Royal Hellenic Navy precisely because some officers and ratings opposed hoisting the national flag on the vessel! Two RHN warships in Alexandria harbour actually lowered their blue and white ensigns and replaced them with red flags. The crew of one of them, the corvette *Apostolis*, refused orders to hunt down a German U-boat that had just sunk a troopship full of American soldiers. The incident prompted a rare outburst from Roosevelt, who in a cable to the British Admiralty condemned what he called 'Greek madmen'.

Aircraftman Vlassis Papingis, a clerk in 13 Mira, was an unremarkable fellow to look at. A former law student, slight in build, he had joined the air force in Gaza as a volunteer and had been placed on administration duties. But unlike other such volunteers, and unbeknownst to anyone else, Papingis was a member of the Central Committee of the KKE, planted in the Greek squadrons for the express purpose of sabotaging their war effort. For months he had operated under deep cover, but in early 1944, when the squadron was planning to move to Italy, he emerged as 13 Mira's unofficial commissar, holding nightly communist indoctrination sessions in his red-flagged tent, and swaggering around the compound showing off his contempt for authority. When orders came through on 6 April for 13 Mira's imminent move to Italy, his KKE masters ordered him to do all in his power to stop it.

The squadron's ground personnel and vehicles were scheduled to depart at first light on 23 April, drive 600 miles to Port Said and embark on two transports. The aircraft and aircrews would fly over later. Papingis put his soviet into high gear. He had already managed to intimidate most of the squadron's officers by affixing the dreaded label of 'fascist' to anyone who even perfunctorily insisted on respect for rank. Squadron Leader Papapanayotou, the 13 Mira CO, knowing the left-leaning inclinations of some of the RHAF brass in Cairo, felt it prudent to play for time. He even agreed to the dissidents' demand to rename the RHAF the Greek Popular Liberation Air Force, as long as it kept the squadron together.

One day Papingis burst into the tent housing the officers' mess and barked: 'All officers on the parade ground!' Some RAF officers present, suspecting imminent violence, discreetly left by a back flap. The rest meekly obeyed Papingis and lined up. One navigator, Captain (later Air Marshal) Tsimbos, observed that Papingis was armed. What happened next remains vague, as 13 Mira's official records for that period were mysteriously destroyed. The officers appear to have been lectured on how their days of power were over, and dismissed.

Fortunately, 13 Mira contained men who were not prepared to be browbeaten by a bunch of red scarf-wearing bolsheviks. One of them, Flying Officer Eleftherios Pantazoglou, an engineer officer, decided to interrupt one of Papingis's tent meetings and have it out with the bumptious aircraftman.

> Look, I don't get involved in politics. But let me tell you something. People have worked hard and even died so that 13 Mira can have the honour of going first to get at the enemy ... If by dropping even a few bombs we can free our country one hour sooner, we shouldn't refuse the chance.

Those words made not the slightest impression on Papingis. On 20 April he called the ground crews out on parade again and delivered a harangue strongly opposing the transfer to Italy. Pantazoglou listened to him, bitterness filling his heart. All the sacrifices they had endured, in the name of their country and their families left behind to an unknown fate – had it all come to this?

On the following day, the eve of the ground crews' departure for Port Said, Flight Sergeant Papageorgopoulos was sweating and cursing trying to fix a troublesome lorry engine, when a slight figure swaggered up to him. 'Flight Sergeant,' Papingis said, 'if you pull a cable from each of the motors, none of them will start in the morning.'

Papageorgopoulos, one of those sturdy NCOs who form the backbone of any military unit, was not in the best of moods. 'Get lost, you nutcase,' he said.

Papingis responded by putting a hand inside his tunic and bringing out a thick wad of red Egyptian banknotes. 'Take this, stupid, and do as I say,' he said. 'Don't be a fool.'

Barely were the words out of his mouth than Papageorgopoulos let him have it with the back of his fist, sending the puny aircraftman sprawling in the dust. Papingis got to his feet and put his hand in his tunic again. This time it came out with a German parabellum pistol in it. 'Now you'll die, fascist,' he snarled. But he was no match for the burly NCO, who disarmed him in a single motion. Papingis's fellows came and took him away.

On the evening of 22 April Pantazoglou was a worried man. He had no idea whether his drivers, many of whom were openly mutinous, would obey orders in the morning. As a precaution, as darkness fell he had all weapons collected and placed under guard. At night the loyal drivers slept in their vehicles to guard against sabotage. 'No sleep tonight,' he wrote in his diary.

Luckily, he had stalwart allies in Papageorgopoulos and Flight Lieutenant Panayotis Savoulidis, in charge of 13 Mira's ground crews. Savoulidis had the idea of announcing the following morning's departure time as eight o'clock while secretly preparing for six o'clock. It was a simple stratagem, but it worked. At five o'clock, in fact, the whole column was ready. Flying Officer Triantafyllos Krikonis jumped into the cabin of the lead vehicle, a fuel tanker, and gave the order to move. In his rear-view mirror was the satisfying vision of eighty vehicles following him out of the compound. Moments later he saw about 100 enlisted men, half-naked and shouting, chasing the lorries, trying to stop the exodus. Luckily they weren't armed. The convoy cleared the gate and was on its way.

Papageorgopoulos, driving one of the lorries, had little reason to relax. Sitting next to him was a communist fitter who had elected to join the convoy. As the truck jolted along, the passenger conspicuously fondled an Italian pistol. The message to Papageorgopoulos was clear – he could be bumped off at any time. But he wasn't about to take any of that, so at one point he slammed on the brakes, throwing the fitter against the windscreen.

'We've been three years out here, eating sand by the mouthful, the flight sergeant snarled, 'and now, because of what I believe and what you believe, they've addled your brain and you're going to kill me?' Papageorgopoulos backed up his words by grabbing the fitter by the collar, seizing his pistol and shutting it in the dashboard compartment.

After a six-hour drive the convoy arrived at Port Said. Men and vehicles boarded two transports, which stayed in port for six days before sailing. But the officers couldn't relax. A good number of drivers and mechanics who came with them were communist sympathizers, and for all anyone knew, could have orders to sabotage the ships. Pantazoglou spent the first night under a lorry in the company of the driver, a known communist. Not surprisingly, he found it hard to get to sleep. But he was dog-tired, so he turned to the driver. 'Listen, mate,' he said. 'If you're going to murder me in the night, so be it. I just want to get some sleep. Goodnight.'

The mutiny among the ground staff of 13 Mira seriously rattled the RAF Middle East command, which naturally demanded explanations. The threat, though unstated, was clear: if 13 Mira proved unreliable, its aircraft would be confiscated, and the only RHAF unit that had fought incessantly since October 1940 would be disgraced and probably disbanded.

Fortunately, political developments in the Greek government-in-exile finally enabled a firm hand to take charge. The new prime minister was George Papandreou, an anti-royalist liberal who, nonetheless, had the wit to see communism for what it was – a deadly menace to flag and country. One of Papandreou's first actions was to sack Group Captain Dimakis, the left-leaning chief of the RHAF, and replace him with Group Captain Alexandris. Papingis and his mutineers were rounded up and sent to the British stockade at Abbasiya near Cairo. Alexandris sent Vladousis to the camp to interview the 110 Greek communists behind the wire. They were sullen and uncooperative, refusing to recognize Vladousis's rank. 'Then who do you want to talk to?' Vladousis asked.

'To Stalin,' one of the men said.

'I'm afraid Stalin has rather more important things to do right now,' Vladousis said.

'Then Roosevelt,' another said.

'I'd say Roosevelt would be even busier,' Vladousis replied. He was ordinarily a patient man, but as the detainees continued to stall, he ended the interview by roundly cursing the lot of them.

Communist agitation had also influenced some of 13 Mira's pilots waiting in Cairo for the order to fly over to Italy. Papapanayotou, the CO, assembled the aircrew in a hall and frankly asked them how many were not prepared to go to Italy. Four pilots and five other aircrew raised their hands. A few later retracted, but the rest were placed under arrest. Sixteen RAF personnel replaced them.

In the aftermath of the May 1944 mutiny, which bid fair to knock out 13 Mira as a fighting force, Alexandris suggested removing one of the grievances that had helped trigger it. Rivalry between the graduates of the Icarus School and EKI on the one hand, and former Army and Navy fliers on the other, was still simmering in the squadrons. Fanis Metaxas, who had come close to disrupting the Rhodesia training programmes in 1942 and was now the RHAF's chief personnel officer, saw his chance at attaining a long-sought goal.

The result, drawn up largely by Metaxas, was Law 3302, passed by the Greek government-in-exile. The law formally separated the 'pure' air force officers – i.e. those who had gone through the air force training schools – from those whose origins lay in the other services. Papandreou, the prime minister, anxious to calm the unrest in the services by any means, signed the law without delay. Yet instead of settling the unrest, Law 3302 may have increased it. It relegated many undoubtedly capable and loyal air force officers to the sidelines, flying empty desks until they could be replaced by the 'pure' set.

Another one who thought he could improve the morale of the RHAF was Tzanetakis, now the RAF's senior maintenance and supply officer in the Middle East. This undoubtedly highly capable engineer officer was typical of those idealistic men caught in the trap of communist propaganda masquerading as liberal politics. He wasn't the only one. Much of Whitehall at the time, not to mention the British press, looked on the Greek partisans with considerable sympathy. After the Battle of El Alamein Tzanetakis had asked the RAF to approve his plan to set up an information bureau to explain to the weary, sand-maddened Greeks just what they were fighting for. He held meetings in the squadrons where political movements were afoot, some on the right and some on the left. He realized, as he put it, that 'the more serious [movements] favoured national unity'.[4]

Others had a less charitable view of Tzanetakis. Flight Lieutenant Nikolaos Platis, an engineer officer, had sat down to one of Tzanetakis's talks when he realized he was listening to an outright communist harangue. As CO of the maintenance base, Platis stopped the speech and asked the speaker to leave. Half the audience – including some left-leaning RAF personnel – rose to noisily support the wing commander. Platis called in the RAF service police and sent the noisiest agitators to stand for hours in the hot African sun. 'I'm ashamed of wearing the same uniform as that man,' Platis told a senior officer in Cairo, referring to Tzanetakis, whose 'enlightening' efforts came to an abrupt end on 30 March when he and eleven other officers handed their pro-EAM petition to the government-in-exile and were arrested for their pains.

The two Greek fighter squadrons, 335 and 336 Mirai, had remained in North Africa while 13 Mira had gone to Italy. Both had their problems with subversives, though they weren't as serious as those in the bomber squadron. Pangalos, the 335 Mira CO, was careful to keep obvious troublemakers out of the unit. In 336 Mira Hatzilakos fretted that communists might sabotage the Spitfires. Ten pilots of 336 Mira had been lost, five in accidents and five in action over Crete, in the twelve months since the squadron had been formed. Margaritis, the CO, exercised a rough and ready face control over new personnel, sending those he didn't like the look of back to Alexandria and Cairo.

Yet the underground network had done its work well. On 23 March the order came to escort a large Italy-bound convoy steaming 100 miles offshore. 336 Mira's Spitfires took to the air in pairs and fours, alternating over the area to be guarded. In the middle of the feverish activity the squadron's ground crews suddenly went on strike. Landing pilots could find no one to refuel and service the aircraft for the next sortie. 'We couldn't even find anyone to tie our planes down so they wouldn't be blown over in the strong wind,' Hatzilakos recalled. 'There were shouts of "Where the hell is everybody?"' The pilots had to refuel their planes themselves.

One who felt particularly threatened by the mutineers was Flying Officer Yannis Papakostas of 335 Mira. 'They're going to get me, I know it,' he had muttered to Anagnostopoulos, shortly before both took off to escort a convoy off Tobruk. He didn't elaborate. Most likely he was one of those loyal officers labelled 'fascist' by the subversives. Ten miles out from Tobruk, at 4,000 feet and in clear weather, Papakostas's engine cut out. Anagnostopoulos told him to bale out, but he elected to ditch. Papakostas's Spitfire sank almost at once on impact with the water, taking its pilot with it.

A search party was unable to take off because the ground crews were still nowhere to be seen. As Margaritis was absent in Cairo, a livid Hatzilakos rounded up Vladousis and as many of his fellow-pilots as he could. Pistols in hand, they burst into the fitters' tent. There they met an astonishing sight. A young engineer flying officer was standing in the middle of a crowd of aircraftmen and NCOs in full indoctrination session. Vladousis walked up to the flying officer, a new man whom no one had seen before. 'Who the hell are you and what are you doing here?' he roared.

'Sir,' an aircraftman piped up, 'this man is giving us instruction and telling us that bastard Papakostas deserved what he got yesterday, and that we need to be rid of all of them.'

The earnest young flying officer and a few other new arrivals were clamped under arrest and sent under guard to Cairo. The KKE's attempts to emasculate the Greek armed forces persisted. In one particularly *opera buffa* attempt, which makes one wonder at the mental faculties of those concerned, as 336 Mira was preparing to move to the base at Mersa Matruh, a group of men under a junior engineer officer called on Margaritis to hand him a petition. The CO glanced at it and called a general assembly of officers and NCOs.

'Gentlemen,' he told them, as the engineer pilot officer stood next to him, 'I've just been given a memorandum which I wish to read to you: "To the Greek government in Cairo. To the governments of Great Britain, France and the Soviet Union (though their embassies) ..."'

The text was essentially the same as what Tzanetakis and his unofficial junta had presented to the authorities in Cairo: a demand to 'democratize' the armed forces and join with EAM (and its master, the KKE) in determining the future of Greece. Margaritis read on: 'Signed, *the President of Greek Airmen, Pilot Officer*—.'

Laughter and catcalls drowned out the last few words. If there is one thing at which the Greeks are masters, it's taking puffed-up characters down a peg or two. There were sarcastic shouts of 'Hey, Prez!' and 'Have you told the Chinese yet?' Whereupon the squadron commander slowly and ceremoniously tore the paper to shreds and walked out. The pilot officer with presidential ambitions stood there, in the words of an eyewitness, 'deflated like a balloon'. He and twenty others were duly loaded on the truck for the barbed wire compound. That, to all intents and purposes, was the end of communism in 336 Mira, thanks to the efforts of Hatzilakos and others who 'without sleep and dropping with fatigue, guns in hand, were resolved not to allow anyone to affect our battle-readiness and fighting spirit.'[5]

Kartalamakis, who devotes a great deal of space to the mutiny in the RHAF ranks, is right to blame it on communist subversion first and foremost. But that's not the whole story. Reading between the lines of his detailed and sometimes emotional account, it becomes clear that the RHAF leadership signally failed to perceive the nature of the threat and confront it before it became unmanageable. Subversion cannot work unless it finds fertile ground to grow in. As the majority of Greek servicemen in North Africa were homesick and completely cut off from their people back home, and rarely given the chance to hit the hated enemy, it was up to the officer corps to maintain morale and inspire the men. Very few – men such as Varvaressos, Vladousis and Vilos come to mind – measured up to the task.[6]

Chapter 15

Back to the Balkans

The engineer and administration officers of 13 Mira were finally able to relax on the pleasant six-day voyage to Bari in Italy, comforted by the sight of the escorting warships. The aircrews and Baltimores began quitting North Africa in stages on 12 May, ending up at Biferno in Italy a week later. On the way they stopped at Catania in Sicily, where, to their considerable satisfaction, they were served by white-gloved Italian mess staff in dinner jackets. The squadron's first operation from Biferno, on 25 May, was to bomb railway stations in northern Italy. A few weeks after that 13 Mira moved to Pescara, on the east coast, as the Germans fell back to the north. A month later the squadron was back at Biferno, its mission switched to Balkan targets. The switch was cheering to the men, who imagined themselves one step closer to home.

A few Baltimores, however, were still being serviced in Benghazi and had to delay their departure. One of them was pronounced ready on 20 May. Tsitsoglou and his crew took off from Benghazi, eager at the prospect of seeing green European fields again after more than two years of stark desert and sea. On the climb-out at 2,000 feet, Tsitsoglou's smile faded as the oil pressure gauge indicated a sudden loss of pressure in the port Wright Cyclone engine. The plane began to drag. Then the oil pressure of the starboard engine began to plummet. On one engine Tsitsoglou could have circled back to base, but with both gone there was no choice but for a forced landing. With its wheels up, the Baltimore pancaked onto soft sand, throwing up a huge dust cloud.

None of the crew, including a British Army captain on sick leave, was harmed. But they were in the middle of the desert, wondering what to do while nibbling at the concentrated emergency food rations and taking sips of water. Under the shade of the wings they sat down and passed the time playing cards, trying to suppress unhappy visions of their desiccated skeletons mouldering by the plane for decades afterwards. A few hours later human shapes were seen on the horizon. The crew fired flares, but the shapes vanished. Two machine guns were detached from the dorsal turret and set up on the sand as a rudimentary defence. Not long afterwards some friendly Bedouin chanced upon them and soon a brisk trade was in progress. The Bedouin supplied chickens, goats, pigeons, milk and bread in return for blankets, towels and shoes – luckily the Batimore had been fully loaded with the equipment needed for the transfer to Italy. Two days later a British patrol picked them up, and they finally reached Biferno on 8 July.

The green fields of Italy were like magic to the crews of 13 Mira. Days after the squadron's arrival at Biferno, Flight Lieutenant Yannis Papantoniou took a stroll by the Adriatic Sea with Savoulidis, the chief engineer officer. The Italian spring was in full bloom, and the two men gazed wistfully at the blaze of wild flowers adorning the low hill at one end of the airfield. 'Pavlo,' Papantoniou said, 'If I ever got killed in an aeroplane, I'd want to crash at such a spot.'

Two days later Papantoniou lifted off in his Baltimore for a practice flight. A mere twenty feet above the runway his plane abruptly levelled off. Instead of climbing, it continued to fly level – straight into the hillside he so admired. The crash remained inexplicable. An investigation suggested that the pilot's harness straps could have been unfastened and might somehow have got tangled in the controls, and even that Papantoniou might have had a heart attack on take-off. Neither theory was convincing.

A major threat to flight safety in 13 Mira, in fact, was the effect of the recent mutiny and subsequent arrests that had depleted air and ground crews. These had to be replaced by men who needed to be freshly trained on the Baltimore and pronounced combat-ready in an impossibly short time. One of the pilots new to bombers was Flight Lieutenant Pericles Liakeas, a veteran of the fighter encounters over the Albanian front. Starting his first bombing operation out of Biferno, he slewed badly on his take-off run, stalled immediately after getting airborne and slammed into an adjacent vineyard, mowing down seven hapless Italian peasants working there. Then the bombs went off, pulverizing plane and crew. Tsimbos, already aloft in one of the lead bombers, saw the accident unfold. 'Liakeas has had it,' he said laconically to his skipper, and the mission went on.

'The Baltimore was not an easy plane to fly,' Kartalamakis wrote later. 'It was untameable. Its mighty engine power demanded alertness on take-off. Even on landing it was sometimes hard to keep inside the runway. It was designed for pilots of a high professional standard.'[1] Tsitsoglou was a great fan of the bomber, precisely because of its cussedness. 'I was in love with that plane,' he said much later. 'It's the aircraft of my youth, of the war I lived through ... I've flown many types of planes, but my love for the Baltimore will never die.'[2]

The squadron was now a part of the so-called Balkan Air Force, under the command of 3 South African Bomber Wing. Flying Officer Yannis Hatzakis enjoyed the satisfaction of looking out of his cockpit at the squadrons of RAF Spitfires flying escort for 13 Mira. 'We bombed pretty accurately,' he said later, 'and had virtually zero losses. We were finally compensating for our earlier lack of experience.'

On 24 June six aircraft took off from Pescara to bomb the San Marino railway station. Flying Officer Byron Frangias, the mission leader, found thick cumulus cloud over the target at 12,000 feet. The bombers nosed into the cloud, which turned out to have a menacing black core of cumulonimbus that bounced the planes about like corks. Hail hammered at the windscreens and lightning flashed incessantly. The bombers loosened whatever formation they had been able to keep and broke cloud in one piece. Shaken by the jolting, the crews went on to bomb their alternative target, the strategic Fano road and rail bridge near Rimini.

At the debriefing back at base Tsimbos, Frangias's bomb-aimer, took a pen and paper to report a near miss. As he was writing an excited warrant officer burst in waving a photograph. 'Congratulations, captain,' the NCO said. 'You've destroyed the bridge!' The squadrons of 3 South African Bomber Wing had been trying to smash the Fano bridge for weeks, without success. Tsimbos that evening was personally feted by the 3 Wing commander who graciously told him: 'Today you gave us a good lesson.' The crew, including an RAF gunner named Pilot Officer Sowden, were cited for valour by the Greek Air Ministry-in-exile.

In the middle of July 13 Mira was given an especially satisfying target – Korce in Albania, last attacked by the RHAF in the heady days of November 1940. On 16 July Hatzakis led six Baltimores on the mission. They met heavy flak over Berat and a shell burst directly in front of the Perspex nose of Flying Officer Yannis Papoutsis's plane; fragments burst through the perspex, slicing a finger off the navigator, Flying Officer Zacharias Arvanitis. Seeing the blood spurting from his navigator's wound, Papoutsis suggested aborting the mission but Arvanitis, bandaging his hand tightly, was in favour of pressing on. The wireless operator, Flight Sergeant Eleftherios Pantzalis, offered to do the bomb-aiming, but Arvanitis refused, knowing that inexperienced or inept bomb-aiming could endanger the other bombers in the mission.

Separated now from the main force, Papoutsis went on to bomb the alternative target at Libofshe, and made an emergency landing at Bari in southern Italy. The bomber was found to be riddled with holes from stem to stern, including the engines. The other five bombers found Korce under thick cloud and turned to unload their bombs on Libofshe as well. When the crews were reunited and Papoutsis's crew was found to be safe, 'great and endless was the consumption of beer' in the mess that night.³

Compared with the merciless desert, life at Biferno was quite comfortable for the crews of 13 Mira. Molyvadas, a veteran navigator, recalled 'getting up at a civilized hour, breakfasting at ten, and flying two or two and half hours hitting targets in northern Italy, mainly bridges ... with no losses.' Morale was soaring. The dark days of costly operations over Crete and the desert mutiny were behind them. The Germans were on the defensive everywhere. But that happy situation was not to last.

There was still serious German resistance to be overcome in Yugoslavia, especially around Sarajevo and Mostar, where the Germans maintained an airfield and transport centre defended by plentiful flak. To get the squadron gradually re-habituated to dangerous operations, it was sent to drop supplies to Tito's partisans and radio transmitters to resistance fighters in the Albanian mountains. These operations indeed had their hazards, and so were flown by volunteers only. Flying Officer Michalis Sotiriou took off on the evening of 20 July to drop a wireless in the Korce area. Dawn found him crossing the Albanian coast, straight into a furious flak barrage. A shell burst in front of the Baltimore, bending one of the propellers and peppering the plane with shrapnel. Sotiriou aborted and turned back, landing safely at Bari despite a serious fuel leak.

The squadron might well bask in its commendable bombing record. But things were to get worse, and suddenly. On 28 July six Baltimores of 13 Mira were ordered to bomb German targets in Sarajevo. Soon after take-off, Flying Officer Makis Kondos's bomber developed engine trouble and turned back. Hatzakis, the mission leader, ordered up a reserve plane. Angelidis, the reserve pilot, flew hard to catch up with the formation, which he finally did at 12,000 feet over the target area. Flak bursts filled the sky. 'Stand by, nearing target,' Angelidis said, making a small course correction for the bomb run. The bomb doors were open when a crew member, probably Pilot Officer Takis Anastasiou, the wireless operator, looked up and saw another Baltimore directly above, its bomb doors open and ready to let its contents go.

A yell told Angelidis of the mortal danger the plane was in. Shaken, he abruptly slewed the bomber to starboard to get out of the way of the other's bombs. The manoeuvre, though, put him in the direct line of flak fire. A shell burst in the starboard engine and sent fuel spurting into the plane. After bombing haphazardly Angelidis gave the order for the crew to bale out. The fuel in the plane began to burn. Anastasiou stumbled through the burning escape hatch, followed by his navigator Molyvadas, who was aflame from head to toe as he jumped. Then an RAF gunner by the name of Flight Sergeant Aldridge jumped, and finally Angelidis himself.

Molyvadas landed in a district controlled by the Chetniks, a Serbian nationalist resistance organization battling Tito's partisans. Blinded by his burns and in pain, he was handed over to the Croats who in turn delivered him to the Germans, from whom he received his first proper medical treatment. He had been in a POW camp in Germany for four days when it was liberated by General George Patton's American tanks.

Anastasiou, after the shock of his burns, experienced another one moments after abandoning the burning plane when he jerked his ripcord handle and it came away in his hand. The nasty moment was mercifully brief. His parachute somehow miraculously blossomed above him, and so he was able to have a grandstand view of the doomed Baltimore slamming into a hillside. He landed in a tree and hung there for some moments until, fumbling with burned fingers, he loosened his harness and dropped to the ground. In short order he found himself ringed by a group of peasants who didn't seem especially friendly, as a couple were pointing antiquated rifles at him. Ordering him to keep his hands up, they divested him of everything he had in his pockets – maps, money, concentrated food, medicine, his pistol and his watch. He was driven to a Serbian first aid station, which sent him on to the German-run military hospital in Belgrade. There he was bound up like a mummy while his burns healed. Some antiseptic ointment got into one eye and blinded it. Just before Christmas he was taken to a POW camp near Frankfurt, where he survived on three boiled potatoes a day and Red Cross parcels until liberation.

Angelidis and Aldridge, the RAF gunner, also landed among the Chetniks, who sheltered them for ten days. Then the partisans were attacked by Tito's forces. As Angelidis watched, Tito's men led the Chetniks in bunches onto a bridge and mowed them all down with machine gun fire. The Greek officer had the presence of mind to remind the Titoist squad leader that as an Allied airman, he was fighting for same cause as Tito, and that could have saved him and Aldridge. On 28 August, 13 Mira was notified that Angelidis was still alive and sent Hatzakis to pick him up. (Two months later, when Athens was liberated, Angelidis was one of the first to be flown there. But the severity of his burns precluded any more service flying.)[4]

The loss of Angelidis and his crew sent a shock through 13 Mira. Not surprisingly, some of the aircrews partook a little too much of Italian wine, enabling the medical officer to approve a few days' rest for 'stomach trouble' to get over the shock. The night that Angelidis failed to return, his tent-mate Krikonis wrote in his diary: 'All alone in the tent. I get up and without thinking, my glance falls on the adjacent bed, like a coffin by my side ... That's the fate of airmen, [that's why] they call us the "fair doomed boys".'[5]

Two days later the good news arrived that Angelidis and his crew had survived. Again the beer flowed copiously, again the mess at Biferno rang with ribald jokes. Amid the merriment, Frangias thought up a practical joke to play on Flight Sergeant Pantzalis. The NCO was called before an assembly of officers and solemnly informed that the King of England had decided to award him the Order of the Garter and that Frangias, in the temporary absence of the squadron CO, had been authorized to pin it on him. Pantzalis stood stiffly to attention, blinking back tears of pride, while Frangias pinned a shred of ladies' garter to his tunic. The onlookers could no longer resist, and when a red-faced Pantzalis realized he'd been had, Frangias had already smartly removed himself from the scene.

Flight Lieutenant Eleftherios Ekonomidis had the reputation of being something of a clairvoyant. He had been one of the 'rebels' in the EKI in Rhodesia, had spent time behind bars for it, and had whiled away the tedious hours of confinement with meditation. Besides his tainted service record, such a quality is not desirable in an aviator. Ekonomidis took off in a six-plane formation with orders to bomb a remote Yugoslav target and land at Brindisi, as there wasn't enough fuel to return to Biferno. The formation, peppered with flak holes, returned intact. Tsitsoglou, who had already landed and was watching the others come in, noticed that Ekonomidis was approaching too fast and too high. Ekonomidis actually leapfrogged the plane in front of him, landed with a bump and rocketed the whole length of the runway, smashing into a pile of construction materials. His Baltimore overturned and burned, incinerating the crew. The fact that Ekonomidis had not requested a go-round suggests to Kartalamakis, who knew the pilot well, that he was under the influence of some trance.

'He was hypnotized,' Kartalamakis wrote, 'by the extreme tension, the heavy flak, the fact that it was his first combat operation with 13 Mira, his exhaustion, and his tendency to sink into self-hypnosis ... On the landing approach he had his eyes glued to the instruments.'[6]

On 11 September Flying Officer Haralambos Paraskakis was sent aloft to test a Baltimore that the previous day had displayed a tendency to yaw. Despite having been checked, the plane slewed to port immediately after take-off, forcing Paraskakis to slam back onto the steel-reinforced runway. Sparks flew from the propeller tips as they scraped across the metal. Fuel gushed from the ruptured lines. Paraskakis tried to open the cockpit canopy, but the lever had bent in the impact. Panicking at the prospect of being burned alive, he hammered his leather-helmeted head against the Perspex with such force that he eventually shattered it, tumbling onto the starboard wing with a ferocious headache and losing consciousness.

A Syrian sapper in the Royal Engineers named Mohammed El-Dorri ran to the burning plane and lifted the Greek pilot from the wing, carrying him on his shoulder to safety. Once Paraskakis was safe, El-Dorri rushed back to the inferno to see if anyone else needed saving. This courageous act, far above and beyond the call of duty, earned Private El-Dorri a medal from the RHAF.[7] Paraskakis, who recovered in an American military hospital, was for ever grateful to the Mohammed who had saved his life.

In the middle of September 1944 the two Greek fighter squadrons, 335 and 336 Mirai, received the long-awaited and happy news that they would finally follow 13 Mira to Italy. It was easy, in that scorching North African summer, to imagine that they had been forgotten while 13 Mira was continuing the war and getting all the Greek glory. To be sure, convoy protection duty was as important as it ever had been, but somehow that didn't compensate for the crews' impression of being relegated to second-class status.

A move did take place – but to El Adem in Libya, twenty miles south of Tobruk. The news caused long faces in both squadrons. They'd suffered through three years of incessant desert, and now more was to come! The RAF, to forestall another possible mutiny, assured the Greeks that Italy was their ultimate destination. Tobruk, though, wasn't all bad. There were the silky beaches, not to mention the nurses in the Allied hospitals who sunned themselves there. But the 335 Mira CO, Squadron Leader Doukas, and Margaritis of 336 Mira hammered away at the demand for Italy until the RAF relented.

Crown Prince Paul himself personally delivered the good news to the squadrons. Most of the ground crews and equipment, and some pilots, assembled at 22 Personnel Transit Camp at Aboukir, while the Spitfires, accompanied by vital technical personnel in Douglas C47 Dakotas, took off for the Balkan Air Force headquarters at Bari. Those men going by sea set sail on the HMS *Union Castle*, escorted by an aircraft carrier, as formations of Spitfires wheeled over Alexandria harbour, speeding them on their way.

The ship docked at Taranto, from where the crews were conveyed to Bari. On their journey north to their designated base at Campo Marino, the men gazed at the war-torn Italian countryside and watched fascinated as USAAF Boeing B17 Flying Fortresses and Consolidated B24 Liberators roared overhead. They had no idea such huge aircraft existed. On 28 September the ground crews arrived at Campo Marino, now the base of 13 Mira as well. On hand to greet them was George Papandreou, the Greek prime minister-in-exile, who delivered a pep talk in the local cinema.

The local Italians looked on the Greek newcomers with some trepidation. They feared the Greeks might take revenge for the Italian invasion of October 1940. Some living near the airfield fled when RHAF billeting officers knocked on doors looking for temporary accommodation. But the Greeks soon put the locals' fears to rest. The two Mediterranean peoples have in common an easygoing willingness to socialize, and so it wasn't long before the local cafes resounded to ragged choruses of 'Regina Campagnola' and other pre-war Italian hits that the Greeks knew as well.

There was little time to relax. 336 Mira was at once put on patrol duties over the Sarajevo area. On the first mission Papaioannou, an experienced ex-instructor, was killed when his Spitfire was slowed down by mud on the runway, stalled on take-off and crashed into a tree. Hatzilakos, next in line for take-off, watched it happen. Getting airborne, out of the corner of his eye Hatzilakos saw the orange flashes and black mushroom cloud rising from Papaioannou's plane – 'a familiar sight in the air force by now, that leaves no doubt as to the finale of the drama.'

The two fighter squadrons managed to see a little action before the weather closed in. Kipouros, hit by flak over Serbia on a train-busting strike, managed to land on the island of Vis, the only free Yugoslav territory, as did Flight Sergeant George Tangalakis, semi-conscious with a bullet lodged in his liver. Then ten-tenths cloud closed in over the whole Adriatic area, and the men of 335 and 336 Mirai became bored again. Margaritis, nonetheless, urged the RAF to authorize operations in such weather on the grounds that the enemy would not be expecting attacks.

Reluctantly, the RAF brass gave in, and so on 7 October Margaritis led a flight of his Spitfires into the clouds to see what they could do. 'We had our fingers crossed,' recalled Kartalamakis, now a flight lieutenant and second-in-command of the operation. As if by some prayer, the heavens unexpectedly cleared. Over the middle of the Adriatic Sea they saw above them and to starboard a large formation of USAAF North American P51 Mustangs on their way to Hungary.

Vis lay under a canopy of cloud, but the sky over the Yugoslav mainland was clear as they arrived at 3,000 feet and the flak came spurting up. Margaritis located a strategic railway line and followed it to carry out 336 Mira's objective of busting whatever trains they could find in motion or in stations with their locomotives steaming. Stationary trains were to be avoided, as the Germans would often use them as decoys to hide flak batteries in. A moving train was spotted in the Zabranica valley and Margaritis descended in wide circles to get into position to hit it. Trying to ignore the flak bursts around them, Kartalamakis and the others followed him down.

Kartalamakis couldn't help smiling as, swooping like a hawk, he lined up the locomotive in his sights. He saw the train driver leap down from the cabin and scurry away while the train kept moving. When he was about 250 yards away Kartalamakis pressed the firing button. The cannon shells hit the base of the locomotive but didn't destroy it. Margaritis went round for his own second try. His first burst hit the locomotive's boiler, sending a plume of steam exploding upwards. Kartalamakis followed him, finishing off the locomotive and shooting the required film of proof. After shooting up the wagons the Spitfires turned for home, only to run into fierce flak from the mountainsides. As they were flying in wide formation, they got through that safely.

By this time it was obvious to everyone that the liberation of Greece was now a matter of days. Thanks partly to the airstrikes in Yugoslavia and Albania, first by 13 Mira and later by 335 and 336 Mirai, the Germans were compelled to pull their occupation forces out of Greece to prevent them being cut off. On 12 October the German columns evacuated Athens, and the blue and white Greek flag was again hoisted on the Acropolis in place of the swastika that had adorned it for three and a half years, and the capital erupted in delirious rejoicing.

Though Allied forced had landed in south-west Greece and were proceeding towards Athens, the Greek airmen in Italy still had their dangerous job to do. On the very day that Athens was freed, Flight Lieutenant Epaminondas Kottas led four Spitfires of 335 Mira on a reconnaissance-in-force over the Zagvod-Nustar-Jablanica road complex in Yugoslavia. Flight Sergeant Lambropoulos was idly gazing at a picturesque village and its copse of mulberry trees when, looking more closely, he excitedly called Kottas: 'Number two to number one, a large column of vehicles under the trees at the entrance to the village!'

Kottas, preocuppied with looking for railway lines, took some time to reply. 'Number one to number two, cannot see column of vehicles,' Kottas replied finally. 'Where are they exactly?'

Lambropoulos, trembling with excitement, slowly and loudly reported the position of the two dozen or so vehicles he'd spotted.

'Okay,' Kottas replied. 'I see the column. All prepare to follow me in to the attack. Maintain normal distances.'

The four Spitfires snapped into a turning dive, their cannon and machine guns pouring fire into the column under the trees. On the way in, the last plane was hit by flak but stayed aloft.

On the climb-out Kottas radioed: 'I don't see any fire. We haven't burned all the vehicles. Prepare for another attack. Normal distances, just like in practice.'

What neither Lambropoulos nor anyone else had noticed was that the German personnel of the column had been relaxing in a nearby inn, and that with the first attack they had run to their anti-aircraft defences. Kottas went in first, followed by Lambropoulos. As Lambropoulos was pulling hard back on the stick to climb out he saw that his leader's plane, also climbing, was on fire. 'Number two to number one, you're burning!' Lambropoulos yelled. Getting no response, he repeated the warning. He didn't have time for a third call before he saw Kottas's Spitfire veer abruptly and crash into the valley below. A charred fragment of parachute floated down into the smoking pyre.

A particularly tragic characteristic of every war is that there always has to be a last man to die. It is as if, on that final day, the gods of war are more malevolent than usual, and demand their pound of flesh even when the larger issue, to all intents and purposes, has been decided. For the duration of a war, violent death acquires a crude acceptance. A soldier can face it better if conflict becomes a habit of life, a more or less 'normal' state of affairs. But let peace again come into view, and the terror of death hits with renewed force. No one wants to be the last to be killed. But the unlucky man who draws that dreaded lottery is, by compensation, to be especially honoured. Flight Lieutenant Epaminondas Kottas – bearing the first name of an ancient Greek military genius – was the seventieth and last Greek airman to die in combat in the Second World War.

Kottas's death threw a pall over an otherwise joyous occasion, and that was the liberation of Athens. Political differences were cast aside as the men of the Greek squadrons hugged one another in relief. In more sober moments, however, many wondered if they would find their loved ones well or even alive; they had been completely without news of them for more than three depressing years. To cap it all the top RHAF brass, in the regrettable way of politically influenced senior officers, made a decision that went against all logic and infuriated 336 Mira from top to bottom: it removed Margaritis as CO and replaced him with Hondros – who, it will be recalled, had a history of obstructionism while 336 Mira was stationed in the Libyan desert and had actually been busted to aircraftman for his insubordination!

Group Captain Alexandris took responsibility for the decision on the grounds that Hondros deserved to be rehabilitated by returning to Greece as a squadron commander! His punishment had supposedly been enough. Therefore a valiant and capable combat officer like Margaritis was sidelined at the very hour of victory. Hatzilakos called it 'a dishonest act' and blamed the nefarious Fanis Metaxas for engineering Hondros's appointment. Less explicable is why Alexandris agreed to it. Margaritis soon returned home to Greece – but anonymously, by ship, while Hondros returned with an aura of utterly undeserved glory at the head of 336 Mira. The arch-mutineer Metaxas, true to form, had shot his arrow at the moment of victory.[8]

Chapter 16

Going Home

Around the middle of October 1944 the honour of being the first Greek airman to set foot again on his native soil went to Vladousis who led four Spitfires – two each from 335 and 336 Mirai – to Greece as escort for C47 Dakotas carrying food to the starving population. As the formation crossed the Greek coast to land at Araxos for refuelling, a mixture of emotions jostled in the pilots' minds. How would they be received? What would they find? What they did find was not quite what they had naively come to expect.

There was already an RAF detachment at Araxos, and while the Spitfires were being refuelled a band of bearded partisans, bandoliers across their chests, sidled up to the crews with sour expressions. 'They approached me like I was the German enemy,' Vladousis recalled.

The guerrillas gestured to the Spitfires' guns. 'What are those?' they demanded. 'Machine guns?'

'We call them cannon,' Vladousis replied shortly.

The tense atmosphere was confirmed later by the RAF commander at Araxos, who warned the Greek airmen that the area seethed with communist partisans none too friendly to the British, or to any of their compatriots who wasn't a leftist. They got more of a taste of what was afoot when they were invited to dinner by the local mayor in the company of the partisan chiefs. For the first time in years, the pilots were able to enjoy the traditional olives and feta cheese of their homeland. But the rafters echoed with communist guerrilla songs. At one point the nervous mayor turned to Vladousis. 'See that mountain?' he whispered. 'Behind it they slaughtered two thousand people.'

The pilots returned to base to find a frantic RAF commander. 'Where the hell have you been?' he demanded. 'You know, they could have sent your heads back here.' He advised them to leave as soon as possible, for their own safety.

The next day they took off for Athens, landing at Hellenikon, the city's main aerodrome. The arrival that was to be so momentous was, in fact, an anti-climax. The air traffic controller at Athens, taken no doubt by surprise (and probably under the control of the partisans), at first refused to authorize them to land. Only when Vladousis claimed that the planes were short of fuel did the controller relent. Once down, the pilots climbed out of their cockpits and knelt to kiss the ground. Yet no cheering crowds surged out to meet them. In fact, they stayed only twenty-five minutes at Athens before returning to Araxos, full of foreboding at what might yet be in store for war-torn Greece.

It wasn't until 4 November that all three Greek squadrons set off for their return home. They flew first to Grottaglie near Taranto, where bad weather kept them grounded for a week. On 11 November all fifty-four aircraft, eighteen Baltimores and thirty-six Spitfires, set out in a wide formation across the Adriatic. After an hour's flight, through a break in the clouds they glimpsed the island of Levkas. To Kartalamakis it was 'as if the aroma of thyme rose up to greet us'.

The formation droned along the Gulf of Corinth, passing the city of Patras to starboard. Lambropoulos's voice broke the silence. 'Somewhere on the right is Kottas's village,' he said. Everyone wondered whether the news of its favourite son's death had reached that village yet. Hatzilakos imagined Kottas's family 'coming out of their house to watch our steel birds go by and wonder whether he was there among them.'[1]

Over Corinth the formation evened out, to make a grand pass over Athens. They flew at low height over the Acropolis and the cone-like Lykavittos Hill to the north. The sight of the Greek flag fluttering on the Acropolis made all the suffering and tragedy worthwhile. Kartalamakis made a few passes over his own neighbourhood – where he looked forward to being reunited with his family – and then with the others landed one by one at Hellenikon. They were home.

But were they? Kartalamakis, for one, found Athens a very different place from that which he left to go to war in 1940, when the cheers of king and country rang in his ears. Seven years later he wrote:

> I had the impression that by walking around in my uniform I would encounter happy faces and smiles of gratitude. But I was bitterly disappointed. Instead, I saw ... people in odd uniforms topped by a paper bag on the head [with the communist acronym on it], regarding me sullenly, with open hatred.[2]

For a few tense months, in fact, to wear a Greek military uniform of any kind was to invite possible murder at the hands of communist extremists.

Nonetheless, on 20 November the RHAF received some encouragement when it paraded in central Athens to lay a wreath at the Tomb of the Unknown Soldier. Thousands of onlookers cheered as flights of 13, 335 and 336 Mirai roared overhead dropping inspiratory leaflets. But all was not well even there. Hatzilakos, leading the marching detachment of 336 Mira, recalled hearing calls for 'an air force of the people' coming from loudspeakers in the crowds. Communist sympathizers inside the RHAF erased the crown from the squadron flags and placed it upside down in the lower right-hand corner when Papandreou ceremoniously inspected the RHAF at Hellenikon shortly afterwards.[3]

Constantine Lambropoulos of 336 Mira, now a flying officer, had an even nastier shock when he flew his Spitfire home to Sedes to see his sister whom he hadn't heard from in four years. He landed at an all-but-deserted base, to be met by a surly fellow in the uniform of a group captain but with a red star where the crown and wings should have been. The 'group captain' and others who were similarly attired ordered Lambropoulos to change out of his uniform and into civilian clothes if he wanted to go into Thessaloniki to see his sister. Wherever he went he was under close surveillance, which he managed to shake off with the help of some friends. He returned to his Spitfire at Sedes, and flew back to Athens.[4] Had his own country, so longed for, suddenly become an enemy?

The retreating Germans had sown the grounds of the old Icarus School at Tatoi with land mines, and an RHAF detachment was sent to clear them. The whole district, however, was under communist control and only with difficulty was Tatoi cleared to be able to resume its training role. Eleusis aerodrome also had to be wrested from communist hands after delicate negotiations; as the national flag was once more raised above the premises, bearded and bandoliered onlookers couldn't hide their hostility.

Greece might have been freed, but the war was still on. On 12 October, the day Athens was liberated and Kottas was killed over Yugoslavia, a Baltimore of 70 OTU crashed on a night bombing exercise at Ismailiya in Egypt, killing the four Greek crew members. The probable cause was the pilot's momentary inattention from the instruments during the release of the flare bomb and subsequent disorientation.

Closer to home, there remained scattered German units in Crete and the Dodecanese, and on the island of Milos in the middle of the Aegean. Milos, defended by two powerful flak batteries, was to be reduced first. Pangalos's Spitfire was hit on his first run in at 6,000 feet. The flak shell exploded under his seat but he wasn't seriously hurt. Margaritis's plane took a hit on the elevators and Pilot Officer Takis Sakellariou's coolant tank was holed; luckily he could land before the coolant leaked away completely.

Squadron Leader Lambros Parisis made his bomb run, but the bomb wouldn't toggle loose from its underwing attachment. Two more runs had the same result. Attempts to jettison the thing over the sea also failed, so he had no choice but to very gingerly land back at base, a highly risky operation and not what the manuals recommended. His wheels had just touched the ground when he heard a thud behind him. The gentle shock of landing had been enough to finally disengage the bomb, which, to Parisis's horror as he looked in his rear-view mirror, was bouncing merrily along behind him. He gave the engine a surge of power to get out of the bouncing bomb's way, ending up at the edge of the runway. The bomb wasn't fused.

Crete remained a tough proposition to the very end. Though it was only a matter of days before the last of the Germans cleared out, there was no sign that the notorious German flak defences had become any weaker. The RHAF crews were willing enough to take another crack at them, but hovering over the plan was a big question mark. An attack on Crete at this stage, however strong or weak the Germans might be, would have little if any strategic value, as the Germans knew they were losing the war and that soon they would have to give up the island. This was the view of Vladousis, who feared that the planned attacks would merely give the German flak gunners more practice and, worse, needlessly sacrifice more Greek pilots.

Nonetheless, the order came down to dive-bomb enemy positions on Crete with Spitfires from a high altitude. On 5 December the raid began. Flight Lieutenant Emmanuel Tingos was reluctant to get out of bed that cold morning, feeling ill, but Volonakis, the mission leader, talked him into getting up. When Tingos climbed into the cockpit of his Spitfire the engine wouldn't start; he went to another Spitfire, but that wouldn't start either. Then the first plane, thanks to the fitters' efforts, burst into life and he went back to it. The five-plane mission refuelled at Heraklion, which Cretan partisans had recently liberated. Early in the attack Tingos's plane was seen plunging straight into the sea with its bombs on board.

Kartalamakis suspects that Tingos's Spitfire, far from being hit by enemy flak, could have been sabotaged by communist partisans in control of Heraklion aerodrome. There can, of course, be no proof of this. However, on the evening of 17 December a Baltimore crew of 13 Mira under Pilot Officer Evanghelos Kostis spent the night at Heraklion before a mission to attack German positions in Crete. Some armed partisans volunteered to guard the bomber through the night, as the crew relaxed, drank and told stories of their North Africa days. The Baltimore took off just before ten o'clock in the morning, circled around the hills a few times, and then set course for the south-west. Moments later, the plane blew up, killing Kostis and his crew, including two RAF men. An investigation concluded that the blast could only have been caused by an explosive device attached beneath the port wing.[5]

On 26 February 1945 Hatzilakos took off with twenty-three other Spitfires under Wing Commander Patrick Woodruff, DFC, to fly over Thessaloniki to mark the arrival in home waters of the *Averof*, a venerable Dreadnought-era battleship that had been the pride of the Greek Navy in Alexandria. After the display the fighters landed to refuel at Sedes when a severe northerly crosswind blew up, grounding all the planes. Woodruff, however, wanted to be back in Athens that evening for 'personal' reasons. Overriding the protests of the pilots, he had them lined up for take-off with aircraftmen holding down the wingtips in the howling wind. Somehow the Spitfires got off. Over Thessaloniki, in order to get into formation, Woodruff noticed that Baltatzis's Spitfire was falling behind and impatiently veered to starboard to link up with it. Baltatzis, noticing the manoeuvre, didn't realize what the mission leader was up to. Woodruff had blocked Baltatzis's view of the rest of the formation, so the Greek pilot put his aircraft into a shallow dive. The result was that his propeller sliced off the whole tail section of Woodruff's Spitfire, sending the Briton straight down in an unrecoverable spin.

'I followed Woodruff down,' Hatzilakos said later, 'in wide circles until he fell into the sea, throwing up a huge spout.' At the same time Hatzilakos and other pilots had to swerve smartly to avoid the tumbling empennage of Woodruff's Spitfire. Baltatzis, his propeller bent, returned to Sedes. He had actually been on the mission in place of Kartalamakis, who hadn't been able to make it. But that wasn't the end of the day's drama.

Approaching the base at Hellenikon, Hatzilakos realized he was falling short of the runway, so he decided to gun the Merlin for a bit more power. He nudged the throttle forward but the engine didn't respond. In fact, the engine had cut out, and the propeller was windmilling helplessly. The roofs of houses were racing up to meet him, so he jerked the stick to starboard, making for an empty space adjacent to the runway. Sliding mere feet above the housetops, skipping left and right to avoid the taller ones, he touched down at stalling speed. The jolt threw Hatzilakos forward violently. His harness seems to have snapped, and he hit his head on the gunsight base, giving him a severe injury above the right eye.[6]

There were also some tragic mistakes. On 27 March 1945 three Baltimores of 13 Mira were ordered to bomb German transports evacuating the island of Kos. The small port of Kos was the trickiest of targets. The bombs only had to fall a few yards wide and the picture-book town itself would be hit. Which is exactly what happened. The plan was to bomb from 12,000 feet. But during the inevitable manoeuvring to evade flak, two strings of bombs fell in the town of Kos, killing twenty-two Greek noncombatants as well as some Germans. That was the last RHAF operation before VE Day. But, unlike most other countries that had taken part in the Second World War and now had a chance to rebuild, there would be little peace for Greece or its airmen.

Epilogue

No Rest for the Weary

The long-suffering people of Athens were given less than two months in which to enjoy their fragile liberty. In early December 1944 the armed KKE made its bid for power by triggering an uprising in the city. The national Greek Army had barely had time to reassemble, having to leave the first phase of the fighting to the gendarmerie that only just saved the day with the timely intervention of British troops and the RAF. When Winston Churchill flew to Athens on Christmas Day he found himself in a war zone.

Order was gradually restored in early 1945, thanks partly to the efforts of the Spitfires of 94 Squadron, which neutralized communist forces in key areas, and of the British Army, which suffered some 2,000 casualties in the process. RAF personnel captured by the communists were subject to severe abuse and near-starvation. Yet a continued RAF presence in Greece was necessary to help the RHAF build itself up to be able to handle the second round of the communist insurrection that broke out in 1946 in the mountains. The civil war lasted more than three years. The RHAF was able to play a decisive role in suppressing the rebellion in the spring of 1949 when it acquired forty-two Curtiss SB2C Helldivers from the United States. The Helldiver was a demanding warbird to fly, but its four machine guns and 900 pounds of bombs made it good at accurate pinpoint attacks on communist positions. The RHAF's Spitfires also did sterling ground-attack work, though their inherent unsuitability for mountain work caused a lot of accidents. Within months the rebellion was defeated, and Greece narrowly escaped being dragged behind the Iron Curtain.

The bomber squadron, 13 Mira, went on to continue its long career. After giving back its Baltimores to the RAF, in 1950 it acquired Douglas C47 Dakota transports modified to carry 5,000 kilos of bombs each. These went to Korea as part of the United Nations force. The squadron also had nineteen Wellingtons acquired in 1945, which served for two years. Training requirements were liberally met by the United States, which delivered at least fifty T6 Harvard trainers.

The RHAF received its first jets in 1952, the year that Greece joined Nato. No fewer than 117 Republic F84G Thunderjets went to equip 335, 336, 337, 338, 339 and 340 Fighter Mirai. In 1973, with the abolition of the Greek monarchy, the RHAF became the HAF. Since the late 1980s the HAF has been getting plenty of practice. Just as, for example, the RAF's reflexes are periodically tested by the irruptions of Russian reconnaissance bombers over northern seas, the Greek fighter *mirai* often scramble their General Dynamics F16s and Dassault Mirage 2000s to confront Turkish manoeuvres over the Aegean Sea. No one seriously foresees a war with Turkey over disputed points in the Aegean area. But there is no doubt that the occasional mock dogfights over the idyllic islands serve to keep the pilots in shape.

After Greece fell Mitralexis, the early hero of the air war, made his way to North Africa to join his fellows, serving in 13 Mira throughout. In 1947, as a squadron leader, he retained enough prestige to be included in an RHAF mission to London to seek RAF help in organizing flying training. On 19 September 1948, now a wing commander, he was a passenger in an Airspeed Oxford on a reconnaissance flight from Rhodes over the Aegean Sea when an engine failed and the aircraft crashed into the sea near the island of Tinos. All on board perished. To this day, the crash remains unexplained. He left behind his widow, Anna, and two infant children.

George Lambropoulos received his pilot officer's commission in June 1945 and continued his service with the Spitfires of 335 Mira, this time against the communist strongholds in the northern Greek mountains. On 1 July 1948 an insurgent anti-aircraft shell penetrated his Spitfire's fuselage just behind his seat, severing the elevator cables. Using his trim tabs alone he managed a hazardous landing at Kozani, earning him a citation from Group Captain Kelaidis and praise from a USAAF colonel who claimed that nothing like it had been accomplished before.

On 26 August 1951 Flight Lieutenant Lambropoulos led two Douglas C47 Dakotas of 13 Mira from Eleusis to the RHAF's most distant mission yet – Korea. They were to replace two other C47s sent the previous November and since lost. The Greek Dakotas acquitted themselves well delivering supplies to and evacuating dead and wounded US marines from the frozen salient at Hagaru-ri. The RHAF lost twelve men in the Korean War, including Wing Commander Frangoyannis, a former warrant officer in the Second World War. With the Korean armistice in 1953, 13 Mira had been almost continuously in action for thirteen years.

In April 1967 the colonels' regime cashiered Lambropoulos for his supposedly liberal views. Now aged fifty, the former group captain and war hero, with sixteen decorations on his tunic, was reduced to driving a school bus in a rundown neighbourhood of Athens. Six years later he was appointed as a state-employed primary school teacher – the job he had given up as a young man when he joined the RHAF! It wasn't until 1987, fourteen years after the restoration of parliamentary rule in Greece, that he was rehabilitated with the rank of air marshal. He died aged ninety-one in 2009.

Ilias Kartalamakis also stayed in the air force, rising to the rank of air vice-marshal in the Air Staff, and retiring in 1967. This left him time to reflect on his kaleidoscopic experiences and amass the wealth of detail for his monumental seven-volume memoir, which serves also as a political and military history of Greece for most of the twentieth century. At the time of this writing he is ninety-five years old and perhaps the most revered man in the air force.

Hatzilakos lives not far away in the staid Athens suburb of Papagou, named after Marshal Papagos and favoured by military retirees. He kept flying into the 1960s, seeing off the last of the RHAF's Spitfires and being one of the first to be retrained on the Thunderjet. In April 1967 he was an air vice-marshal serving as Greece's air attaché in Washington when the military junta that had seized power in Greece that month offered him a senior Air Staff position at home. He declined, on the grounds that as an officer he had taken an oath to serve the Greek constitution, not a bunch of usurping Army colonels.[1] For his views he was cashiered with the rank of air marshal. Now ninety-two, he works indefatigably on energy projects of his own devising, surrounded by his family, his wartime photographs and dozens of models of the aircraft he has flown. He remains chairman of the Athens branch of the Royal Air Force Association.

Vladousis, after attending senior staff courses in Britain after the war, was appointed commandant of the Icarus School in 1949. Though the government forces had just defeated the communists in the Greek civil war, communist agitation in the military continued. One day in 1952 a cadet at Tatoi had a landing accident in his T6 Harvard. The accident was blamed on alleged sabotage to the plane's landing system. This led several overzealous senior officers to suspect communist sabotage. However, the case quickly got out of hand, triggering a lamentable political witch-hunt in the RHAF officer corps and Icarus School. Dozens of undoubtedly patriotic war veterans and experienced fliers found themselves summarily dismissed from the air force as 'communist sympathizers'. Several were even brutally tortured. In the vast majority of cases, the charge was outrageously false. Vladousis was considered guilty of negligence and suspended for six months. Another investigation, however, cleared his name and he took up a position as professor in the National Defence College. In 1955 he was posted to Naples as senior RHAF officer in the Nato southern command, and retired in 1959 with the rank of air marshal. He died in August 2010 at the age of ninety-five.[2] In his last interview, just before his death, Vladousis quoted the official Greek air force motto, adopted around 1975 and taken from the lyric of an ancient Spartan war dance: *Ames de g'esometha pollo karrhones*, or, 'we will be a lot better than you'. In his last photograph he smiles out at us, his frail form spruce in a double-breasted jacket, squadron badge pinned on his lapel, in the company of three Icarus School cadets, two of whom are women.

Notes

I use the following abbreviations for five key sources:

AFHM: Air Force Historical Museum
IK3 for Kartalamakis: *The Air Force in the 1940 War*
IK4 for Kartalamakis: *Flying in Foreign Skies*
IK5 for Kartalamakis: *The Air Force in the Civil War*
33M for Mermingas: *The Fairey Battle and 'Pirates' of 33 Mira, 1940–41*
OAF for Mermingas: 'The Organization of the Air Force on 28 October 1940'

Preface
1. Montgomery of Alamein, *A History of Warfare*, London: Collins 1968, 545.
2. For a more general view of the Allied air campaign in the Balkans, see Shores, *et al.*, op. cit.

Prologue
1. Cervi, 26–35.
2. *Ibid.*, 28.

Chapter 1
1. Quoted in IK3, 34–40.
2. Hatzilakos to author.
3. 33M, 4.
4. IK3, 27–30.
5. Hatzilakos to author.
6. IK4, 196.
7. IK3, 31.
8. *Ibid.*, 28–33.
9. *Ibid.*, 42–43.
10. Personal recollection of Kouziyannis, quoted in IK3, 78.
11. OAF, 5.
12. IK3, 35–36; Cervi, 123. Kartalamakis cites Ciano's courage in contrast to Cervi.
13. OAF, 5–6.
14. 33M, 85–87.

Chapter 2
1. Harousis, H. in 'Sedes Aerodrome', *Battles and Soldiers*.
2. Moutousis eventually rose to become Greece's military attaché in Sofia in 1927. He ended his career as Chief of Staff of the Engineer Corps and died in 1956, aged seventy-one.
3. AFHM, *op. cit.*
4. Located north of Thessaloniki international airport, Sedes is now the home of the HAF's 305 Guided Missile Wing with two *mirai* of Patriot missiles.
5. The present Athens international airport, opened in 2001, bears the name of Venizelos in recognition of his contributions to Greek military and civil aviation.
6. Harousis, 9; AFHM, *op. cit.*
7. Words of Admiral Alexander Sakellariou, Chief of the Naval Staff, quoted in 33M, 9.
8. AFHM, 172.
9. *Ibid.*, 105; 172–174.
10. Woodhouse, C.M., *The Story of Modern Greece*, London: Faber and Faber, 1968, 236.

Chapter 3
1. Harousis, 6.
2. OAF, 4; 33M, 20.
3. 33M, 21.
4. OAF, 1.
5. Christofilis, 35.
6. *Ibid.*, 12.
7. 33M, 9–11.
8. Cited in Harousis, 6–7.
9. Harousis, 18–25.
10. *Ibid.*, 26–41.
11. 33M, 70–77.
12. *Ibid.*, 80.
13. IK3, 419–420.

Chapter 4
1. Cervi, 64–69.
2. Quoted in Cervi, 81, 304.
3. Harousis, 42–47.
4. Dialogue in Cervi, 63.
5. Harousis, 90.
6. Quoted in Cervi, 106.

Chapter 5
1. Quoted in IK3, 46–47.
2. Cervi, 128–129; IK3, 68.

3. Cervi, 127–128.
4. *Ibid.*, 120.
5. *Ibid.*, 129–130; 134–138.
6. Quoted in IK3, 107–108; 33M, 109–110.
7. IK3, 99–103; 33M, 103.
8. OAF, 7.
9. 33M, 118.
10. *Ibid.*, 123.
11. Wing Commander Pandelis Vatakis, 'Meeting with a Veteran', in *Ikaros*, winter 2010–2011.
12. IK3, 127–128.

Chapter 6
1. IK3, 180–185.
2. Cervi, 158–164.
3. Term used by Gabriele Casini, quoted in IK3, 189. See also Shores *et al.*, op. cit.
4. OAF, 8.
5. IK3, 192–195; see also Shores *et al., op.cit.*
6. IK3, 195–196.
7. 33M, 135.
8. Harousis, 81.

Chapter 7
1. Quoted in IK3, 204.
2. IK3, 230–232.
3. 33M, 150.
4. On the history of Kamberos, see AFHM, 28–37.
5. IK4, 117–119.
6. IK3, 245–247; Harousis, 70.
7. IK3, 252–253; Shores, *et al.*, op.cit.; Lamb, 159.
8. Harousis, 70.
9. IK3, 262–264.
10. *Ibid.*, 268–270; Wisdom, *op. cit.*
11. IK3, 280–288.
12. Cervi, 203.
13. Harousis, 72.
14. 33M, 163. The two Greek airmen are believed to be buried at an unknown location in Albania. The sole evidence is an old photograph of a rough gravestone for unnamed 'Greek airmen'. Stathakos's red leather wallet remains in his family's possession.
15. *Ibid.*, 167–168.
16. Quoted in IK3, 332.
17. Personal communication by Mermingas to author.

Chapter 8
1. Harousis, 73.
2. Quoted in IK3, 336.
3. *Ibid.*, 360–361.
4. *Ibid.*, 428–431.
5. *Ibid.*, 432–434.
6. *Ibid.*, 363–366.
7. *Ibid.*, 377.
8. *Ibid.*, 387–388. Kartalamakis thinks the Germans concentrated on the Gladiators because they thought they were British.
9. Kartalamakis's phrase, in IK3, 389.
10. Wisdom, *op. cit.*
11. 33M, 177.
12. IK3, 423–425.
13. *Ibid.*, 2.
14. Harousis, 90–94; 33M, 180.

Chapter 9
1. IK3, 449.
2. *Ibid.*, 432–455.
3. *Ibid.*, 546–547.
4. IK4, 24–25.
5. AFHM, 129.
6. IK4, 30–34.
7. *Ibid.*, 42–43.
8. *Ibid.*, 49.
9. Now the site of Cairo international airport.
10. IK4, 76.
11. Quoted in IK4, 90.
12. Mermingas to author.
13. IK4, 70–71.

Chapter 10
1. The poem was kept by his fellow cadet Constantine Valavanis. Quoted in IK4, 95, and translated by the author.
2. IK4, 98–99.
3. *Ibid.*, 125.
4. *Ibid.*, 122–123.
5. *Ibid.*, 139.
6. *Ibid.*, 150–155.
7. *Ibid.*, 176.
8. A full, if somewhat rambling, account of the Rhodesia mutiny can be found in IK4, 148–178.
9. Tedder quoted in IK4, 180; also, letter from Markou to Kartalamakis.

10. IK4, 179–185.
11. *Ibid.*, 205–207; written up by H. Morris in *The Salisbury Times*, undated 1944.

Chapter 11
1. IK4, 230–232.
2. *Ibid.*, 247.
3. *Ibid.*, 261–266.
4. Kartalamakis to author, March 2011.
5. IK4, 278.
6. Mermingas to author.

Chapter 12
1. IK4, 326–361; Kartalamakis devotes considerable space to the communist-led subversion of the RHAF, in his view 'the darkest page in the air force's history'.

Chapter 13
1. IK4, 369.
2. Skliris to Kartalamakis, in IK4, 369–370.
3. IK4, 401.
4. Quoted in IK4, 402–404.
5. Hatzilakos, quoted in IK4, 415–419.
6. Dakoronias, quoted in IK4, 420–422.
7. Mermingas to author.
8. The term 'power-mad' is Kartalamakis's, in IK4, 430.
9. As told to Kartalamakis in IK4, 430–432.
10. Noted by Aphrodite Katsanevaki, a local journalist, and quoted in IK4, 437–438. Author's translation and italics.
11. Quoted in IK4, 439.
12. *Ibid.*, 442–460.

Chapter 14
1. Montgomery, *op. cit.*, 518.
2. IK4, 463–464; Manglinis, *op. cit.*
3. Full text of the petition in IK4, 475.
4. Quoted in IK4, 523–524.
5. *Ibid.*, 527–524.
6. *Ibid.*, 467–534; Kartalamakis cites Flight Sergeant Constantine Manikas, a left-wing sympathizer, as confirming that Papingis was a KKE Central Committee member. Papingis himself, in a letter to Kartalamakis dated 22 July 1993, termed himself an 'anti-fascist' rather than a communist agitator, and claimed to have been acting 'under duress' at the time.

Chapter 15
1. IK4, 555.
2. Quoted in Manglinis, *op. cit.*

3. IK4, 540.
4. *Ibid.*, 544–549; Manglinis, *op. cit.*
5. Quoted in IK4, 550.
6. *Ibid.*, 554–557.
7. Citation text in IK4, 560–561.
8. *Ibid.*, 565–568.

Chapter 16
1. IK4, 587–591.
2. IK5, 48.
3. *Ibid.*, 50–53.
4. *Ibid.*, 53–54.
5. *Ibid.*, 109–117.
6. *Ibid.*, 118–122.

Epilogue
1. Hatzilakos to author.
2. Vatakis, 'Meeting with a Veteran'.

Appendix I

Targets and Losses of the RHAF, 1941–1944

13 Light Bombing Mira

Sorties	Combat hours	Bomb load dropped
3,151	9,576	1,300 tonnes

Operations: 2 U-boats sunk, 5 possibly sunk, 3 damaged. 6 railway lines destroyed, 1 ammunition dump, 9 port facilities, 3 road bridges, 7 railway stations, 3 factories, 7 fuel dumps and 5 concentration camps.

Losses: 18

335 Pursuit Mira

Sorties	Combat hours
5,550	8,000

Operations: Italian HQ at El Alamein destroyed, plus miscellaneous road and rail vehicles. Two German aircraft shot down and 2 more destroyed on the ground.

Losses: 14

336 Pursuit Mira

Sorties	Combat hours
3,250	5,180

Operations: Targets identical to 335 Mira. One German aircraft shot down.

Losses: 12

(Source: Ilias Kartalamakis)

Appendix II

Scores and Victories

The subject of just how many enemy aircraft were destroyed by the RHAF in the war up to the end of April 1941 is a vexed one, as is the related issue of which Greek airmen, if any, are entitled to 'ace' status. Many official squadron records were either lost or destroyed in the chaos of the war and German occupation. Individual reminiscences, of course, are not necessarily trustworthy. To complicate matters further, the RHAF at the time had no systematic 'kill' reporting procedures in place. Successes were hastily reported in log books with no apparent effort to check their accuracy

Nonetheless, serious efforts to get at the truth have recently been made, most notably by an ex-naval officer, Nikolaos Christophilis, who in an exhaustive study (*Weapons and Victories of the Greek Air Force, 1940–41*) comes up with a mimimum of sixty-eight confirmed kills and twenty-three probables between 28 October 1940 and the end of April 1941. The figures are derived from a comparative evaluation of data supplied by the Hellenic Air Force Historical Museum and those of the late Air Marshal Kelaidis, who as a group captain at the time headed Greece's fighter command. To this figure may be added three confirmed victories against Luftwaffe aircraft in the few days before the Greek capitulation.

Italian loss figures are especially hard to ascertain, as in many cases RHAF and RAF pilots claimed joint credit. The RAF claimed 150 Italian aircraft shot down – an almost certain exaggeration, as the Italians' own loss figure comes to 65, though they state their 'damaged' figure at a rather startling 495.

Figuring out who was Greece's 'ace' pilot in that period is equally problematic. Christophilis gives the accolade to Flight Lieutenant Andreas Antoniou of 22 Pursuit Mira, credited with four confirmed personal kills and at least a couple of possibles, which, with a bit of generosity, would probably get him the traditional five-kill qualification for ace. The number two spot goes to Flight Lieutenant Yannis Kellas of 21 Mira and number three to Flight Sergeant Epaminondas Dangoulas of 22 Mira.

Bibliography and Related Works

Air Force Historical Museum, *The Road to a Unified Air Force*, Athens: AFHM 2010 (in Greek).
Beldecos, G. *Hellenic Wings*, Athens: HAF Historical Branch 1999.
Cervi, M. *Storia della Guerra di Grecia*, 2nd edition, Milan: RCS Libri 2000 (in Italian).
Christofilis, N. *Weapons and Victories of the Greek Air Force, 1940–41*, Athens: Doureios Ippos 2010 (in Greek).
Harousis, H. *The Greek Air Force in the 1940–41 War*, Athens: A Line Defence 2007 (in Greek).
Harousis, H. 'Sedes Aerodrome', *Battles and Soldiers*, December 2010 (in Greek).
Kartalamakis, I. *The Air Force in the 1940 War*, Athens: (self-published) 1990 (in Greek).
Kartalamakis, I. *Flying in Foreign Skies*, Athens: (self-published) 1993 (in Greek).
Kartalamakis, I. *The Air Force in the Civil War*, Athens: (self-published) 1999 (in Greek).
Karykas, P. *Greek Wings 1912–2005*, Athens: Strategic Publications 2005 (in Greek).
Lamb, C. *To War in a Stringbag*, New York: Bantam Books 1980.
Lambropoulos, G. *The Sky, My Life*, Athens: Zaharakis 2009 (in Greek).
Manglinis, I. 'With the Baltimores over the Mediterranean', *Air History*, issue 26, December 2003–January 2004 (in Greek).
Mermingas, G. 'The Organization of the Air Force on 28 October 1940', (unpublished monograph) (in Greek).
Mermingas, G. *The Fairey Battle and 'Pirates' of 33 Mira, 1940–41*, (unpublished work) 2008 (in Greek).
Mermingas, G. 'Greek Airmen's Mediterranean Tour', *Mani* issue 45, October–December 2010 (in Greek).
Shores, C., Cull, B. and Malizia, N. *Air War Over Yugoslavia, Greece and Crete, 1940–41*, 2nd edition, London: Grub Street Publications 1992.
Wisdom, T.H. *Wings Over Olympus: The Story of the Royal Air Force in Libya and Greece*, London: G Allen & Unwin 1942.

Index of Names

The names of military personnel are followed by the rank with which they first appear in the book. Some, of course, received promotions during and after the war. For example Flight Sergeant Hatzilakos became a pilot officer in 1943 and rose to air marshal in later years.

Aidonopoulos, Adamantios, Plt Off, 79
Aitken, Max, Wg Cdr, 121
Aldridge, Flt Sgt, 147
Alexandra of Kent, Princess, 92
Alexandris, George, Gp Capt, 113, 139, 152–3
Alexopoulos, Constantine, WO, 85
Anagnostopoulos, Yannis, Plt Off, 105–6, 141
Anastasiou, Takis, Plt Off, 146–7
Angelidis, Angelos, Fg Off, 147–8
Anninos, Dimitrios, Lt, 12
Antoniou, Andreas, Flt Lt, 48, 50, 60, 171
Arnidis, Frangoulis, Sgt, 35
Arvanitis, Zacharias, Fg Off, 145
Ataturk, Kemal, 20
Athanasakis, Eleftherios, Plt Off, 120–1
Averof, Nikolaos, Wg Cdr, 53, 68, 88–90

Babas, Evanghelos, Plt Off, 79
Badoglio, Pietro, Marshal, 24–5, 118
Balbo, Italo, Marshal, 26
Bales, Anastasios, Sgt, 125
Baltatzis, Sophocles, Flt Lt, 34, 57, 158
Barbas, Spyros, Flt Sgt, 64–5
Bardavillias, Anastasios, Fg Off, 50–1
Bassi, Livio, Lt, 44
Bevington-Smith, Eric, Plt Off, 44
Bousios, Patroklos, Fg Off, 4
Brooks, G.N., Sgt, 40
Buckler, John, Cmdr, 60
Byron, Lord, 39

Cavallero, Ugo, Gen, 47, 55, 59
Chamberlain, Neville, 15
Christakos, Sotirios, Plt Off, 131–3
Christidis, Christos, Flt Sgt, 37–8
Chrizopoulos, Constantine, Flt Sgt, 54
Churchill, Winston, xv–xvi, 33, 39, 49, 53, 112, 118, 134–6, 160
Ciano, Galeazzo, Count, 8, 24, 26, 29, 47
Constantine, Crown Prince of Greece (later King Constantine I), 11

Dakopoulos, Spyros, Sqn Ldr, 73–4, 79
Dakoronias, Loukas, Flt Lt, 101
D'Albiac, John, Air Cdre, 39–40, 44–5, 47, 52–3
Dangoulas, Epaminondas, Flt Sgt, 50, 171
Daravingidis, George, WO, 35
Dasios, George, Plt Off, 84
Davakis, Constantine, Fg Off, 73, 80
Davis, 'Fuzzy,' Fg Off, 95–6
Dedes, Vlassis, Flt Sgt, 94
Depountis, Spyros, Flt Sgt, 54, 102
De Robilant, Maurizio, Capt, 45
Diamantopoulos, Dimitrios, Midshipman, 63–4
Diamantopoulos, Spyros, Flt Lt, 111, 116, 121–3, 130
Dietrich, Sepp, Maj Gen, 70
Dimakis, Yannis, Gp Capt, 112–3, 139
Dimakopoulos, Andreas, Sgt, 94–5
Dimitrakopoulos, Ilias, Flt Lt, 50
Dimitriadis, Dimitrios, Fg Off, 74, 79
Douglas, Sholto, ACM, 120

Douhet, Giulio, Maj, 26
Doukas, George, Fg Off, 3, 5, 149
Drenas, Leonidas, Plt Off, 78, 100
Dritsas, Dimitrios, Sqn Ldr, 126–7
Duke, Lord, Sqn Ldr, 114

Eden, Anthony, 54, 92
Ekonomakos, Panayotis, Maj Gen, xvi, 48–9
Ekonomakos, Vasilios, Plt Off, 117
Ekonomidis, Eleftherios, Flt Lt, 148–9
Ekonomidis, Yannis, Flt Sgt, 94
Ekonomopoulos, Panayotis, Fg Off, 60
Ekonomou, Yannis, Flt Lt, 64–5
El-Dorri, Mohammed, Pvt, 149
Erbach-Schoenberg, Victor zu, Prince, 59–60
Exarhakos, Constantine, Fg Off, 69–70, 94

Falkonakis, George, Gp Capt, 3
Filis, Dimitrios, Sgt, 1
Finlayson, Gordon, Sqn Ldr, 44
Franco, Francisco, Gen, xv
Frangias, Byron, Fg Off, 145, 148
Frangos, Pelopidas, Flt Lt, 37–8
Frangoyannis, Panayotis, WO, 110, 161
Frederica, Princess (later Queen), 81

Galanakos, Dimitrios, Flt Sgt, 73
Gavotti, Giulio, 2d Lt, 11
Gazis, Theodore, Flt Sgt, 117
Georgakopoulos, George, Sqn Ldr, 91
George II, King of Greece, xv–xvi, 54, 67, 70, 78, 92, 106, 112, 120, 130, 135–6
Georgopoulos, Yannis, Plt Off, 134
Germanos, Byron, Flt Sgt, 77
Giannaris, Evanghelos, Plt Off, 4
Grant, Ulysses S., Lt Gen, xii
Grazzi, Emanuele xiv–xvi, 1, 25, 29
Gyzas, Yannis, Flt Sgt, 116–17

Hadjioannou, Byron, Flt Sgt, 88, 105
Hadjioannou, Kleanthos, Plt Off, 4, 44–5
Hartokolis, Nikolaos, Fg Off, 124–5
Hatzakis, Yannis, Fg Off, 145–7
Hatzilakos, Constantine, Flt Sgt, xii, 2–3, 20, 111, 124, 132, 140–2, 150, 152, 155–6, 158, 162
Hellbig, Joachim, Col, 85, 87
Hickey, William, Sqn Ldr, 40, 43
Hinaris, George, Fg Off, 35

Hitler, Adolf, 15, 22, 24–5, 44, 49, 55, 57, 70
Hondros, Constantine, Flt Lt, 103, 105, 107, 152–3

Ioannou, Christos, Flt Sgt, 108–9

Jellicoe, Lord, 118

Kamberos, Dimitrios, Sqn Ldr, 14, 48–9
Kanellopoulos, Panayotis, 102
Kapsambelis, Yannis, Flt Lt, 33
Karakitsos, Dimitrios, Plt Off, 31
Karathanasis, Stamos, Flt Lt, 132
Karnavias, George, Flt Lt, 6–7, 35, 44
Kartalamakis, Ilias, Fg Off, xi–xii, 37, 71, 74, 83, 86–7, 89, 91, 99–105, 116, 118, 120, 124, 126, 128, 133, 142, 144, 150–1, 155, 157–8, 162
Karydis, Evanghelos, Plt Off, 87, 129
Katasos, Friderikos, Plt Off, 31
Katsarellis, Leonidas, Flt Sgt, 66
Katsaros, Yannis, Plt Off, 30, 32, 100
Katsoulas, Yannis, Sgt, 31
Kavourinos, Nikolaos, Sgt, 73
Kelaidis, Emmanuel, Wg Cdr, 42, 53–4, 161, 171
Kellas, Yannis, Sqn Ldr, 41, 45, 49–51, 61, 65–8, 101–7, 171
Kinatos, Menelaos, Wg Cdr, 56
Kipouros, Yannis, Plt Off, 34, 48, 57
Kleiamakis, Doros, Plt Off, 3, 94
Koliopoulos, Christos, Flt Sgt, 114–15
Kokkas, Constantine, Plt Off, 120–1, 133
Kondos, Makis, Fg Off, 146
Kontidis, Miltiades, WO, 35
Koryzis, Alexander, 53–4, 59, 70–1
Koskinas, Nikolaos, Fg Off, 127
Koskoros, Nikolaos, Flt Lt, 78
Kostis, Evanghelos, Plt Off, 157–8
Kostorrizos, Nikolaos, Flt Sgt, 50–1
Koudounas, Argyrios, Sqn Ldr, 3
Koumanakos, George, Capt, 110
Kounoupas, George, Sgt, 95
Kourdis, Vasilios, Flt Sgt, 73–4
Koutroumbas, Pericles, Flt Sgt, 61, 65
Koutsoukos, Ilias, Flt Lt, 31
Kouyoufas, Agryris, Flt Lt, 63
Kouyoumtzoglou, Yannis, Sgt, 4
Kouziyannis, Lambros, Flt Lt, 6–8
Kovatzis, Spyros, Plt Off, 7–8
Krikonis, Triantafyllos, Fg Off, 138, 147

Index of Names   175

Kyriazis, Yannis, Fg Off, 37
Kytariolos, George, Plt Off, 70

Lambropoulos, Constantine, Flt Sgt, 1–2, 156
Lambropoulos, George, Sgt, 75–6, 93, 151–2, 155, 161
Leonidas I, King of Sparta, xvi, 67
Liakeas, Pericles, Flt Lt, 144
Linos, Pantelis, Flt Lt, 51, 64
Longmore, Arthur, ACM, 39–40, 54

Mademlis, George, Flt Sgt, 129
Malakis, Alexander, Plt Off, 36–7, 41
Manavis, Panayotis, Fg Off, 80
Manias, Yannis, Sqn Ldr, 112–13
Margaritis, Constantine, Fg Off, 9, 34, 78, 131, 141, 149–53
Markou, George, Flt Lt, 78, 88–9
Marmaras, Anastasios, Fg Off, 135
Merifield, John, Sgt, 39
Metaxas, Ioannis, xiv–xvi, 6, 9, 14–15, 18–19, 21, 25, 29, 36, 39–40, 44–5, 47, 49–50, 52–3, 57, 80, 89
Metaxas, Theophanes (Fanis), Sqn Ldr, 89–91, 112, 128, 139, 153
Michelli, Enrico, Sgt, 45
Mitralexis, Marinos, Plt Off, 1–2, 32–3, 36, 50–1, 161
Mokkas, George, Sgt, 66
Molinari, Edoardo, Capt, 41, 43, 57
Molyvadas, Stephanos, Flt Sgt, 90, 146–7
Mondini, Luigi, Lt Col, xiv–xv, 29
Montgomery of Alamein, FM, xi, 102–3, 106, 119, 134
Morris, H., Sqn Ldr, 95–6
Moutousis, Michalis, Lt, 11
Mussolini, Benito, xi, xiv–xv, 19, 24–6, 28–30, 32–3, 43, 47, 55–6, 70, 103, 118
Mussolini, Bruno, 9
Mussolini, Vittorio, 9

Nanopoulos, Spyros, Flt Lt, 47–8
Nasopoulos, Alexander, Fg Off, 94, 127
Nikitidis, Nikolaos, WO, 34, 44

Orphanidis, Panayotis, Flt Lt, 34

Palairet, Michael, xvi
Paleologou, Constantine, Flt Sgt, 62–3
Paliatseas, Dimitrios, Sqn Ldr, 48

Panagopoulos, Constantine, Fg Off, 70, 85–6
Panagopoulos, Kyriakos, Flt Lt, 103, 105, 113, 117
Pangalos, George, Flt Lt, 62, 107, 156
Pantazoglou, Eleftherios, Fg Off, 137–8
Pantzalis, Eleftherios, Flt Sgt, 145, 148
Papadakis, Yannis, Sqn Ldr, 44
Papadimitriou, Yannis, Flt Lt, 68
Papadopoulos, Sgt, 30
Papadopoulos, Spyros, Flt Sgt, 62–3
Papageorgiou, Dimitrios, Fg Off, 4, 34
Papageorgiou, Ilias, Flt Sgt, 117
Papageorgopoulos, Stephanos, Flt Sgt, 115, 137–8
Papagos, Alexander, Lt Gen, 5, 29, 31, 53, 58, 67, 162
Papaioannou, Alexander, Fg Off, 4
Papaioannou, George, Flt Sgt, 86, 150
Papakostas, Yannis, Fg Off, 141
Papamichail, Lazaros, Plt Off, 4
Papandreou, George, 139, 150, 156
Papantoniou, Yannis, Flt Lt, 144
Papapanayotou, Panayotis, Sqn Ldr, 128, 136, 139
Papatheou, Haralambos, Flt Lt, 53
Papatsoris, Alexander, Wg Cdr, 113–14, 117
Papingis, Vlassis, Aircraftman, 136–9
Papoutsis, Yannis, Fg Off, 145–6
Pappas, Aristophanes, WO, 35
Paraskakis, Haralambos, Fg Off, 148–9
Parisis, Lambros, Sqn Ldr, 157
Park, Keith, AVM, 99–102, 130
Passialis, Christos, Sqn Ldr, 74
Pattas, George, Fg Off, 125–6
Pattle, Marmaduke 'Pat', Flt Lt, 40–1, 43, 54–5, 60–1, 68–9, 79, 103
Patton, George, Gen, 147
Paul, Crown Prince, later King Paul I of Greece, 81, 90, 101, 149
Peter of Yugoslavia, Prince, 92
Philippas, Stephanos, Gp Capt, 6, 75–6
Pitsikas, Dimitrios, Flt Lt, 35, 57
Pitsilis, Gerasimos, Sqn Ldr, 90
Plastiras, Philip, Plt Off, 83
Platis, Nikolaos, Flt Lt, 140
Platsis, Constantine, Wg Cdr, 78, 81, 88, 90, 92–4, 101
Pleionis, George, Plt Off, 107–8
Pongis, Renos, Sqn Ldr, 112–3
Portal, Charles, MRAF, 92–3, 101

Potamianos, Haralambos, Sqn Ldr, 4, 45, 71
Pricolo, Francesco, Gen, 25–6, 28–9, 32–3, 55–7, 72
Psilolignos, Constantine, Plt Off, 129

Ranza, Ferruccio, Gen, 28, 32, 56, 59
Razelos, Pelopidas, Gp Capt, 90
Roatta, Mario, Gen, 24–6
Rommel, Erwin, Gen, 79, 82, 91, 99–103, 106
Rossi, Carlo, Gen, 31

Sakellariou, Takis, Plt Off, 157
Sakellariou, Yannis, Fg Off, 30
Sakis, George, WO, 4
Sarafis, Constantine, Plt Off, 35
Sarsonis, Dimitrios, Flt Sgt, 129
Sarvanis, Alexander, Plt Off, 31
Savellos, Michalis, Flt Lt, 49
Sioris, Constantine, Flt Sgt, 61, 65
Skaltsoyannis, Dimitrios, Flt Lt, 54
Skatzikas, Sarandis, Fg Off, 9, 21, 34, 48, 69, 123
Skatzikas, Sotirios, Plt Off, 121, 123
Sklavos, Panayotis, Flt Sgt, 108
Skliris, Marios, Flt Sgt, 117, 123
Skourbelos, Nikolaos, Fg Off, 54
Smuts, Jan, Gen, 81
Smyrniotopoulos, Eleftherios, Flt Sgt, 60–1
Soddu, Ubaldo, Gen, 33, 43, 47
Soufrilas, Dimitrios, Flt Sgt, 105–6, 123, 131, 133
Sowden, Plt Off, 145
Spentzos, Christos, Sgt, 64
Spyridonos, Dimitrios, WO, 132
Stalin, Josef, 90, 118, 134–5, 139
Stathakos, Dimitrios, Sqn Ldr, 56–7
Stavraetos, George, Fg Off, 51
Stavropoulos, Haralambos, WO, 119–20, 122–3
Stratis, Michalis, Fg Off, 56, 114, 119, 125–8

Tangalakis, George, Flt Sgt, 150
Tedder, Arthur, ACM, 91–2, 102–3, 106
Theodoropoulos, Grigorios, Sqn Ldr, 35, 49, 67
Theophanopoulos, Theophanes, Plt Off, 83
Tilios, Stergios, Gp Capt, xvi, 5, 16
Tingas, WO, 64
Tingos, Emmanuel, Flt Lt, 157

Toumbakaris, Nikolaos, Flt Lt, 51, 63–4
Trenchard, Lord, 102
Troupakis, Nikolaos, Plt Off, 6–7
Tsarpalis, Vasilios, AVM, xvi
Tselos, Epaminondas, Maj, 70
Tsimbos, Andreas, Capt, 110, 137, 144–5
Tsirikoglou, Panos, Fg Off, 127
Tsitsas, Constantine, Plt Off, 41–2
Tsitsoglou, George, Plt Off, 128, 143–4, 148
Tsolakoglou, George, Lt Gen, 70
Tsotsos, George, Fg Off, 133
Tsouderos, Emmanuel, 92
Twain, Mark, xii
Tzamtzis, Efthymios, Flt Sgt, 135
Tzanetakis, George, Wg Cdr, 68, 135, 140–1
Tzovlas, Evanghelos, Flt Sgt, 56

Valavanis, Constantine, Plt Off, 108–9, 114
Vale, William, Plt Off, 43
Valkanas, Grigorios, Sgt, 36
Varvaressos, Xenophon, Sqn Ldr, 74–7, 82–3, 85–7, 89, 99, 101, 107, 142
Venizelos, Eleftherios, 11–13
Vercellino, Mario, Gen, 43
Vilos, Panayotis, Wg Cdr, 13, 49, 77–8, 80–1, 89–92, 101, 107, 112, 142
Visconti Prasca, Sebastiano, Gen, 24–5, 31–3
Vladousis, Anastasios, Plt Off, 7, 35–6, 76, 111, 114, 131, 133, 139, 141–2, 154–5, 157, 162–3
Volonakis, Nikolaos, Fg Off, 51, 102, 157
Voutsas, Dimitrios, Flt Sgt, 96–8
Voutsinas, Dimitrios, Plt Off, 70, 116

Wavell, Archibald, FM, 49, 54, 57, 79
Wilhelm II, Kaiser of Germany, 11
Wilson, Henry 'Jumbo', Maj Gen, 67
Wisdom, T.H., 69
Woodruff, Patrick, Wg Cdr, 158
Woodward, Vernon, Fg Off, 69

Xanthakos, George, Plt Off, 124
Xydis, Emmanuel, Flt Sgt, 101
Xydis, Stratis, Plt Off, 119

Yakas, Dimitrios, WO, 35
Yannikostas, Constantine, Fg Off, 36
Yemenetzis, Constantine, Sgt, 4

Zannas, Alexander, 12